AN INTRODUCTION TO MAMMALS

AN INTRODUCTION TO MAMMALS

By

H.S. Bhamrah

Kavita Juneja

Edited by

Balvinder K.

ANMOL PUBLICATIONS PVT. LTD.

NEW DELHI - 110 002 (INDIA)

ANMOL PUBLICATIONS PVT. LTD.
4374/4B, Ansari Road, Daryaganj
New Delhi - 110 002

An Introduction to Mammals

First Edition, 1990
Reprint, 1991, 1992, 1994
Second Revised Edition. 2002

ISBN 81-261-0707-3

PRINTED IN INDIA

Published by J.L. Kumar for Anmol Publications Pvt. Ltd., New Delhi - 110 002 and Printed at Mehra Offset Press, Delhi.

Contents

Preface

We feel pleasure in bringing out the second revised edition of the present book on the instance of our learned teachers. Besides rectifying the errors of first edition, new material is added here and there in the light of recent development and researches in the field.

This text is designed to approach the morphology, anatomy, physiology and development of the *Mammals* in a coherent way since it is most natural for a student in studying the architectural elements of an animal body in the quest to know how they function. This text intends, therefore, to enable the student, through his own natural appetency, to correlate form and function so that he possesses for subsequent work in either anatomy or physiology a firm foundation for a real edifice of knowledge.

The book features both a text and a laboratory guide. It deals with the structures and physiological phenomena of each system. Origin, adaptative radiation and other general topics are also dealt in details. It is hoped that this book will not only meet the requirement of Indian students but will also be useful as a guideline to the teachers in their teaching.

There can be no claim to originality except in the manner of treatment and much of the information has been obtained from the books and scientific journals available in different libraries.

We express our thanks to our friends and colleagues whose constant inspiration have initiated them to bring out this book.

The authors are also grateful to Dr. J. Bahadur, Professor and Head, School of Studies in Zoology, Jiwaji University Gwalior, Dr. A.K. Pandey, Professor & Head, Vikram University, Ujjain for their valuable suggestions.

All the constructive criticisms and suggestions for improvement from learned teachers and scholars are welcome.

H.S. Bhamrah
Kavita Juneja

1

Mammalia : Characters and Classification

CHARACTERS

(A) Integumentary characters

1. The skin is more or less clothed with hairs.
2. Sweat glands or sudorific glands are present, whose function is to cool down the body surface by exuding water taken from the blood stream. Evaporation of water cools the surface.
3. Oil or sebaceous glands are present which keeps the hair and skin soft and pliable by releasing its secretion.
4. Presence of mammary glands, which produce milk to nourish the young ones.

(B) Characters of teeth

5. Teeth are heterodont i.e. differentiated into incisors, canines, premolars and molars.
6. They are thecodont i.e. embedded in alveolar sockets of jaw.
7. Diphyodont condition i.e. only two sets of teeth, a milk set which is later replaced by permanent set.

(C) Skeletal characters

8. Skull is dicondylic i.e. two occipital condyles for the articulation with the atlas vertebra.
9. Lower jaw is made up of only a pair of bones, the dentaries, for articulation with squamosal of skull.
10. The articular and quadrate bones, which help in articulation in lower vertebrates, are transformed into two ear-ossicles, malleus and incus of ear apparatus.
11. Turbinal bones are introduced into the nasal passages, probably to warm up the in breathed air and to catch bacteria and dust.
12. Long bones have epiphyses and diaphyses, that aid in the growth of bones.

13. Ribs are double headed, capitulum and tuberculum for articulation with vertebrae.
14. The body of vertebra is composed of three pieces, the centrum and two epiphysis.
15. Cartilaginous discs or intervertebral discs septate the centra of adjacent vertebrae.
16. Neck with 7-cervical vertebrae, few exceptions are there.
17. Except monotremes, the coracoid and precoracoids are reduced in all other mammals.
18. The tympanic bones are fused to form the periotic which is further modified into tympanic bulla.

(D) Blood vascular system

19. The heart is completely four chambered.
20. The red blood corpuscles are biconcave and enucleated (without nuclei).
21. Left aortic arch is present, however, right one disappears.

(E) Brain

22. The cerebrum and solid cerebellum are highly developed and have much grey matter in them.
23. Corpus callosum, a massive bundle of fibrous tracts connect the two cerebral hemispheres together. It is absent in monotremes and rudimentary in marsupials.
24. There are four optic lobes.

(F) Auditory mechanism

25. The external ear or pinna is present is mammals except in monotremes and aquatic mammals.
26. The external auditory meatus is present.
27. Except monotremes, the internal ear is elongated and is in the form of a spirally coiled cochlea.
28. Connecting the ear drum with the internal ear, there are three ear-ossicles: *malleus*, *incus*, and *stapes*.

(G) Urino-genital system

29. Kidneys are metanephric.
30. The ureters open into the urinary bladder instead of cloaca, which is present only in monotremes.
31. A male copulatory organ or penis is always present.

(H) Egg and mode of reproduction

32. The eggs are microscopic and with little or no yolk.
33. The eggs mature in Graffian follicles.
34. Two oviducts fuse to form a common uterus or paired uteri.
35. Except monotremes, which lay eggs, uterine gestation is the rule .
36. Except in monotremes and most of the marsupials, allantoic placenta is present which supplies nourishments to the embryos.
37. Mostly viviparous except monotremes.

(I) Miscllaneous characters

38. Abdominal and thoracic cavities are separated by a muscular diaphragm. It helps in breathing.
39. Homiothermous i.e. warm blooded animals. Constant or nearly constant high body temperature.
40. The opening of trachea into the buccal cavity is guarded by epiglottis.

CLASSIFICATION

Class Mammalia has been divided into three sub-classes.

1. Sub-class =Prototheria
2. Sub-class=Allotheria
3. Sub-class=Theria.

Sub-class-1. Prototheria

1. Oviparous mammals, found in Australia, Islands of Tasmania and New Guinea.
2. The eggs are provided with large amount of yolk.
3. Mammary glands without nipples or teats.
4. The coracoid and precoracoid are well developed in pectoral girdle.
5. The epiphyses are absent or poorly developed.
6. Corpus callosum is absent or poorly developed in brain.
7. Epipubic bone is present in pelvic girdle.
8. Cloaca is present.
9. The testes are abdominal and scrotum is absent.
10. The posterior part of the oviducts do not fuse to form the uterus and vagina.
11. They are not fully homoiothermous i.e. unable to keep body temperature constant.

Sub-class Prototheria is divided into three orders.

1. Triconodonta 2. Symmetrodonta 3. Monotremata.

Order-1. Triconodonta

1. Extinct and recorded from upper *Triassic* to the lower *Cretaceous.*
2. They were small in size with a very small brain comparatively.

Examples : *Tricodon, Priacodon.*

Order-2. Symmetrodonta

1. Extinct. They were found from the beginning of the *Jurassic* to middle *Cretaceous.*

Examples : *Peralestes*

Order-3. Monotremata

(Gr. *Monos* : single, *treme* : opening)

1. The general characters are same as that of its sub-class.
2. This class includes two families -*Ornithorhynchidae* and *Echidnidae.*

Examples : *Ornithorhynchus* and *Echidna.*

Sub-class 2. Allotheria

1. They are extinct and were found during *Jurassic* until *Eocene.*
2. The molar teeth had two or three longitudinal rows of tubercles with 2-5 cusps in each row.
3. Canines were absent. One lower and three upper incisors were present.
4. They were herbivores

Only one order Multituberculata

Examples : *Plagianlax, Ctenacodon*

Sub-class 3. Theria

It includes some extinct forms, and all the modern mammals.

1. Viviparous mammals i.e. give birth to young ones.
2. Ears with external pinnae.
3. Teeth found in both adults and young ones.
4. Mammary glands with nipples or teats.
5. Each oviduct in female differentiated into upper fallopian tube and lower uterine part.

Subclass Theria is divided into three infra-classes

1. Pantotheria 2. Metatheria 3. Eutheria

Infra-class -1. Pantotheria

1. Includes all the extinct forms of *Mesozoic* era. It is divided into two orders.

Order-1. Dryolestoidea

1. They occurred in *Jurassic* period.
2. Jaws were very small reaching to a maximum of 4 cms.

   Example : *Amphitherium.*

Order-2. Docodonta

1. They occurred in upper *Jurassic*.
2. They resemble Dryolestoidea except in arrangement and structure of teeth.

   Example : *Docodon.*

Infra-class -II Metatheria

1. Well developed marsupium or brood pouch is present is females.
2. Mammary glands are sebaceous, and present in marsupial pouch.
3. Epipubic bone or marsupial bone is usually present and attached with the pubis. It supports the marsupium.
4. Ribs are double headed.
5. Corpus callosum poorly developed or absent.
6. Double vagina in females and bifid penis in males.
7. Ovoviviparous, young ones are born premature after very short gestation and after birth, young ones usually get matured in marsupial pouch.
8. Cloaca is present but it is not completely developed.
9. Yolk sac placenta is developed.

   Infra-class Metatheria is divided into single order.

Order-1. Marsupialia

1. Incisor teeth 4-5 in upper jaw but their number is less in lower jaw.

   Examples : *Macropus* (Kangaroo), *Parameles* (Bandicoot), *Didelphis* (Opposum), *Phascolarctus* or Australian Teddy Bear.

   Order *Marsupialia* is divided into two sub-orders :

Sub-order (i) - Didactyla

1. All the digits are free.
2. Including carnivorous forms.

   Example - *Didelphys* (Opossum), *Motoryctes* (marsupial mole).

Sub-order- (ii) Syndactyla

1. Few carnivorous and rest are herbivorous.
2. The second and third toes are bound together.

   Examples : *Macropus* (Kangaroo), *Petaurus* (flying opossum).

Infra-class -III Eutheria

1. Marsupial pouch is absent and the epipubic bone is also absent in pelvic girdle.
2. Mammary glands with well developed teats or nipples.
3. Cloaca is absent.
4. Corpus callosum is well-developed in brain.
5. Single vagina and penis.
7. Testes are extra-abdominal contained in scrotal sacs.
8. Viviparous with allantoic placenta. The young ones are born in advanced stage, as there is a long gestation.

Infra-class Eutheria is divided into following orders :

Order-1. Insectivora

1. Small sized, mostly nocturnal with elongated snout and teeth adapted for insectivorous diet
2. Skin usually covered with soft fur, but sometimes with spines.
3. Give multiple births.

Example : *Erinaceus* (Hedge-hog), *Talpa* (Mole), *Hemiechinus* (Indian hedge-hog).

Order-2. Chiroptera

1. Small to large sized mammals.
2. Only mammals with true flight. The organs of flight are lateral extensions of the skin, the *patagia* supported by the fore-limbs.
3. Keeled sternum for attachment of powerful flight muscles.
4. Testes are abdominal.
5. Mammary glands are thoracic.
9. They produce only one or sometimes two young ones.

Order Chiropetera is divided into two suborders (i) Megachiroptera, and (ii) Microchiroptera

Sub-order (i) Megachiroptera

1. Feed on fruits.
2. Bear claws on the first two digits of fore-limb.
3. Lack of tail.
4. Snout is elongated.
5. External nares are without nose leaves.

Example : *Pteropus.*

Sub-order (ii) Microchiroptera

1. Feed on insects, except few that suck blood.
2. Bear a claw only on the first digit of the fore-limb.
3. Tail is present.
4. External nares may be surrounded by leaf-like appendages called nose leaves.

   Example : *Scotophilus*.

Order-3. Dermoptera

1. They are nocturnal, arboreal and herbivores.
2. All the limbs are of equal size.
3. A fold of skin extending along either side of body from neck to tail and enclosing the limbs called *patagia*.
4. They only glide from branch to branch and do not fly.

   Example : *Galaeopithecus* (Flying lemur).

Order-4. Edentata

1. Teeth present or absent, if present only premolars and molars. Incisors and canines are absent.
2. Feet have well developed claws.
3. Testes are abdominal.
4. Clavicle is present.
5. Coracoid unites with acromian.
6. Extra articulating surfaces between the lumbar vertebrae.

   Order Edentata is divided into two suborders.

   (i) Pilosa (ii) Loricata

Suborder-(i) Pilosa

1. This includes edentates with powerful claws.
2. The snout may be long with protrusible sticky tongue in ant eater or flat as in sloths.

   Example : *Myremacophaga* (ant eater) and *Bradypus* (sloth).

Suborder-(ii) Loricata

1. This includes armoured edentates.
2. They are nocturnal insectivorous animals.

   Example : *Dasypus* (armadillo).

Order-5. Pholidota

1. Nocturnal and burrowing in habit, sometimes arboreal.

2. Body covered by large over-lapping horny scales.
3. Hairs are found between scales.
4. The snout is elongated, teeth are absent.
5. Tongue is long, sticky and protrusible.
6. Claws are very large.
7. Pinnae are reduced.

Example : *Manis* (Pangolin or scaly ant-eater)

Order-6. Primates

1. Generally arboreal mammals.
2. They are plantigrade and have long limbs, each bearing 5-digits protected by nails.
3. The first digit of each limb (pollax and hallax) can be brought opposite the remaining digits to make hands and feet grasping organs.
4. Orbits are directed forward and surrounded by bony rings.
5. Clavicles are present.
6. The femur without third trochanter.
7. The cerebral hemisphere are large and highly convoluted, and completely or incompletely cover the cerebellum.

Order Primates is divided into three suborders:

(i) Lemuroidea (ii) Tarsioidea (iii) Anthropoidea

Suborder-(i) Lemuroidea

1. Head is usually produced into a snout.
2. Some toes bear claws and others nails.
3. Tail is long and non-prehensile.
4. Fore limbs shorter than hind limbs.
5. Orbits are not surrounded by bones behind but open into temporal fossa.
6. Fur is usually thick and wooly.

Example : *Nycticelrus* (lemur), *Loris* .

Suborder-(ii) Tarsioidea

1. Nocturnal, arboreal and insectivorous.
2. Eyes are very large, being directed more forwards.
3. Ears are large.
4. Hind limbs are larger than forelimbs.
5. The tail is longer than body with a tuft at the tip.

6. Second and third toes bear claws.

   Example: *Tarsius*

Suborder-(iii) Anthropoidea

1. Terrestrial or arboreal, and diurnal.
2. Hands and feet are prehensile except in man.
3. Digits bear flat nails.
4. Teeth are 32-36 in number.
5. Mammae restricted to thoracic region.
6. Pinnae are reduced.
7. Upper lip is protrusible.

   Anthropoidea falls into two categories or series

   (i) Catarrhina (Old world monkeys)

   (ii) Platyrrhina (New world monkeys)

   Series (i) Catarrhina : Old world monkeys are found in Asia and Africa. Cheek pouches are present. Tail is nonprehensile. Have thick coloured pads, the ischial callosities on the buttucks. They sit on these pads. Bony external auditory meatus present. They have only two-premolars.

   Example : *Macaca* (Rhesus monkey), *Presbytes* (Langur), *Pongo* (Orang utan), *Pan* (Chimpanzee), *Gorilla* and *Homo* (Man).

   Series (ii) Platyrrhina : New world monkeys are found in central and south America. The cheek pouches are absent. Tail is prehensile. The ischial callosities are absent. The number of premolars is three. The bony external auditory meatus is absent.

   Example : *Callithrix* (Marmoset), and *Ateles* (Spider monkey).

Order -7. Lagomorpha

1. Includes rabbit and hares.
2. The pinnae are large.
3. Two pairs of incisors in the upper jaw, but canines are absent.
4. Strongly built hind limbs for leaping.
5. Tibia fused with fibula.
6. Soles of feet are hairy.

   Example : *Lepus* (Hare), *Oryctolagus* (Rabbit).

Order-8. Rodentia

1. Usually small sized mammals.
2. Limbs with five toes and claws.

3. The canine teeth are absent. The incisors are long and sharp. The space between canines and premolars is called *diastema*.
4. Testes are usually abdominal.
5. In porcupine, the hairs are modified into spines.

   Example : *Funambulus* (Squirrel), *Mus* (House mouse), *Rattus* (House rat), and *Hystrix* (Porcupine).

Order -9. Cetacea

1. Medium sized to very large sized aquatic mammals.
2. Body is spindle shaped and fish like.
3. Head long and pointed without neck.
4. Hairs are reduced in adults, only few bristles on the snout.
5. Eyes and ear openings are minute.
6. Nostrils are placed on the top of head.
7. Fore-limbs are modified into paddles, digits without claws and are enclosed in a common integument.
8. Hind-limbs are absent.
9. Tail is long ending in two broad transverse fleshy flukes notched in the mid-line.
10. A thick layer of fat called *blubber* is present beneath the skin.
11. Bones of skull are spongy and contain fat.
12. Stomach consists of 3 or 4 chambers.
13. Testes are abdominal in position.
14. Teeth are often lost.

   Cetacea is divided into two suborders.

   (i) Odontoceti (ii) Mystacooceti.

Sub order-(i) Odontoceti

1. Nostril is single and olfactory sense is poor.
2. They feed on fishes and cuttle fishes.
3. Teeth are present,and are homodont.

   Example : *Dolphins*

Sub-order-(ii) Mystacoceti

1. Paired nostrils.
2. Teeth are absent.
3. Feed on small crustaceans.

   Example : *Whales*

Order-10. Carnivora

1. They are very powerful flesh eaters.
2. Their teeth are adapted for tearing and cutting the flesh. Three incisors are present. Canines are large and pointed. Premolars have sharp cutting edges.
3. The digits are never less than four and are clawed.
4. Clavicles are incomplete or absent.
5. Mammae are abdominal.
6. Tympanic bulla large and rounded.

   Order Carnivora is divided into three suborders:

   (i) Fissipedia (ii) Pinnipedia (iii) Credontia (extinct).

Sub-order-(i) Fissipedia

1. Terrestrial carnivorous.
2. The digits are clawed and separate.
3. Canines are always very large and strong.
4. The last premolar in the lower jaw known as *carnassial* teeth and two molars are crushing teeth.
5. The clavicle is small and sometimes quite rudimentary.

   Example : *Panthra leo* (Lion), *Panthra tigris* (Tiger), *Prionalurus* (leopard), *Vulpus* (Fox), *Canis* (Wolf), *Herpestes* (Mangoose), etc.

Sub-order-(ii) Pinnipedia

1. It includes marine carnivorous secondarily adopted for aquatic life.
2. The hand and feet are webbed.
3. Thick tuft of sensory hairs is provided on the upper lip.
4. Tail is very short and helpful in swimming.
5. External ears are small or degenerated.

   Example : *Phoca* (Seal), *Odobenus* (Walrus).

Order-11. Tubulindentata

1. They are shy and nocturnal animals living in burrows.
2. Body stout, somewhat pig like.
3. They are ant eaters with slender snout and long protrusible tongue.
4. The skin is thick and covered with sparse hairs.
5. Pinnae are long, erect and pointed.
6. Milk teeth numerous but permanent teeth are few.

   Example : *Orycteropus*

Order-12. Hyracoidea

1. Small rabbit like animal, and body covered by fur.
2. Herbivorous, and found in Africa.
3. Four digits in fore limbs, and three digits in hind limbs.
4. Clavicles are absent.
5. Testes are abdominal.
6. Six pairs of mammae or mammary glands, four pair inguinal and two pairs axillary.

   Example : *Hyrax.*

Order-13. Proboscidea

1. This group includes large sized terrestrial animals.
2. Skin is thick and covered with sparse hairs.
3. Head is large with a long prehensile proboscis. Nostrils are placed at the tip of proboscis.
4. Five functional digits are present on each fore and hind-limbs. The limbs are massive pillar like.
5. The incisor teeth of upper jaw are greatly elongated and form the tusks.
6. Molars are lophodont and canines are absent.
7. Clavicles are absent.
8. Skull bears cavities.
9. Testes are abdominal.
10. Two pectoral mammae.

    Example : *Elephas* (elephant).

Order-14. Sirenia

1. Sirenia includes marine forms which are commonly known as sea-cows.Herbivorous.
2. Body is stream-lined,short necked and thick skinned without hairs.
3. Pinnae are absent.
4. Fore limbs are modified into paddles for swimming, and hind limbs are absent.
5. Tail possesses candal fin.
6. Clavicles are absent.
7. Testes are abdominal.
8. Nostrils are on the upper surface of the snout.

   Example : *Halicore* (Dugong), *Trichechus* (Manatee).

Order-15. Perissodactyla

1. Large sized, hoofed mammals.
2. The middle digit is well developed and carries most of the weight of the body.
3. Teeth are lophodont having enamel ridges.
4. Dorso-lumbar vertebrae are 23.
5. Mammae are inguinal.

   Example : *Equus* (Horse), *Rhinoceros* (Rhino).

Order-16. Artiodactyla

1. Herbivorous, terrestrial or semi-aquatic large-sized mammals.
2. Fore-and hind-limbs bear two, rarely four digits.
3. Teeth are bunodont or solenodont.
4. Dorso-lumbar vertebrae are 19.
5. Stomach is simple.
6. Some of them have horns on their heads.

   Order Artiodactyla is divided into three sub-orders.

   (i) Suiformes (ii) Tylopoda (iii) Ruminantia.

Sub-order-(i) Suiformes

1. They have two or four hooves.
2. Some forms are semi-aquatic.
3. Stomach may be simple or 3 chambered.
4. The teeth are bunodont.

   Example: *Sus* (Pig), *Hippopotamus*.

Sub-order-(ii) Tylopoda

1. It includes cud-chewing mammals.
2. The limbs are long without 2nd and 5th toes.
3. Molars are solenodont,one pair of incisors in upper jaw, and canines in both the jaws.
4. Stomach three chambered with water cells.

   Example : *Camelus* (Camel), *Lamas*.

Sub-order-(iii) Ruminantia

1. It also includes the cud-chewing mammals.
2. Teeth are solenodont.
3. Stomach is four chambered.
4. The horns are unbranched or in some cases branched, and are called *antlers*.

Example : *Axis axis* (cheetal), *Moschusmoschiferous* (Musk deer), *Giraffa*, *Bos indicus* (Cow), *Ovis* (Sheep), *Capra* (Goat), *Antelope*, etc.

TACHYGLOSSUS (ECHIDNA)

Phylum	-	Chordata
Group	-	Vertebrata
Sub-phylum	-	Gnathostomata
Class	-	Mammalia
Sub-class	-	Prototheria
Order	-	Monotremata
Genus	-	*Tachyglossus*
Species	-	*aculeata*

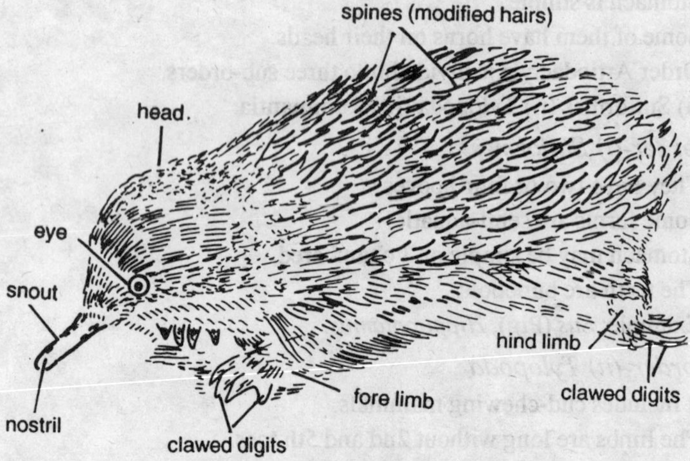

Fig. 1.1. *Tachyglossus aculeatus*.

1. It is commonly called as 'spiny ant eater'. It is nocturnal. It is also called a connecting link between reptiles with mammals.
2. The body is covered by strong pointed spines.
3. Snout is long and tapering like a bird's bill.
4. The tongue is long, and protrusible and is provided with sticky salivary secretion.
5. Claws are very powerful and long modified for digging.
6. Teeth are not developed throughout life. Pinnae are absent.

7. The tail is rudimentary.
8. Mammary glands without nipples or teats.
9. A fold of skin near the mammary glands forms a temporary marsupium in which eggs are kept and young ones retained for some times.
10. A cloaca is present.
11. Body temperature is not constant i.e. poikilothermal. Tarsal spurs are present in each hind limb of male.
12. They are found in Australia, Tasmania and New Guinea.

ORNITHORHYNCHUS

Phylum	-	Chordata
Group	-	Vertebrata
Sub-phylum	-	Gnathostomata
Class	-	Mammalia
Sub-class	-	Prototheria
Order	-	Monotremata
Genus	-	*Ornithorhynchius*
Species	-	*anatinus*

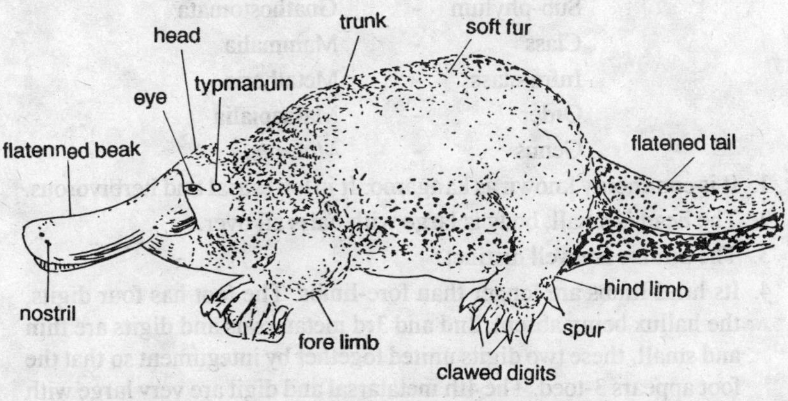

Fig. 1.2. *Ornithorhynchus anatinus.*

1. It is commonly called as "duck-billed platypus", and is nocturnal.
2. Semiaquatic beaver like mammal found in burrows on the bank of rivers and pools.
3. The body is covered by soft brown fur.
4. The feet are five toed, webbed for swimming purpose, and clawed for digging.

5. The upper jaw is produced into a depressed beak, like that of duck, and adapted for burrowing in mud. Eyes are small and have nictitating membranes.
6. The young one possesses a set of milk teeth, all molars which are 8-10 in number. However, teeth are absent in adult and replaced by horny plates.
7. The tail is large, and dorso-ventrally flattened and is used as a rudder when swimming in water.
8. External ears or pinnae are absent.
9. Male bears a scent gland on the under surface of the neck.
10. It is carnivorous and feeds mainly on fresh water insects, worms and crustaceans.
11. The eggs are laid by females in a nest of grasses to the number of 2 or 3.
12. They are found in Tasmania and Southern Australia.

MACROPUS

Phylum	-	Chordata
Group	-	Vertebrata
Sub-phylum	-	Gnathostomata
Class	-	Mammalia
Infra-class	-	Metatheria
Order	-	Marsupialia
Genus	-	*Macropus*

1. It is commonly known as kangaroo. It is terrestrial and herbivorous.
2. The head is small, body is large with hairs all over.
3. The pinnae are well distinct.
4. Its hind-limbs are longer than fore-limbs. The foot has four digits, the hallux being absent, 2nd and 3rd metatarsals and digits are thin and small, these two digits united together by integument so that the foot appears 3-toed. The 4th metatarsal and digit are very large with a strong claw which is used in fighting. The 5th toe is small.
5. The tail is long, round and thick at the base and is used for locomotion and rest.
6. Cervical ribs are absent.
7. Pectoral girdle has large scapula with a spine, coracoid is reduced.
8. Clavicles are large, interclavicle is absent.
9. The young develops in the uterus with only yolk sac placenta.

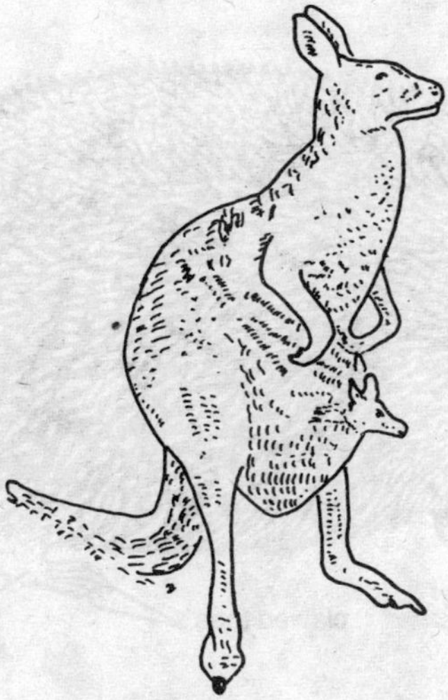

Fig. 1.3. *Macropus.*

10. Well developed marsupium, supported by epipubic bone.
11. Mammary glands with nipples, present in the marsupium.
12. Dental formula is i 3 / 1, c 1/0, pm 2/2, m 4/4 x 2 = 34.
13. They are found in Australia, New Zealand, Tasmania and New Guinea.

ERINACEUS

Phylum	-	Chordata
Group	-	Vertebrata
Sub-phylum	-	Gnathostomata
Class	-	Mammalia
Infra-class	-	Eutheria
Order	-	Insectivora
Genus	-	*Erinaceus*

1. It is commonly known as " hedge-hog".
2. The dorsal and lateral sides of the body are covered with spines which are backwardly directed.
3. The ventral side has soft fur.
4. External ears or pinnae are small.
5. Nocturnal in habit and feeds on insects, worms, and also on fruits and roots of plants.

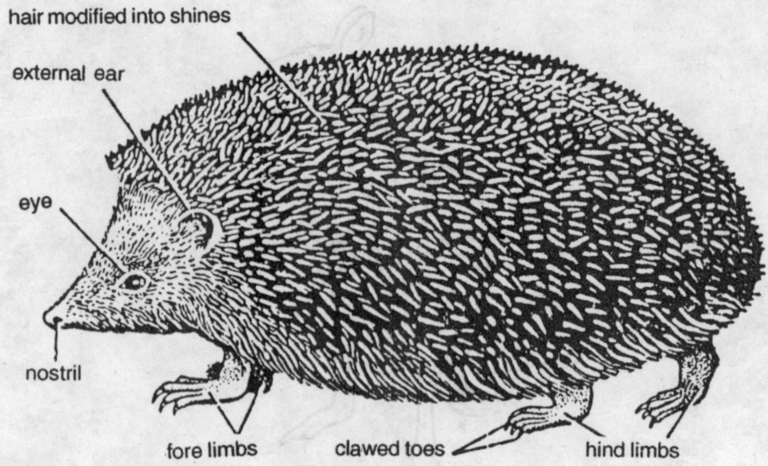

Fig. 1.4. *Erinaceus.*

6. It has a small head with a pointed snout.
7. The dental formula is i. 3/2, c. 1/1, pm. 3/ 2, m. 3/3 x 2 = 36.
8. The tail is very small.
9. The animal rolls up into a ball when in danger, the spines covering the head and tail also.
10. It is immune to snake bite.
11. It hibernates in winter.
12. It is found in Asia, Africa and Europe.

SOREX

Phylum	-	Chordata
Group	-	Vertebrata
Sub-phylum	-	Gnathostomata
Class	-	Mammalia
Infra-class	-	Eutheria
Order	-	Insectivora
Genus	-	*Sorex*

1. It is commonly called as 'shrew', or'chuchunder' in Hindi.
2. It is nocturnal.
3. Snout is elongated and body is covered with silky fur.
4. Eyes and pinnae are small.

Fig. 1.5. *Sorex* (Shrew).

5. First pair of incisors are very long and the dental formula is i. 3/2, c. 1 /0, pm. 3/ 1, m. 3/3 x 2 = 32.
6. Limbs have five clawed digits.
7. They feed on cockroaches, insects, small invertebrates and rodents.
8. Imparts a light musky odour. There is a poisonous substance in the saliva of shrew, which helps it to capture prey.
9. They are found in Asia, Europe and North America.

PTEROPUS

Phylum	-	Chordata
Group	-	Vertebrata
Sub-phylum	-	Gnathostomata
Class	-	Mammalia
Infra-class	-	Eutheria
Order	-	Chiroptera
Sub-order	-	Megachiroptera
Genus	-	*Pteropus*

1. It is commonly called as 'flying fox' or "fox bat".
2. It is large bat with a wing spread over five feet though the body is only about a foot in length.
3. The body is covered with brown fur.
4. The snout is long and without nose leaf.
5. The snout is elongated like a fox.
6. Eyes are large. Ears are oval and the two edges of the ear are in the contact at the base.

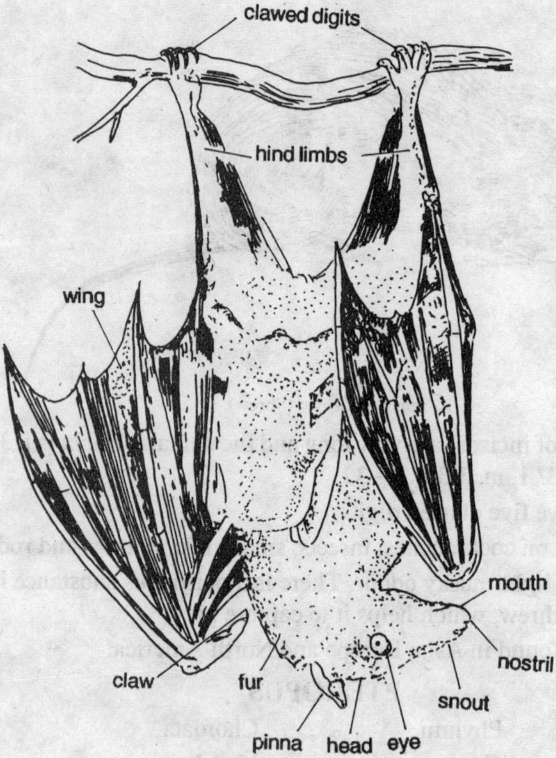

Fig. 1.6. *Pteropus medius* (Flying fox).

7. Tail is absent.
8. The dental formula is i. 3/2, c. 1/1, pm. 3/2, m. 2/3, x 2 = 32.
9. They are frugivorous and feed on figs and guava.
10. It is found in India, Sri Lanka, Australia, Africa and Medagasear.

DESMODUS

Phylum	-	Chordata
Group	-	Vertebrata
Sub-phylum	-	Gnathostomata
Class	-	Mammalia
Infra-class	-	Eutheria
Order	-	Chiroptera
Sub-order	-	Microchiroptera
Genus	-	*Desmodus*

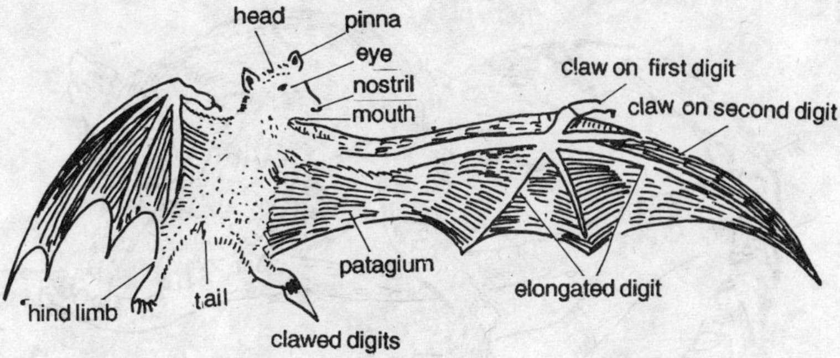

Fig. 1.7. *Desmodus.*

1. It is commonly called 'bat'.
2. It is small animal and the body is covered with soft fur.
3. A small snout with or without nose-leaf.
4. Pinnae are large and often provided with flags, serving as tactile organs and also in making the power of hearing more acute.
5. Eyes are small, the visual rods are poorly developed.
6. Tail is long and included in the inter-femoral membrane.
7. Insectivorous, occasionally frugivorous or sanguivorous (blood sucking).
8. Gregarious, living in temporary groups of thousands.
9. They are cosmopolitan in distribution.

LEMUR

Phylum	-	Chordata
Group	-	Vertebrata
Sub-phylum	-	Gnathostomata
Class	-	Mammalia
Infra-class	-	Eutheria
Order	-	Primates
Sub-order	-	Lemuroidea
Genus	-	*Lemur*

1. These are arboreal in habitat and nocturnal in habit.
2. Body is small, hairy with elongated head.
3. The eyes are rounded and are directed side ways, there is no binocular vision.

Fig. 1.8. *Lemur* (Lemur).

4. Tail is long, bushy and non-prehensile.
5. Dental formula is i. 2/2, c. 1/2, pm. 3/3, m. 3/2 x 2 = 36.
6. Mammary glands are thoracic and inguinal.
7. The penis has an *os penis* bone and the same is also found in clitoris.
8. It eats fruits, eggs, and insects.
9. It is found today only in Medagaskar.

DASYPUS

Phylum	-	Chordata
Group	-	Vertebrata
Sub-phylum	-	Gnathostomata
Class	-	Mammalia
Infra-class	-	Eutheria
Order	-	Edentata
Genus	-	*Dasypus*

1. It is commonly known as 'armadillo'.
2. It is nocturnal, fossorial and omnivorous.
3. Head is short, broad and depressed. There is a long protrusible tongue for feeding on insects.
4. In adults incisors and canines are absent.
5. Eyes are small, and external ears are large.
6. Limbs provided with claws for digging.
7. They have an armour of bony dermal plates or osteoderms which are

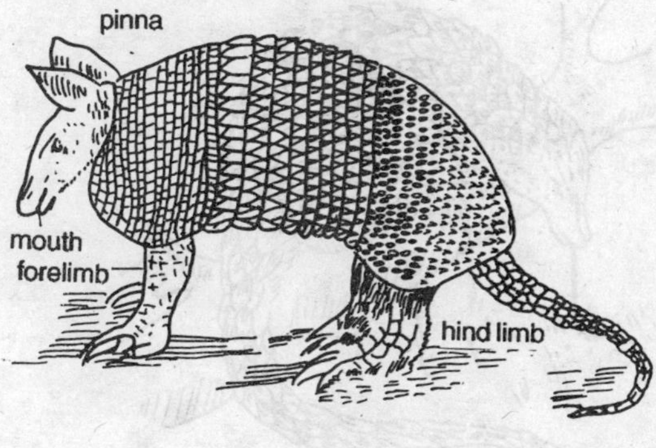

Fig. 1.9. *Dasypus.*

covered with horny epidermal scales or scutes. Ventral side has no armour.

8. The dental formula is i. 0/0, c. 0/0, pm. 2 / 2, m. 2/ 2 x 2 = 16.
9. They give birth to 4 to 8 young ones at one time. All the young ones are developed from one egg hence *monozygotic*, and the sex is same. This is due to *polyembryony*.
10. They are found in Central and South America.

MANIS

Phylum	-	Chordata
Group	-	Vertebrata
Sub-phylum	-	Gnathostomata
Class	-	Mammalian
Infra-class	-	Eutheria
Order	-	Pholidota
Genus	-	*Manis*

1. It is commonly called as 'pangolin' or 'scaly ant-eater'.
2. It is nocturnal and burrowing in habit.
3. It feeds on ants and termites.
4. Body is covered with large, rounded horny epidermal overlapped scales.
5. Head is small with a short pointed snout.
6. Eyes and pinnae are small.
7. Limbs are short and strong with 5 digits.
8. The tongue is elongated, sticky and protrusible.

Fig. 1.10. *Manis.*

9. Skin is devoid of sebaceous glands.
10. It is found in India, Africa and Asia.

HERPESTES

Phylum	-	Chordata
Group	-	Vertebrata
Sub-phylum	-	Gnathostomata
Class	-	Mammalia
Infra-class	-	Eutheria
Order	-	Carnivora
Genus	-	*Herpestes*

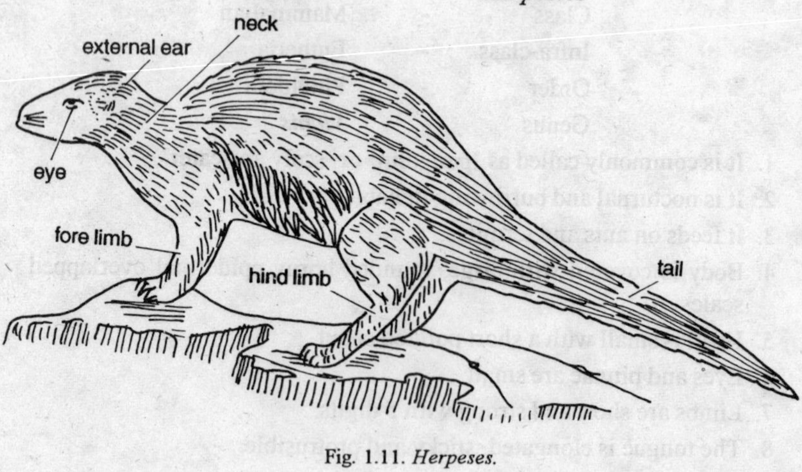

Fig. 1.11. *Herpeses.*

1. It is commonly called as 'mangoose' or 'nyola' in Hindi.
2. Body is elongated and covered with yellowish grey fur.
3. Head is elongated and possesses pointed snout.
4. Eyes are small and pinnae are small.
5. Tail is long.
6. Fore-and hind-limbs have five clawed digits.
7. The incisors and canines are large and pointed. Premolars are sharp.
8. It is famous for its ability to kill snake and to suck its blood.
9. It is found in Ethiopian and Oriental regions. In India it is represented by *H. bengalensis. H.edwardsii, H.fuscus,* and *H.vitticolis.*

HYSTRIX

Phylum	-	Chrodata
Group	-	Vertebrata
Sub-phylum	-	Gnathostomata
Class	-	Mammalia
Infra-class	-	Eutheria
Order	-	Rodentia
Genus	-	*Hystrix*

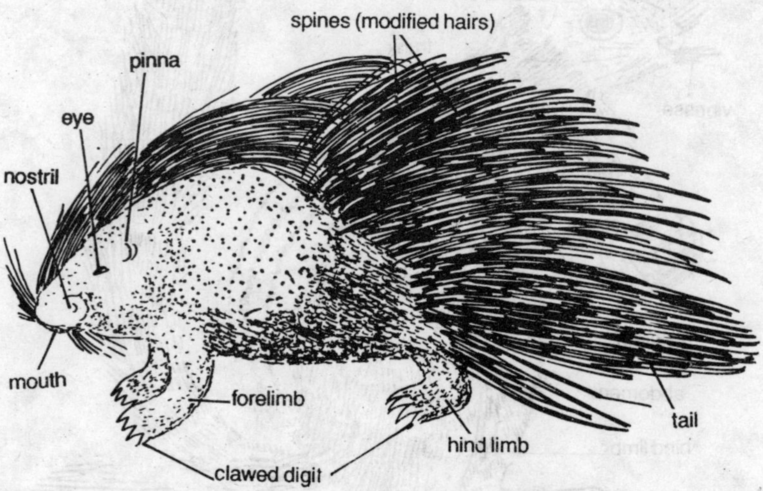

Fig. 1.12. *Hystrix.*

1. It is Indian porcupine commonly known as 'sahi'.
2. It inhibits in the bushes and holes near the fields and hairs. It is nocturnal and herbivorous.

3. Body is covered with long erectile spines which are modified hairs.
4. Eyes and pinnae are small.
5. Tail is short and non-prehensile.
6. The sole of foot is smooth and not covered with rough tubercles.
7. The spines are weapons of offence.
8. Dental formula is i. 1/1, c. 0/0, pm. 1/1, m. 3/3 x 2 = 20.
9. It is found in East Indies, Africa, Europe and India.

FUNAMBULUS

Phylum	-	Chordata
Group	-	Vertebrata
Sub-phylum	-	Gnathostomata
Class	-	Mammalia
Infra-class	-	Eutheria
Order	-	Rodentia
Genus	-	*Funambulus*

Fig. 1.13. *Funambulus*.

1. It is commonly called as 'squirrel' or 'gilhari' in Hindi.
2. Body is elongated and covered with fur.
3. It is arboreal as well as terrestrial and leads an active life on trees and ground. It is diurnal.
4. Five longitudinal stripes of dark colour are present on the back.
5. Tail is long and bushy.
6. The eyes and pinnae are large.
7. The fore-limbs have an inconspicuous thumb.
8. The hind limbs have four clawed digits.
9. The soles of fore-limbs are nacked while that of hind-limbs are hairy.
10. The dental formula is i. 1/1, c. 0/0, pm. 0/0, m. 3/3 x 2 = 16.
11. They are found all over the world except Australian region.

RATTUS

Phylum	-	Chordata
Group	-	Vertebrata
Sub-phylum	-	Gnathostomata
Class	-	Mammalia
Infra-class	-	Eutheria
Order	-	Rodentia
Genus	-	*Rattus*

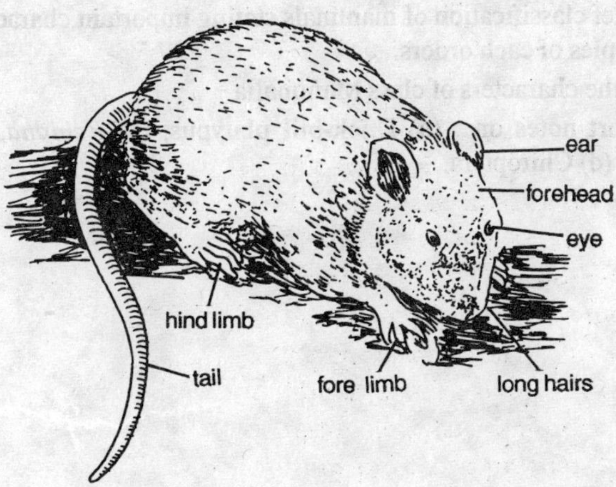

Fig. 1.14. *Rattus rattus.*

1. It is commonly known as 'black rat'.
2. The body is long, cylindrical and covered with small soft hairs.

3. Protruding from the sides of the face are long, bristle-like hairs called *vibrissae*.
4. The snout is elongated like squirrel, and the tail is long without hair.
5. Limbs are short and digits ending into claws.
6. Canines are absent and the dental formula is i. 1 /1, c. 0/0, pm. 0/0, m. 3/3 x 2 = 16.
7. Most successful mammals exhibit a wide range of adaptations viz. terrestrial, subterrestrial, cursorial, jumping, aquatic and volant.
8. Feed on avarity of plant and animal substances.
9. Carrier of several disease-germs like, cholera, plague, jaundice and trichinosis of swine.
10. It is cosmopolitan in distribution.

Revision Questions

1. Give an account of distinguishing characters and outline classification of mammals.
2. Give a brief classification of mammals stating important characters and examples of each orders.
3. Describe the characters of class Mammalia.
4. Write short notes on : (a) Duck-bill platypus, (b) *Echidna*, (c) Pangolin, (d) Chiroptera.

2

Rabbit (Oryctolagus)

Kingdom	-	Animal
Sub-kingdom	-	Metazoa
Phylum	-	Chordata
Sub-phylum	-	Vertebrata
Class	-	Mammalia
Sub-class	-	Theria
Order	-	Lagomorpha
Genus	-	*Oryctolagus*
Species	-	*cuniculus*

Distribution

It is now cosmopolitan (world-wide) in distribution although their original home was Western Europe and Africa but gradually they were spread all over the world by man. They increase in number wherever they found favourable condition and become harmful to the agriculture.

Habits and Habitat

The rabbit occurs in the fields, grass-lands and open-wood-lands. It is a *fossorial* animal i.e. it lives in burrows which, it digs into the ground with the help of claws of fore-limbs. The burrow often has several side passages and may have more than one outlet or exit. It is called the *warren*.

They are nocturnal in habit and they feed on green vegetation, carrots etc. i.e. *herbivorous.* For feeding they come out of their burrows in dim light, such animals are called *crepuscular. Coprophagy,* an interesting feature in feeding, is that the food is passed twice through the alimentary canal. It eats its semiliquid faeces passed in night. They are *gregarious* as they often move about in groups.

They are fast runners and cover about 32-40 kms in an hour. The average life-span of a rabbit is about eight years. It sexually matures within six months and it breeds four times a year and gives rise to 5-8 young ones in each litter. The gestation period is about 30 days. It is *polygamous* i.e. one male lives in the company of many females.

The female shows parental care as the newly born young ones are deaf, blind and naked (without hairs) helpless creatures. Then mother feeds them with milk and they develop eyes, ears etc.

Its natural enemies are men, dogs, cats, snakes, jackals, owls etc. On seeing an enemy, it thumps its hind-limbs on ground producing a warning sound to others for hide.

Economic Importance

It is harmful as well as useful animal. As harmful animal it spoils the fields by making burrows, damages crops and vegetables, and grass of the lawns. They befoul the grass of the lawns and pasture with their excreta. On the other hand it is useful in the sense as it provides a good fur for gloves, purses etc. Their meat is palatable which is very delicious. They are also used for various biological and medical researches in hospitals and educational institutions. It is a good pet and is domesticated.

Important Adaptations

Although rabbits are defenceless and have several enemies, yet they are capable of maintaining their existence. This is due to several adaptations found in them, some of the adaptations are :

1. Protective colouration and burrowing mode of life.
2. They are fast runners and always remain alert.
3. They are *crepuscular* i.e. they feed and move about in dimlight.
4. Senses of smell and hearing are keen.
5. They have got a wide field of vision.
6. They can live in different environmental conditions.
7. The rate of reproduction is very high. .
8. Parental care is taken by mother.

RABBITS AND HARES

Rabbits and hares are closely related to one another hence for a long time they were kept together in the genus *Lepus*. But both show a number of differences hence are given separate generic names, *Oryctolagus* for rabbit and *Lepus* for hare.

A number of species of *Lepus* are found in different parts of world. *L ruficandatus* is found in North India, it is red-brown in colour; *L.nigricollis,* black napped hare found in plains; *L. dayanus* is found in the deserts of India. The points of differences are :

Oryctolagus	*Lepus*
1. It is comparatively small in size, the colour is brown and is a pet animal.	1. Comparatively large, the colour on dorsal surface is brown while that of ventral surface is white. It is wild animal.
2. It digs burrows like branching tunnels having several exits.	2. It does not forms a burrow and lives alone beneath the grasses bushes in pits.
3. It is crepuscular in nature i.e. comes out of burrow in dimlight	3. It is nocturnal and comes out in dark.
4. The body is adapted for living in burrows, so that the snout is narrow, ears and limbs are short and the digits are provided with powerful claws.	4. Its body is adapted for fast running hence the snout is broad, ears are big, hind-limbs are very large for leaping and the claws are weak.
5. The colour of ears is the same as that of rest of the body.	5. The tips of ears are black.
6. It is *gregarious* i.e. lives in groups.	6. It is *solitary* in habit and does not live in group.
7. It runs at a speed of 32-40 km/hr.	7. It runs at a speed of about 56-72 km/hr. So the nasal passage are comparatively large.
8. A distinct inter-parietal bone is present in skull.	8. Inter-parietal bone is found fused with supraoccipital.
9. As soon as there is a danger of enemy it gives thumping on the ground by its hind legs, erects its tail to show its white hairs. This is a warning signal.	9. It gives warning signal by rubbing its teeth and also erects its tail.
10. It gives birth to 5-8 children at a time.	10. It gives birth to only two babies at a time.
11. When young ones are born, they are weak, blind, deaf naked (without hair).	11. The young ones born are strong, covered with hair and their both eyes are opened.
12. Just infront of the incisors there is a deep notch (hare-lip) in the upper lip.	12. The notch is absent in *Lepus*.

EXTERNAL FEATURES

Shape, size and colour

It is a quardruped, about 46 cm in length and weighted about 2.25 kg., average 1.8 kg. Its body is pointed anteriorly and broad posteriorly which is covered with short, soft, close-set woolly fur. Fur keeps body temperature constant by preventing an undue loss of heat. The body temperature remains 101.8°F or 38.8°F. The colour of european wild rabbit, *Oryctolagus cuniculus* is brown on the dorsal and lateral sides and the ventral side is white whereas the domesticated verieties may be white, black, white with black patches etc.

Divisions of body

The body of rabbit is divisible into four regions. The *head, neck, trunk* and *tail.*

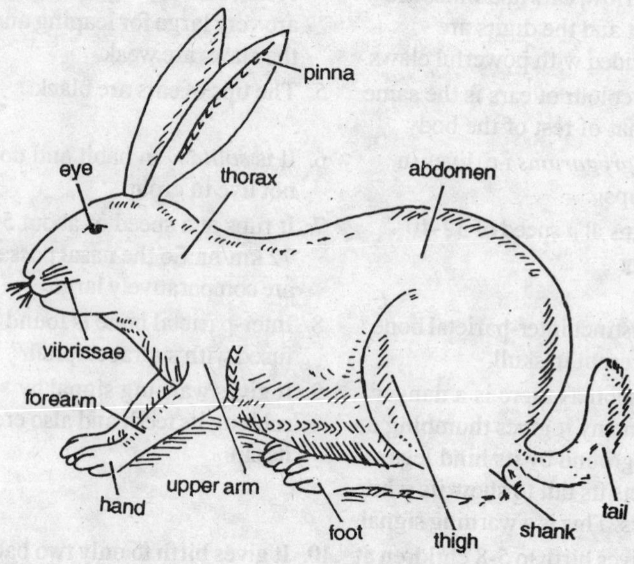

Fig. 2.1. *Oryctolagus.* External features.

Head

Head is large some what ovoid and flattened, and extends anteriorly into a blunt *snout* or *muzzle.* The snout is made up of long upper and lower jaws. Head is situated at an angle with the rest of the body and has a terminal *mouth* at its anterior end. The mouth is a transverse slit-like aperture bounded by two soft, movable hairy *lips,* the *upper* and *lower.*

The upper lip is divided in the middle into right and left halves due to a vertical cleft which is continuous upto nostrils, such a condition is known as *hare-lip* from this cleft long, front teeth, *the incisors* are exposed. Just above the mouth there are two oblique, oval openings of *external nares,* situated under the fleshy tip of snout. From the sides of upper lip thick, tactile hairs or feelers or *vibrissae* or *whiskers* project outwards. These are sensory in function as they have nerve-endings at their bases. A pair of large, prominant eyes are situated above the nares and are laterally placed. Each eye is provided with movable *upper* and *lower eyelids* with few eye-lashes, and a small third eye-lid or *nictitating membrane*. The nictitating membrane is also movable, white in colour and is situated at the inner or anterior end of the eye. At the top of the head, a pair of large, movable trumpet-shaped *external pinnae* or *ears* are situated. Each pinna has an *external auditory meatus* and the tympanic membrane, is situated at the end of external auditory meatus.

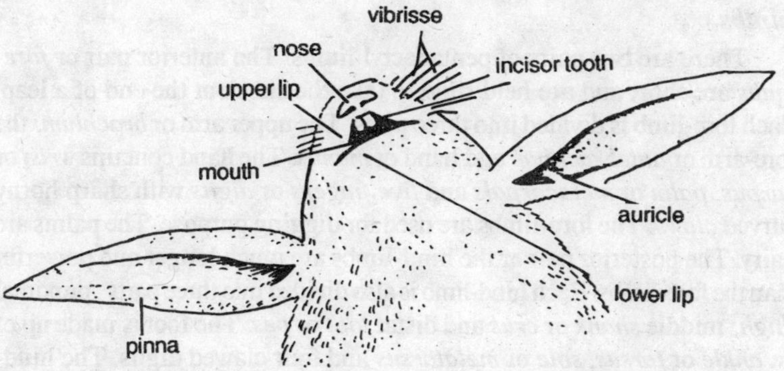

Fig. 2.2. Showing the position of mouth.

Neck

The neck connects the head and trunk. It permits the animal to turn its head about. It is short, therefore, the ears are long and flexible so that they can be turned in any direction to catch the sound.

Trunk

Following neck is the trunk region. It is somewhat cylindrical and divided into two parts : anterior narrow *thorax* and posterior broad *abdomen*. The thorax is firm due to presence of ribs and sternum in its wall. It protects the heart and lungs which are present in its thoracic cavity. On the ventral side of abdomen and thorax there are 4-5 pairs of *nipples* or *teats* or *mammae* on which milk glands or *mammary glands* open out. Teats are also found in males but they are non-functional or vestigial. The abdomen is devoid of ribs and sternum. Its cavity is called *abdominal cavity.* At the posterior end of the body, between trunk and tail, there is anus. In front of anus lies a *urinogenital aperture.* This part where anus and urinogenital openings are found is called *perineum.* In the male, urinogenital aperture is situated at the tip of *penis.* Penis is a cylindrical structure covered with a fold of loose skin, the *prepuce.* On either side of penis, there is an oval pouch of skin, the *scrotal sac* containing the testes. In female, the urino-genital aperture is slit-like and is called *vulva.* There is a rod-like structure situated at the anterior margin of the vulva, called *clitoris,* which is homologous to penis of male. In both the sexes, there is a pair of hairless depressions on the sides of the anus. These are called *perineal pouches.* Each pouch possesses a papilla on which opens the *perineal gland.* The secretion of the perineal glands has a strong odour, characteristic of rabbit.

Limbs

There are two pairs of pentadactyl limbs. The anterior pair or *fore-limbs* are short and are held rigid to take the shock at the end of a leap. Each fore-limb is divided into three parts. The upper arm or *brachium;* the fore-arm or *antebrachium* and hand or *manus.* The hand contains *wrist* or *carpus*, *palm* or *metacarpals* and *five fingers* or *digits* with sharp horny curved *claws.* The fore-limbs are used for digging purpose. The palms are hairy. The posterior pair or the hind-limbs are much longer and powerful than the fore-limbs. Each hind-limb is also divided into three parts : proximal *thigh;* middle *shank* or *crus* and distal *foot* or *pes.* The foot is made up of an *ankle* or *tarsus*, *sole* or *metatarsus* and four clawed digits. The hind-limbs are main locomotory organ. The sole is hairy.

Tail

A short, bushy tail is found at the end of trunk. It is usually curved upwards. In the wild-rabbit, its lower side is white which is used for warning signal to other rabbits when danger approaches.

LOCOMOTION

The mode of locomotion in rabbit may be of three types, *walking running* and *leaping.*

3

Mammalian Skin

The vertebrate integument consists of the skin and its derivatives. It may be considered a compound organ. Morphologically it is compound because it is structurally double, being made up of *epidermis* and *dermis* or *corium.* Embryologically it is compound organ because epidermis arises from the *ectoderm* and the dermis arises from the *mesoderm.* Physiologically the integument is also a very versatile organ, since it performs a number of functions that it may be quite approciately termed as, "Jack of all the trades".

EPIDERMIS

It is the outermost layer of skin or integument and present above the dermis or corium. The cells of epidermis are arranged in stratified layers as follows :

(i) Stratum germinativum or Stratum Malpighii or Malpighian layer (in honour of Malpighi, 1628-1694).

It is the lowermost layer, thick and wavy in appearance. Its lowermost cells are columner and receive nutritive substances from the dermis. These cells divide continuously due to which new cells are formed, they push old cells upwards. In old cells the cytoplasm shows some changes, their shape is also changed first oval then flat. Their walls become thicker at the expense of the cytoplasm.

(ii) Stratum granulosum

It is sevêral layers in thickness next to Malpighian layer. It is called granulosum because upon the break down of Malpighian nuclei of the old cells of stratum Malpighii, *keratohyalin* granules are formed in cytoplasm which give it an appearance of greater density.

(iii) Stratum lucidium

It is apparently homogenous lies just outside the stratum granulosum and is derived from it. The keratohyalin of stratum granulosum becomes changed into a different chemical compound called *eleidin*. This layer is absent where the skin is particularly thick but it reaches a conspicuous development in the nails.

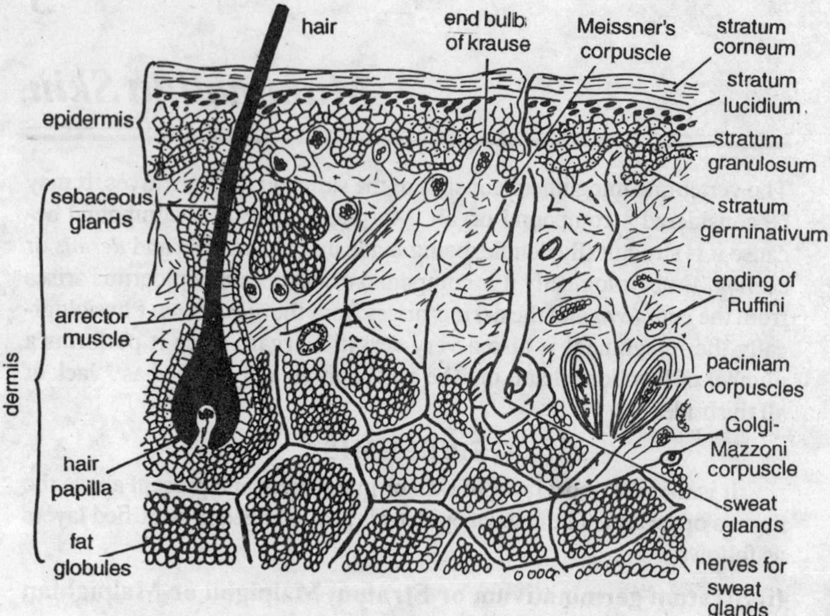

Fig. 3.1. V.S. of skin of a mammal.

(iv) Stratum corneum

Eleidin is finally changed into *keratin*. The cells having lost their nuclei, become scale-like and dry forming the outermost layer i.e. stratum corneum. The process of keratin formation is called *keratinization* or *cornification*. Keratin is a protein having large amount of sulphur, containing aminoacids like cystine and methionine. Keratin is insoluble in water, so that it makes a protective covering of the body. Besides it helps in the formation of hair, nails, horns and hoofs (exoskeleton elements). The cornified cells are not dead and recent researches have shown that they secrete several hormonal substances which retard the cell-division in the stratum Malpighian layer. To keep keratinization active, cornified cells have to be got rid off.

Many pigment cells, *melanophores*, are found among the cells of stratum Malpighii which give colour to the skin. The melanophores have many branches and processes. They *synthesize melanin* pigment for colour. The colour of skin depends upon two factors:

(a) transparency which permits the underlying capillaries to show through as blushing, and, (b) by the presence of pigments, the melanin.

Hairs are found on epidermis, sweat glands open out through minute pores near the hairs. The epidermis is richly supplied by nerve-endings often forming tiny *Merkel's discs.*

DERMIS

It is the vascular and flexible layer beneath the epidermis. It is much thicker than epidermis and remains closely attached to the stratum Malpighii on the upper side. The dermis is formed largely of collagen and elastic fibrous tissue and connective tissue cells like fibroblast, histiocytes and mast cells. In certain regions of the body such as finger-tips, the outer part of the dermis, just under the epidermis, is thrown up into rows of tiny projections or papillae, that form ridges. This is called *papillary layer* of corium or dermis. The roughened papillary layer helps possibly to hold the corium and epidermis together at points on the skin where pressure or friction is frequently applied. There are two types of papillae, *nutritive* and *sensory*. The nutritive papillae containing capillay knot where as sensory papillae occupied by a sensory nerve ending. The remaining fibrous part of dermis is called *reticular layer*. The deeper part of corium forms the *sub-cutaneous layer* characterized by the inclusion of masses of soft fat-cells or *adipose tissue* forming a layer of cells *panniculus adiposus*.

Among many structures embedded in the corium are capillaries, lymph vessels, nerve endings, migrating pigment cells,deposits of glycogen and fat,sweat glands, hairs, sebaceous glands and smooth muscle fibres.The hair, sweat glands and sebaceous glands being down-growth from the epidermis. Derivatives of skin in the mammalian integument are the hair and sweat glands. Sebaceous glands are associated with hair follicles.

HAIRS

Nearly all mammals are covered with hairs developed in *hair-follicles*. Hair follicle is a tube-like invagination of the epidermis formed by stratum Malpighii and lies in the dermis. Each hair is a slender rod, and is composed of two parts: a long slender *shaft* piercing out through the skin and a bulb-like swollen base called *root* remains fixed in the follicle.The dermal cells form a raised structure below the follicle called *dermal papilla*. The papilla is richly supplied by fine blood vessels carrying nourishment which diffuses into the root of the hair. The cells of root constantly divide and the growth of hair takes place. As the new cells are being formed by division, the old cells keep on moving upwards the shaft. Their cytoplasm is changed into keratin and push the shaft from below. Shaft is composed of such keratinized and dead cells, while the root has active cells.

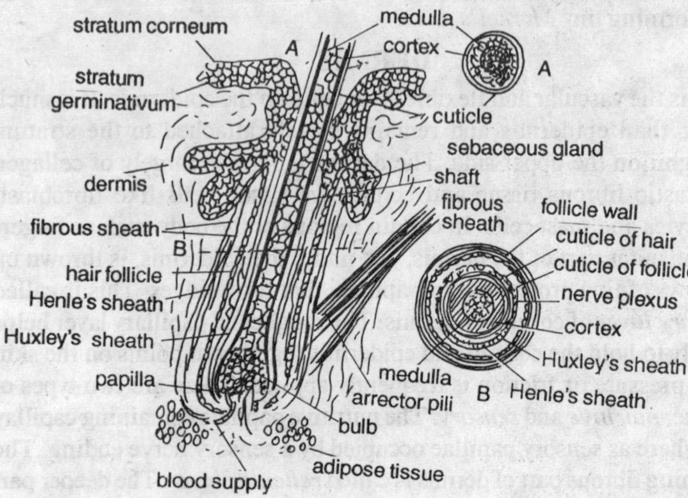

Fig. 3.2. Structure of hair and its follicle.

Three regions can be recognized in the transverse section of shaft. The small cells in the centre are very closely packed so that they have no space between them, this rod-like structure is called *medulla*. Medulla is surrounded by *cortex* formed of flattened cells, often containing pigment granules. The cortex is surrounded by *cuticle* formed of much flattened, scale-like cells.

Between the follicular wall and the shaft are present a few layers of cells-on the outside of cuticle of shaft is a thin layer of follicular cuticle, next to it on outside are thin *Huxley's* and *Henle's layers* and a plexus of nerve fibres between them. The outer most is the follicular wall made up of stratum Malpighii, outside of which is fibrous dermal sheath of the follicle. Near the follicles are present *sebaceous glands*, which are round and multi-cellular structure. These glands open into the follicle. The oily secretion of this gland is called *sebum*, which spreads over the shaft and skin surface keeping the hair supple and skin waterproof. Sebaceous glands are absent on the surface of palm and sole. They are also present where the hairs are absent like lips and glans of penis. Recent investigations show that the formation of vitamin D by the action of sunlight occurs in sebaceous glands.

Attached to hair is a bundle of unstriped muscle fibres, the *errector pili*. Hair is eractile due to action of this muscle which is innervated by the sympathetic nervous system. Thus hair, 'stand on end' during extreme fear, 'goose flesh' are raised in cold and specific emotional stress or hair can be raised as a heat conservation mechanism during cold weather.

Shedding of hair is more or less periodical in certain mammals where as it is slow but steady process in others. New hair is developed from the old papilla and keeps pace with shedding. In addition to sebaceous glands, following glands are also found in the skin of mammals.

Sweat glands or sudorific glands

They are tubular and coiled glands which are found deep in the dermis. Glandular cells are present in the coiled part of the gland which secrete a fluid called *sweat*. The sweat contains salt water. From each gland, a duct arises which extends through dermis and epidermis to open on the surface of skin. These structures thus act as accessory kidneys.

The sweat glands are not uniform in distribution being more numerous on the palms and soles than elsewhere and attaining a notable greater size under the arm-pits. In rabbit they are maximum in lips. In human being it has been estimated that there are two and a half million of sweat glands in the skin, each with separate pore. Sweat glands are absent in *Echidna* (egg-laying mammal), some insectivores and water living Sirenia and Cetacea. Previously it was believed that the sweat glands are absent in dogs, but not it has been confirmed that very few sweat glands are present in hairy parts. They do not help in regulation of body temperature by protecting the skin from an excessive raise in temperature (*Aoki* and *Wada*, 1951). The coiled sweat glands are of two types :

1. *Eccrine glands*. These are thermoregulator eccrine glands of epidermal in origin, whose cells secrete continuously into a duct (merocrine secretion).
2. *Apocrine glands*. These are thermoregulator and scent types arise as an outgrowth of hair follicles, possess storage sacs and secrete by cellular budding or disintegration into the duct (apocrine secretion).

Eccrine sweat is a hypotonic solution of sodium chloride, potassium, urea, lactic acid, little protein and mucopolysaccharides. Apocrine, secretion is thicker which may contain some fat and pigment in addition to other normal constitutents.

The main function of sweat glands is to regulate body temperature.

Mammary glands

Found in mammals alone, they are modified sweat glands and produce milk. They are highly branched and apocrine. When not active they consist of thin ducts which receive many excretory ducts. During pregnancy when the stratum Malpighii lining the excretory ducts, begins to divide quickly producing tiny *sacs* or *alveoli* at the blind end. A number of alveoli constitute a lobule of the gland and many such lobules make up the mammary glands. Excretory ducts from the lobules unite to form large ducts. Large ducts meet with each other forming the main duct. These main ducts open outside separately. The skin at such places is raised to form *nipples*. The nipples are abdominal in rabbit but thoracic in human. The number of nipples varies from two in man, horse, elephant, monkey to twenty five in opposum. The number of main ducts in the nipples also varies. In mice, ruminant and insectivores, there is only one duct in each nipple, 2 or 3 in pigs, and 20 ducts in man which open separately. The nipples are absent in egglaying mammals, here the mammary glands resemble sebaceous glands and the ducts of glands open the surface or in a skin-pouch over the abdominal region.

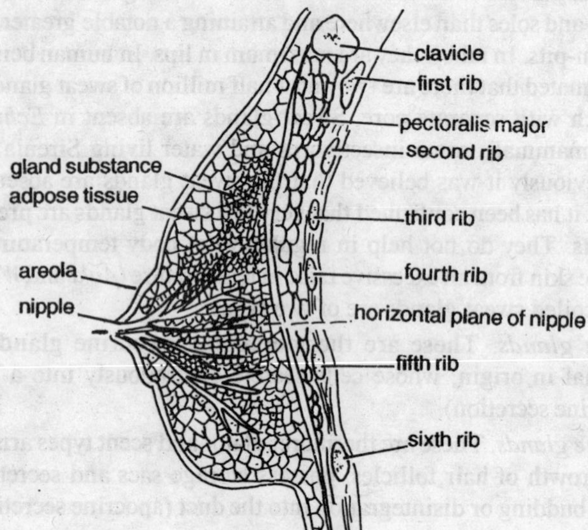

Fig. 3.3. The mammary gland.

When the mammary glands are active in males, the condition is known as *gynecomastia*. Sometimes milk is present in new-born baby called '*witch's milk*'.

Meibomian or Tarsal glands

Along the edge of each eyelid there is a line of modified sebaceous glands,called meibomian glands or tarsal glands. In man there are about 30 glands in upper eyelid and 20 in lower eyelid. They secrete an oily substance which lubricates the cornea to keep it smooth.

Preputial glands, vulval glands and scent glands

These integumentary alveolar glands are associated with sexual activity in various mammals. Preputial glands in male and vulval glands in female are found in the genital organs. The scent glands act as an allurement to the opposite sex. The scent glands are located near the anus as in musk deers, dogs, foxes etc called *civet glands.* In rabbit they are present between the anus and penis or vulva and are called *inguinal glands.* Their structure is similar to that of sweat glands (apocrine type).They secrete an odorous substance which gives the characteristic odour of particular animal.

Wax glands or Ceruminous glands

These glands are present in the passage of external ear. They are tubular glands with their inner ends coiled like the sweat gland. In function they resemble sebaceous glands. They produce a waxy or gummy substance more or less like oil than sweat. They serve to arrest sand particles.

Zeis glands

These are sebaceous glands associated with the follicles of eye lashes. Their secretion keeps the eye lashes smooth and oily.

Functions of Integument

Shape. It helps in maintaining a characteristic shape of the body.

Protection. It protects the body from mechanical injuries due to friction, from harmful bacterial entry etc. It prevents the excessive loss of water due to evaporation. In aquatic animals it prevents the absorption of excess water. In some animals skin protects the animal from its enemies by changing the colour. Claws, nails etc. are derivatives of skin help in defending them.

Regulation of body temperature. The sweat glands of skin help in regulation of body temperature by evaporating sweat. Many structures such as hair and layers of fat are present in the skin to prevent the heat loss from the body.

Removal of waste products. Metabolic wastes of body are removed along with sweat. The shedding of keratinized dead cells of the epidermis is a sort of excretion.

Storage of reserve food. Fat is stored in the form of sub-dermal fat in the skin. In whales such a fatty layer is called *blubber*.

Secretion of useful substances. The mammary glands secrete milk, sebaceous glands secrete sebum and meibomian glands secrete oily substance which are useful to the animals.

Bone formation. The dermis gives rise to the dermal bones of the skull. In some reptile (turtle) it forms the dermal long plates.

Locomotion. The skin is elastic, therefore, it allows different types of locomotory movements. In some mammals like bat, the skin forms *patagium*, which is nearly a fold of skin, and helps the animals in flight. Same structure is also seen in *Draco* (flying lizard). In frog, web of hind-limb helps in locomotion.

Transmission of stimuli. The fine nerve-endings and tectile corpuscles provide sensory function to skin. It receives stimuli to touch, pain, temperature etc. and convey them to the central nervous system.

Absorption. It serves to absorb oil and ointment to certain extent.

Formation of vitamin-D. Sebaceous glands help in the formation of vitamin-D. Vitamin-D is synthesized in human skin under the influence of solar rays in ultra violet region of the spectrum (wave-length 290-320 nm) that convert the provitamin 7-dehydrocholesterol. One square centimetre of human skin can synthesize upto 8 I.U. of this vitamin in three hours (only 0.01-2.5 mg per day is synthesized).

Sexual attraction. It helps in sexual selection. The colour of skin and the secretion of perineal glands help in attraction of opposite sex during breeding season.

Respiration. Very slight exchange of gases may occur through the skin (frog).

4

Endoskeleton

The endoskeleton is chiefly made up of bones with very little cartilage. Bones may be *cartilaginous* or *replacing* formed from the cartilage and *membranous* or *dermal bones* which are formed by the ossification of connective tissue. Patella or knee bone is a *sesamoid bone* formed by the ossification of certain tendons.

The endoskeleton can be studied under two headings.

I. *Axial skeleton*. which includes the *skull, vertebral column, ribs* and *sternum*. It lies along the longitudinal axis of the body.

II. *Appendicular skeleton*. includes the *girdles* and *limb-bones*.

AXIAL SKELETON

Skull

Broadly the skull of rabbit can be divided into (1) Cranium, (2) Sense capsules, (3) jaws and (4) Hyoid apparatus.

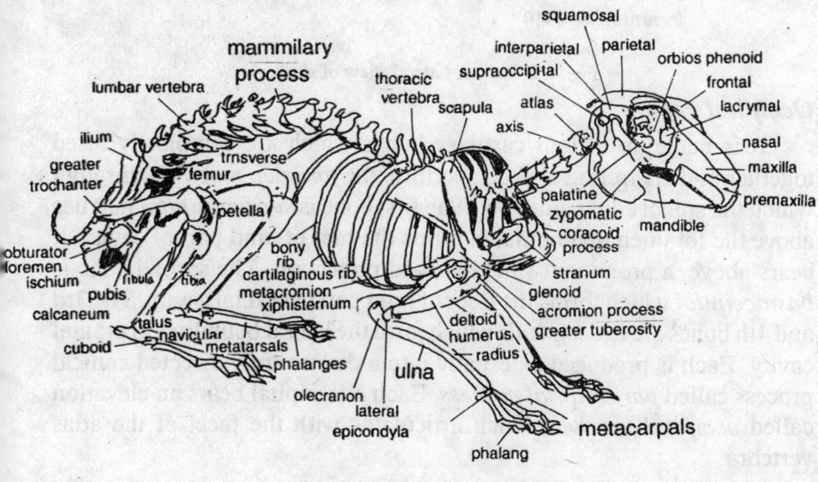

Fig. 4.1. Skeleton of a rabbit.

1. Cranium

The cranium forms the posterior hollow part of skull, containing brain in it. It is made up of 15 bones and these bones are arranged in three regions:

(a) posterior *occipital region*
(b) middle *parietal region*
(c) anterior *frontal region*

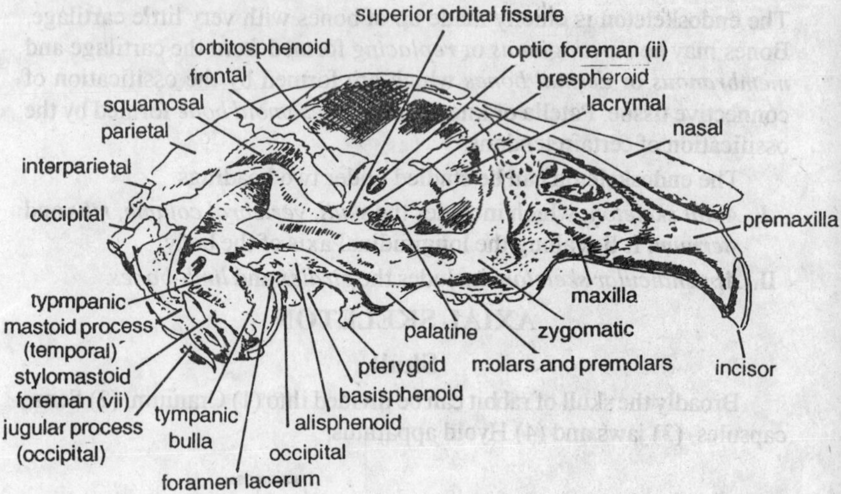

Fig. 4.2. *Rabbit.* Lateral view of skull.

Occipital region

It is made up of four cartilage bones which are completely fused together and encircling a large aperture, the *foramen magnum*, through which the spinal cord comes out. The first bone is *supraoccipital* that lies above the foramen magnum and forms the roof of hind part of cavity. It bears above, a prominent shield-shaped projection. The second bone is *basioccipital* which forms the floor of hind part of cranial cavity. The 3rd and 4th bones are *exoccipitals* which form the lateral boundries of cranial cavity. Each is produced externally into a downwardly directed conical process called *paroccipital process*. Each exoccipital bears an elevation called *occipital condyle* which articulates with the facet of the atlas vertebra.

Parietal region

This region joins the occipital segment dorsally as well as ventrally but separated laterally due to presence of *auditory capsule* and *squamosal*. It is made up of six bones *basisphenoid* -which is a median triangular bone united behind with basioccipital by a cartilage. Basisphenoid forms the floor of middle part of cranial cavity.*Alisphenoids* are paired, semivertical, irregular bones forming the ventro-lateral walls of the cranial cavity. The *parietals* are paired on the dorsal side forming roof of cranial cavity. They are squarish bones and meet together along the mid-dorsal line by sutures. The *interparietal* is small and triangular bone which

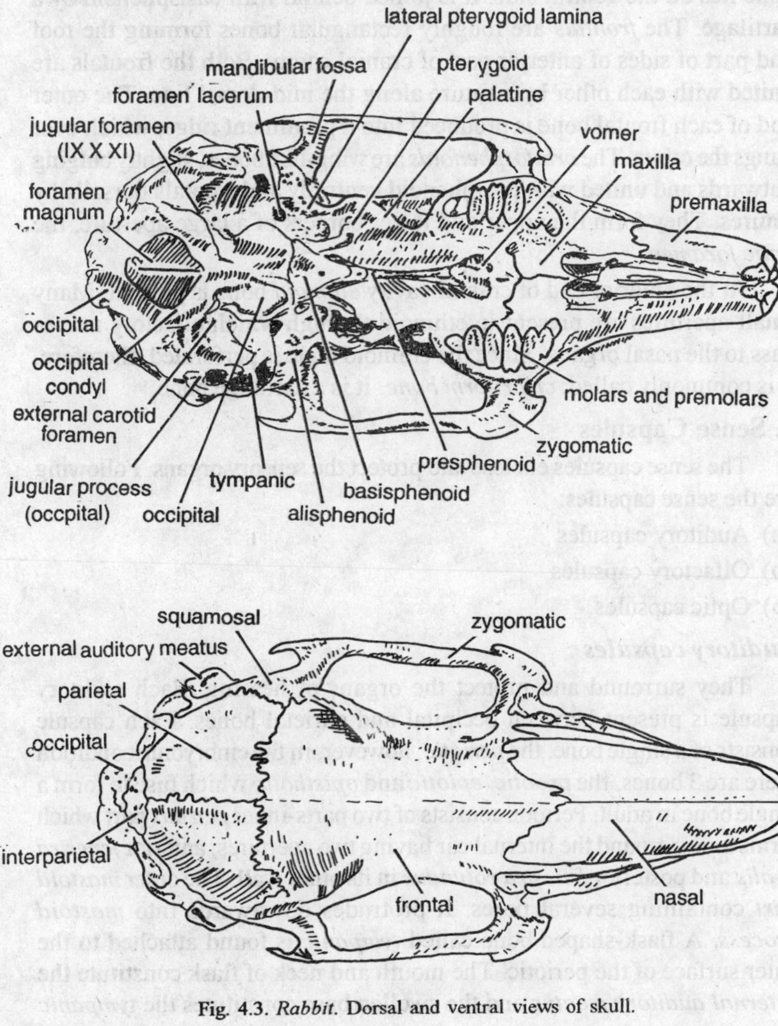

Fig. 4.3. *Rabbit*. Dorsal and ventral views of skull.

separates the parietals from supraoccipitals. The former three bones are cartilagenous where as the remaining three i.e. two parietals and interparietal are membranous bones.

Frontal region

It is the largest of cranial segment and consists of five bones, a *presphenoid bone*, ventrally located; two *orbitosphenoids*, and two *frontals*, dorsally situated. Presphenoid is a median, laterally compressed bone lies on the ventral side. It is joined behind with basisphenoid by a cartilage. The *frontals* are roughly rectangular bones forming the roof and part of sides of anterior part of cranial cavity. Both the frontals are united with each other by a suture along the mid-dorsal line. The outer end of each frontal bone is produced into a prominent ridge, which over hangs the orbits. The *orbitosphenoids* are wing-like bones, slightly bulging outwards and united with presphenoid ventrally and frontals dorsally by sutures. They form the upper and lower borders of a large aperture, the *optic foramen.*

At the anterior end of cranial cavity *ethmoid* bone is present. Many small apertures are present in ethmoid through which olfactory nerves pass to the nasal organs. Since the ethmoid bone is perforated, therefore, it is commonly called, *cribriform bone*. It is a cartilage bone.

2. Sense Capsules

The sense capsules enclose and protect the sensory organs. Following are the sense capsules:

(a) Auditory capsules

(b) Olfactory capsules

(b) Optic capsules

Auditory capsules

They surround and protect the organs of hearing. Each auditory capsule is present between occipital and parietal bones. Each capsule consists of a single bone, the *periotic*, however, in the embryonic condition there are 3 bones, the *prootic, epiotic* and *opisthotic* which fuse to form a single bone in adult. Periotic consists of two parts-inner *petrous* part which forms a ring around the internal ear having two apertures, anterior *fenestra ovalis* and posterior *fenestra rotundus* in its outer wall. The outer *mastoid part* containing several pores. It protrudes downwards into *mastoid process.* A flask-shaped bone called *tympanic* is found attached to the outer surface of the periotic. The mouth and neck of flask constitute the *external auditory meatus* and the swollen base constitutes the *tympanic bulla*. The pinna is attached on the mouth of tympanic bone. The tympanic bulla contains a cavity called *tympanic cavity*. An incomplete ring of cartilage is present a little inside the tympanic cavity. A tympanic membrane is attached on this ring. On the inner side of this membrane are attached *ear ossicles* i.e. *malleus, incus* and *stapes*.

Optic capsules

The optic capsules or *orbits* are present in the frontal segment of cranium. Each orbit is open on three sides and two orbits are separated from each other by *inter-orbital septum* which is a thin and vertical partition.There is an *optic foramen* in the inter-orbital septum for optic nerves. Inter-orbital septum is formed of the orbitosphenoids above, presphenoid below and ethmoid in front. Each orbit is bounded dorsally by *frontal*, antriorly by *maxilla* and *lacrymal* bones, posteriorly by *squamosal* and *alisphenoid* and externally by *zygomatic* arch.

Olfactory capsules

They are situated in front of cranium enclosing the organs of smell. Each capsule is formed of four bones, *vomer*, a pair of *nasals, premaxillae* and *maxillae*. A long and thin vomer is present on the ventral side. A pair of long and flat nasals are found on dorsal side. Premaxillae and maxillae are present on the lateral sides. The two olfactory chambers are separated from each other by a median, vertical bone, the *mesethmoid*. Its anterior part is cartilaginous called *nasal septum* and posterior bony called *ethmoid*. Three pairs of twisted turbinal bones are projected in nasal chamber from ethmoid, nasals and maxillae hence they are called *ethmoturbinals*, *nasoturbinals* and *maxilloturbinals*. They increase the surface area of capsules.

3. Jaws

There are two jaws, the upper jaw and lower jaw.

Upper jaw

The upper jaw forms the roof of snout and consists of two halves or rami, which meet together anteriorly in the middle line. Each ramus is made up of six bones, *premaxilla, maxilla, jugal, palatine, pterygoid* and *squamosal*.

The premaxilla and maxilla form the nasal part of upper jaw. These are joined together by sutures. Premaxilla gives off a *nasal process* on the dorsal and a *palatine process* on the ventral side. The nasal process runs backwards between the nasal and maxilla to meet the frontal. The palatine process of premaxilla passes backwards along with the palate in contact with its fellow of the opposite side. The premaxillae bear incisor teeth at their anterior end. *Maxilla* is a large, irregular bone situated behind premaxilla. A flat *palatine process* is given out from the ventral surface of each maxilla and meets its fellow of the other side to form middle part of hard palate. A flat process from the posterior part of each maxilla passes backwards and joins with the similar forwardly directed process of the squamosal, forming the *zygomatic arch*. The maxillary processes are known as *zygomatic processes*. The *jugal* is a laterally compressed bone forming the middle part of zygomatic arch.The pterygoids are small, irregular, bony plates situated behind the palatines and are joined with the alisphenoids. The *squamosal* is a large irregular bone lying on the lateral sides of the cranium in front of periotic. It gives off two processes, the zygomatic process runs forwards and forms the posterior part of zygomatic arch. It bears on its lower side an articular facet for the lower jaw. The other process is known as *post tympanic process*, which arises from the hind end of squamosal and extends downwards behind the tympanic bone.

Lower jaw

Like upper jaw, lower jaw is also composed of two equal halves or rami, united anteriorly in the middle line by *mandibular symphysis*. Each ramus is a single vertical plate of bone, narrow anteriorly and broader at the posterior end. It is called *dentary*. The anterior half of the dentary is very stout and bears sockets for the attachment of teeth like *premolars, molars* and *incisors*. The posterior half is much thinner and bears three processes (i) The *condyle*: It is highest point of the dentary and articulates with the zygomatic process of the squamosal of upper jaw, (ii) *Coronoid*

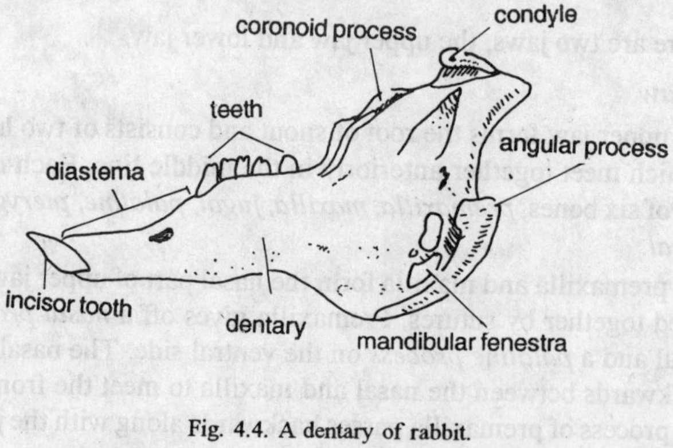

Fig. 4.4. A dentary of rabbit.

process: It is present in front of condyle and forms the outer border of the groove between the grinding teeth and condyle, (iii) *Angular process:* It is present at the posterio-ventral angle of the dentary. The canine teeth are absent in rabbit that is why there is a gap between the incisors and premolars called *diastema*, *Inferior dental foramen* is present for the passage of blood vessels and nerves.

4. Hyoid

It is a bony structure in rabbit consists of a stout body, the *basihyal* and two pairs of horns or *corunae*, the anterior coruna and posterior coruna. The anterior coruna is situated below the tongue and made up of a series of small bones namely-*ceratohyal, epihyal, stylohyal* and *tympanohyal*. The posterior coruna consists of a single bone called *thyrohyal*.

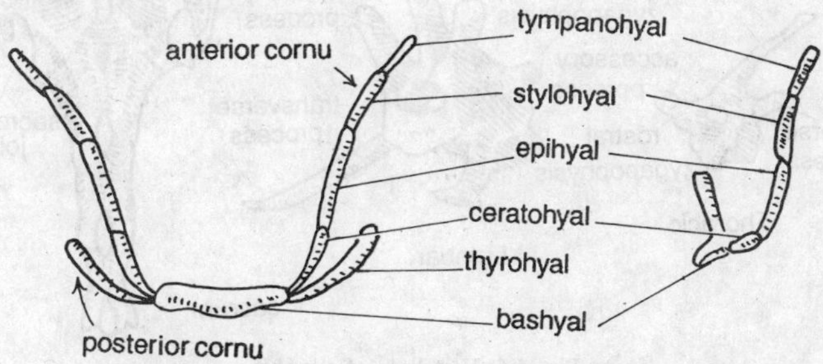

Fig. 4.5. Front and side view of hyoid of rabbit.

Vertebral Column

Vertebral column consist of a large number of vertebra, about 45 in number. Vertebrae are amphiplatyon and inter-vertebral discs are present between the centra of two adjacent vertebrae. Vertebrae are grouped as follows:

1. Cervical vertebrae

There are seven cervical vertebrae present in neck region.

(i) Atlas or first cervical

The first cervical vertebra is called as *atlas*. It is a ring shaped vertabra with broad and horizontal *transverse processes*. *Neural canal* is very large but *neural spine* is very short. On its anterior face are present two concave articular facets called *condylar facets* which receive the two condyles of the skull. This mechanism is helpful for the movement of head on the atlas. *Centrum* and *zygapophyses* are absent. Odontoid process of second vertabra fits with space below the neural canal in atlas. At the base of transverse process a *foramen transversium* is present for the passage of the vertebral artery and vein.

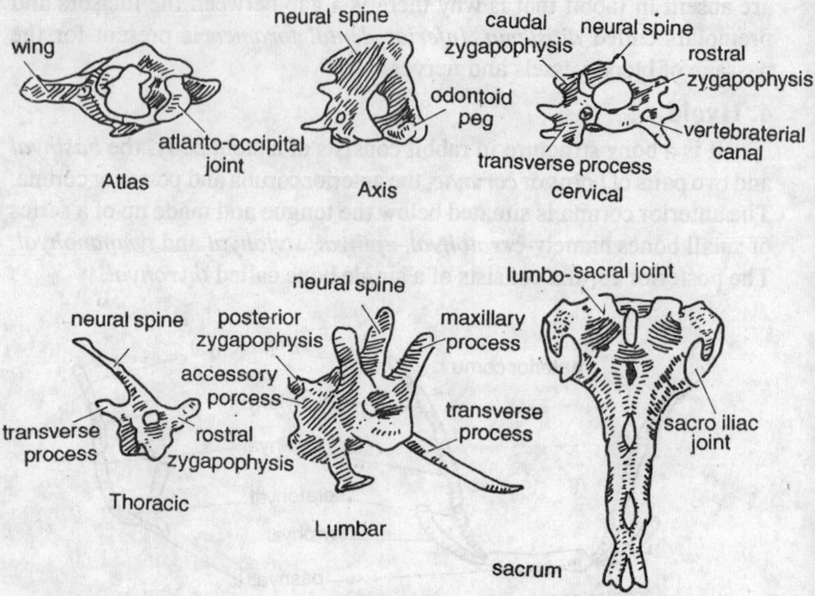

Fig. 4.6. Vertebrae of a rabbit.

(ii) Axis or 2nd cervical

Broad and flat centrum forms *odontoid process* for articulation with the atlas at the anterior end. The neural spine is flat ridge like. The transverse processes are small. The *vertebrarterial canals* or foramen transversium are present. *Prezygapophyses* are absent but two postzygapophyses are present.

(iii) Typical cervical vertebra. (3- 6th cervical)

It is broad and has a small flattened centrum. A large neural canal and a small neural spine are present. Zygapophyses are well developed. Transverse processes are short. The foramen transversium or vertebrarterial canal is present. The crevical ribs are much reduced and more or less incorporated in the vertebra.

(iv) 7th cervical vertebra

It differs from rest of the vertebrae in having a large neural spine. It bears a small concave semilunar facet at the posterior edge of the centrum for the articulation of thoracic ribs. The vertebrarterial canals are absent.

2. Thoracic vertebrae

There are 12 thoracic vertebrae present in chest region. First 6-7 are called *anterior thoracic* and remaining are *posterior thoracic.*

(i) Anterior thoracic

Each vertebra consists of a long neural spine directed backward, neural arch with prezygapophyses (facing downwards and inwards) and postzygapophyses (facing upwards and backwards). Transverse processes are small, bearing ventrally facets for articulation of thoracic ribs. Centrum is short and thick. There are two demifacets. (a) anterior cranial costal (b) posterior caudal costal. The caudal demifacet of one vertebra and the cranial costal demifacet of next vertebra together form a depression which serves for the articulation of capitulum of thoracic rib.

(ii) Posterior thoracic

Possesses well-developed centrum, small neural spine, reduced transverse processes and well developed pre-and post-zygapophyses. The transverse processes do not bear tubercular facet but have complete capitular facet. *Metapophyses* are present

3. Lumbar vertebrae

There are 6-7 lumbar vertebrae. First 2 are called *anterior lumbar* and remaining are posterior.

(i) Anterior lumbar

Prominent neural arch and neural canal, strong neural spine points forward. Large and stout transverse processes point downwards, outwards and forwards. Above the neural arch are two upwardly directed metapophyses, each of which has a pre-zygapophysis. Below post-zygapophysis lies backwardly directed *anapophysis*. *Hypapophysis* is median ventral process of centrum.

(ii) Posterior lumbar

They are similar to anterior lumbar except that they do not bear the hypapophyses.

4. Sacral vertebrae

Containing 3 or 4 vertebrae which fuse to form the *sacrum*, only first articulates with ilium of pelvic girdle. It is believed that only first vertebra is the sacral vertebra and the remaining 3 are the *anterior caudals.* However, each vertebra of sacrum possesses a long and upright neural spine, tubercle like-projections on the upperside representing *zygapophyses*. The first vertebra has large, stout and flattened transverse processes formed by the fusion of rib and transvere processes. Metapophysis is reduced and anapophysis is absent. On the boundaries between the fused sacral vertebrae, three pairs of sacral foramina are present on ventral and dorsal side for the passage of dorsal and ventral rami of the sacral spinal nerves.

5. Caudal vertebrae

There are about 15 or 16 caudal vertebrae. Only the anterior are provided with well developed neural spines, neural arches and zygapophyses. They gradually decrease in size posteriorly until the last vertebra near the end of tail is only left in form of centrum, transverse processes are absent.

Ribs

Ribs are slender, curved like elbow and stout bones which movably articulate with thoracic vertebrae above and unite with sternum below so as to form a basket like framework in the thorax for the protection of internal organs like lungs, heart etc. There are 12 pairs of ribs in rabbit, sometimes there may be 13 pairs. The first rib is short but progressively increase in size upto 6th and again decrease. Each rib is made up of two parts (a) *vertebral part* and (b) *sternal part.*

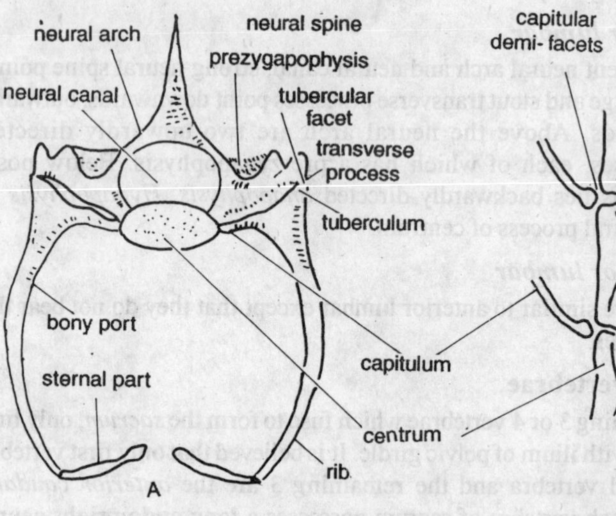

Fig. 4.7. Showing ribs.

(a) Vertebral part

It is the dorsal bony part of a rib, directed outwards, downwards and backwards. In first 9 pairs of ribs, the upper part is forked into a *capitulum* which articulates with the *capitular facets* on the adjacent centra and *tuberculum*, which articulates with the tubercular facet on the underside of transverse processes. Besides, there is a small projection above the tuberculum for the attachment of ligament. This projection is absent in first pair and last 4 pairs of ribs.

(b) Sternal part

It is a small cartilaginous ventral part of ribs directed inwards, downwards and forwards. The sternal part of first seven pairs of ribs are directly attached to the sternum hence these are called *true ribs* while next two pairs i.e. 8th and 9th pairs of ribs are ventrally attached to the 7th pair and are called *false ribs*. Remaining 3 pairs of ribs are free ventrally and are known as *floating ribs*.

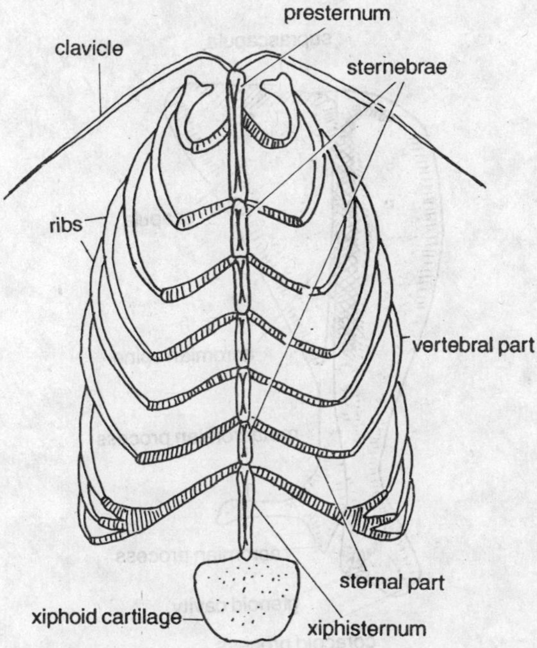

Fig. 4.8. Sternum and ribs of rabbit.

Sternum

It forms the ventral axis of the thorax. It also forms the mid-ventral part of the bony basket in the thoracic region along with ribs and thoracic vertebrae. It is made up of seven bony pieces, called *sternebrae*, lying in a row one behind the other. The sternum is divided into three parts:

(i) *Pre sternum* is in the form of long bone and is also called *manubrium*. It is slightly expanded anteriorly and is produced ventrally into a longitudinal ridge or *keel* the costal part of Ist thoracic rib is attached to it.

(ii) *Mesosternum.* It is constituted by 5 small bones. First four sternebrae are almost of equal size. The last sternebra is very small.

(iii) *Xiphisternum.* It is the 7th sternebra. It is long and slender. Posteriorly, it bears a broad, horizontal plate of cartilage, the *xiphoid cartilage*.

APPENDICULAR SKELETON

It includes girdles and limbs bones.

Girdles. There are two girdles-pectoral and pelvic.

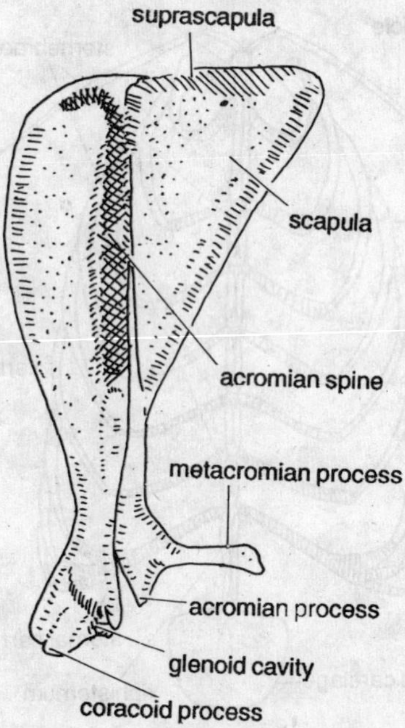

Fig. 4.9. Left half of pectoral girdle of rabbit.

Pectoral girdle

The pectoral girdle lies obliquely outside the ribs and is attached to the axial skeleton by muscles and ligaments. It consists of two similar halves which are separate and each half *osinnominatum* is known as *pectoral arch.* Each half consists of two main elements the *scapula* and *coracoid.* The scapula is thin, flat and triangular bone. Its apex is directed downwards and forwards and the base facing upwards and backwards. A *glenoid cavity* for the articulation of head of *humerus* lies in apex. Overhanging the glenoid cavity is a hook-like process known as *coracoid process.* Coracoid fuses with scapula infront of glenoid cavity. Scapula at its broad base bears a thin strip of cartilage called *suprascapula*. Scapula also bears a prominent *ridge* or *spine* on its outer surface which terminates into an *acromian process*. From acromian a backward process is given which is known as *metacromian*. Both the processes are free. The spine, acromian and metacromian process serve for the insertion of muscles.

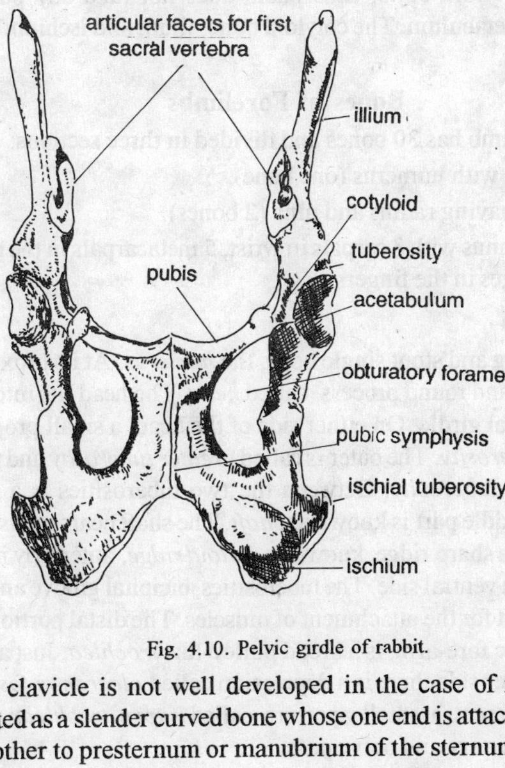

Fig. 4.10. Pelvic girdle of rabbit.

The clavicle is not well developed in the case of rabbit and it is represented as a slender curved bone whose one end is attached to acromian and the other to presternum or manubrium of the sternum.

Pelvic girdle

Like pectoral girdle, pelvic girdle is also made up of two similar halves. Each half is called *osinnominatum* which consists of three bones. Both the halves are firmly articulated above with the sacrum and unite with each other in mid- ventral line. This joint is called *pubic symphysis*. Each half encloses a wide aperture called *obturator foramen*. The three bones are *ilium, ischium* and *pubis.*

The ilium forms the anterior part of osinnominatum. It is narrow behind and expanded in front to articulate with the sacrum. The ischium forms the posterior and dorsal boundary of the obturator foramen. Its hinder end is expanded and thickened to form the *ischial tuberosity*. The pubis is small and situated mid-ventrally forming anterior and ventral boundary of obturator foramen. At the junction of all the three bones there is a cup-shaped cavity, the *acetabulum* for the articulation of head of femur bone. In rabbit between the pubis and acetabulum there is a small bone, *cotyloid bone*, thus pubis does not take any part in the formation of acetabulum. The cotyloid bone, ilium and ischium take part in its formation.

Bones of Forelimbs

Each forelimb has 30 bones and divided in three sections:

1. Upper arm with humerus (one bone).
2. Fore-arm having radius and ulna (2 bones).
3. Hand or manus with 8 carpals in wrist, 5 metacarpals in the palm and 14 phalanges in the fingers.

1. Upper arm

It has a long and stout single bone, the *humerus*. At its proximal end it bears a large and round process, called *head*. The head fits into glenoid cavity of pectoral girdle. On either side of the head, a small projection is present, the *tuberosity*. The outer is called *greater tuberosity* and the inner is called *lesser tuberosity*. Between the two tuberosities is a *bicipital groove*. The middle part is known as *shaft*. The shaft bears on its anterior convex surface a sharp ridge, known as *deltoid ridge,* anteriorly it reaches upto the head on ventral side. The tuberosities, bicipital groove and deltoid ridges are meant for the attachment of muscles. The distal portion, which is attached to the fore-arm, is a broad pulley-like *trochlea*. Just above the trochlea on either side there is a depression called *olecranon fossa*. Near this fossa is present a small aperture called *supra trochlear foramen* through which artery and nerve pass.

2. Fore-arm

There are two bones in fore-arm (i) *Radius* and (ii) *Ulna*. Both these bones are curved like bow. The *radius* is smaller and inner bone. Its proximal half lies in front of the ulna and the distal on the inner side of ulna. At the proximal end of radius is a depression in which the sides of trochlea fit. Its lower end is much expanded and articulates with two carpal bones. Proximally the *ulna* is prolonged beyond the radius and

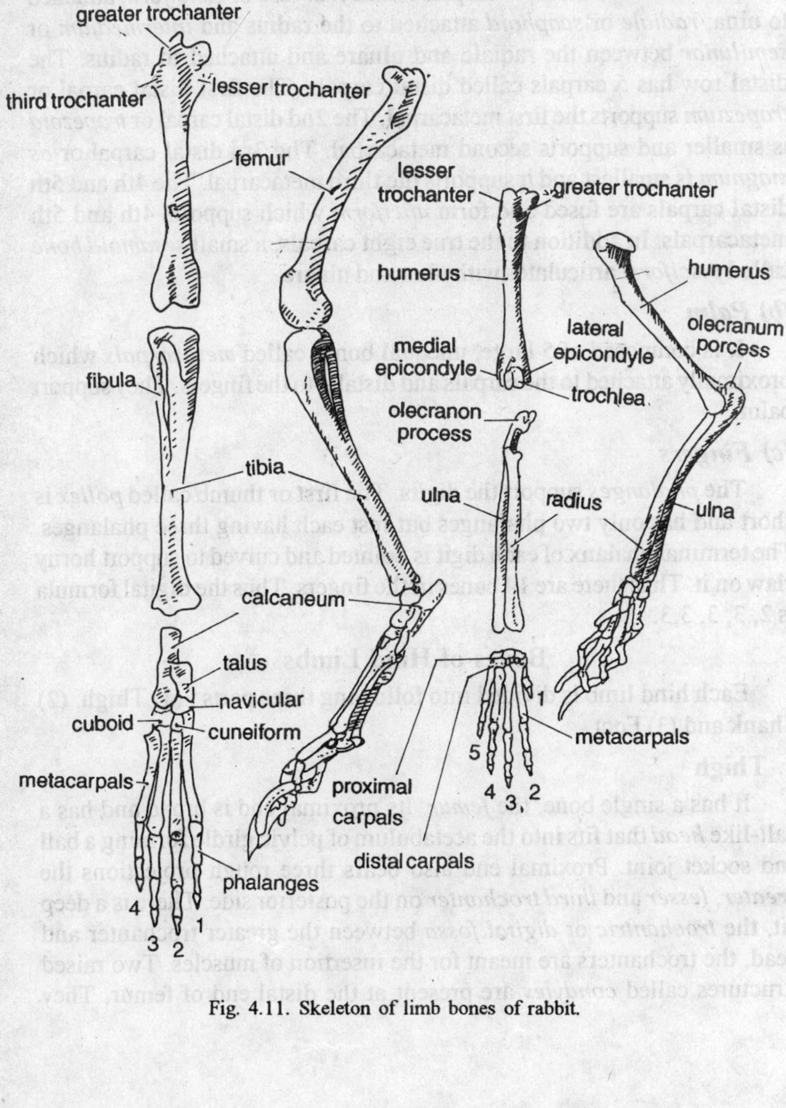

Fig. 4.11. Skeleton of limb bones of rabbit.

form *olecranon process* which bears a deep notch called *sigmoid notch*. The sigmoid notch articulates with the trochlea. The distal end is less expanded and articulates with only one carpal.

3. Hand or manus

It is composed of three parts (a) *wrist,* (b) *palm* and (c) *fingers.*

(a) Wrist

Contains 8 carpals arranged in two rows: the *proximal* and *distal*. The proximal row has three carpals namely: *ulnare* or *cuneiform* attached to ulna; *radiale* or *scaphoid* attached to the radius and *intermedium* or *semilunar* between the radiale and ulnare and attached to radius. The distal row has 5 carpals called distal carpals. The first distal carpal or *trapezium* supports the first metacarpal. The 2nd distal carpal or *trapezoid* is smaller and supports second metacarpal. The 3rd distal carpal or *os magnum* is smallest and it supports the third metacarpal. The 4th and 5th distal carpals are fused and form *unciform* which supports 4th and 5th metacarpals. In addition to the true eight carpals, a small *sesamoid bone* called *pisciform* articulates with ulna and ulnare.

(b) Palm

It is composed of 5 large, unequal bones called *metacarpals* which proximally attached to the carpals and distally to the fingers. They support palm.

(c) Fingers

The *phalanges* support the digits. The first or thumb called *pollex* is short and has only two phalanges but rest each having three phalanges. The terminal phalanx of each digit is pointed and curved to support horny claw on it. Thus there are 14 bones in the fingers. Thus the digital formula is 2, 3, 3, 3,3.

Bones of Hind Limbs

Each hind limb is divided into following three parts : (1) Thigh, (2) Shank and (3) Foot.

1. Thigh

It has a single bone, the *femur*. Its proximal end is broad and has a ball-like *head* that fits into the acetabulum of pelvic girdle forming a ball and socket joint. Proximal end also bears three rough projections the *greater*, *lesser* and *third trochanter* on the posterior side. There is a deep pit, the *trochantric* or *digital fossa* between the greater trochanter and head, the trochanters are meant for the insertion of muscles. Two raised structures called *condyles* are present at the distal end of femur. They enclose a deep notch, the *inter-condylar groove* between them. The condyles articulate with the bones of shank. The inter condylar groove is continuous round the edge of the bone with another groove, called *patellar groove*, which is present on the front side of femur. A bone, *patella* or *knee cap* slides in the pateller groove. Patella is attached to the tibia by ligaments.

2. Shank

It is provided with two bones *tibia* and *fibula*. The tibia is the inner bone which is well-built, stout and strong than the fibula. The fibula is short and slender bone on the outer side. The proximal end of tibia is broad and has two depressions, called *proximal epiphyses*, in which the condyles of femur fit. On the dorsal surface of the proximal end of tibia is a ridge-like projection called *cnemial crest* which provides the surface for attachment of thigh muscles.

3. Foot

It is divisible into three parts:

(a) Ankle

It is made up of 6 bones called *tarsals* arranged in three rows, proximal, middle and distal. Proximal row consists of two tarsals, inner small called *astragalus* and outer large called *calcaneum*. Astragalus articulates above with the tibia. The calcaneum articulates with the fibula. The proximal end of calcaneum is produced backwards in the form of a *calcaneal process* which forms the heel. The *middle row* has only one tarsal, the *central* or *navicular*. It is shifted from its normal position to the inner side of tarsus so it lies infront of the astragalus.

The *third row* possesses three bones. The first distal tarsal is called *entocuneiform* is absent due to absence of first digit or *hallux*. The second distal tarsal or *mesocuneiform* is smallest and supports the second metatarsal. The third distal tarsal or *ectocuneiform* is large and supports the third metatarsal. The 4th and 5th distal tarsals are fixed to form *cuboid* to support 4th and 5th metatarsals.

(b) Sole

The sole has 4 long, slender bones called metatarsals proximally attached to distal tarsals and distally to the toes.

(c) Toes

There are 4 fingers containing 12 phalanges, three in each digit. Small nodule like sesamoid bones are developed on the underside of the foot in connection with joints between metatarsals and phalanges (first, second and third). The last phalanx of each toe possesses a horny curved claw. The digital formula of hind limb is 0, 3,3, 3,3.

5

Coelom and Viscera

COELOM

In the vertebrates, the trunk contains a large mesodermal body cavity or coelom. In other words, 'The space which lies between the body wall and visceral organs which is formed by the splitting of mesoderm is called coelom.' It is lined by coelomic epithelium which is extended as epithelial sheets or mesenteries to cover the visceral organs. The outer epithelium that lines body wall is known as *parietal peritoneum* and the inner epithelium that surrounds the viscera is called as *visceral peritoneum.* The coelom containing a coelomic fluid which protects and allows movement of the visceral organs.

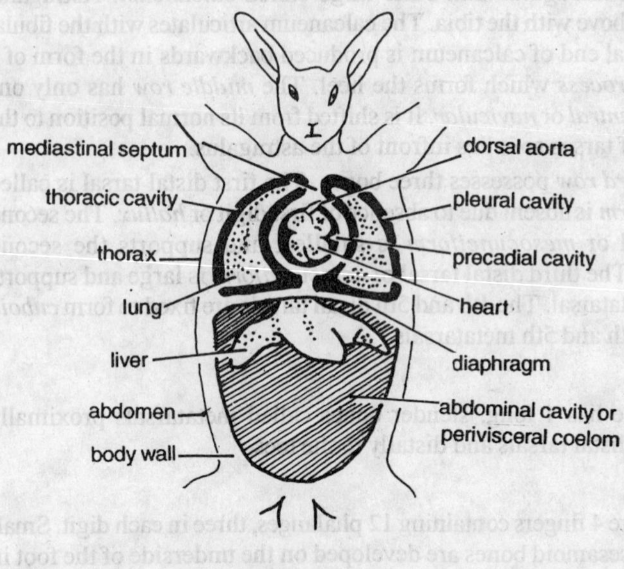

Fig. 5.1. Division of coelom or body cavities in rabbit.

In mammals, *diaphragm*, which is a transverse muscular partition, divides the coelom into two compartments, the anterior is thoracic cavity and the posterior which is very large is abdominal cavity. The thoracic cavity is further divided into three parts, two lateral *pleural cavities* which lodge the lungs and a median *pericardial cavity* in which the heart lodges. In the abdominal cavity digestive system, excretory system and reproductive system are present.

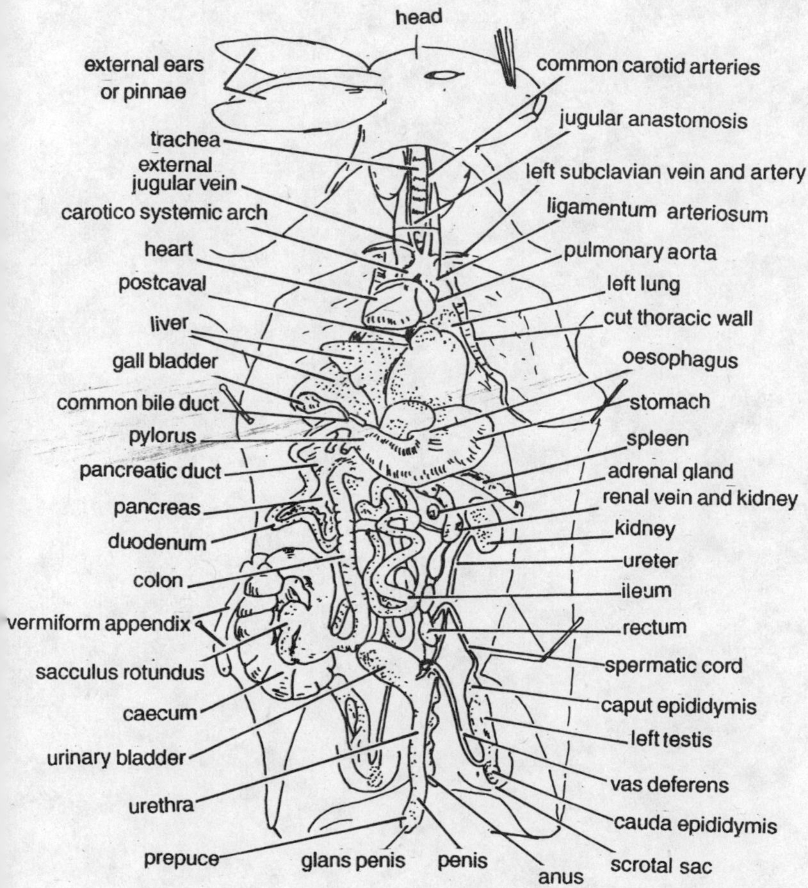

Fig. 5.2. Rabbit showing general anatomy.

VISCERA

The delicate internal organs of the body are collectively called as *viscera* or *visceral organs.* The heart lies in pericardial cavity. Lungs are present in pleural cavities while oesophagus and trachea are present in the thoracic cavity.

Liver lobes are attached to the posterior surface of diaphragm and are situated in the abdominal cavity along with digestive and urino-genital systems etc.

6

Digestive System

In the living organism, while energy is being released by the oxidation of the tissues, it is necessary that replacement may be made from outside sources, or in other words, the food be obtained. It is simply not enough, however, to get food, since energy containing substances can not be utilized until they are liquified and transformed so that they may be taken into blood, to be forwarded to the needy tissues where the actual oxidation of food materials occurs. To accomplish these transformations, digestive system is necessary. All the vertebrates have digestive system comprising a tubular alimentary canal and associated digestive glands.

ALIMENTARY CANAL

The rabbit is a herbivorous animal which feeds on grasses, green leaves and green vegetables. Its alimentary canal is long and coiled tube of varying diameters. It can be divided into following zones:

1. *Ingressive zone* - including mouth and buccal cavity.
2. *Progressive zone* - includes pharynx, oesophagus and stomach.
3. *Degressive zone* - including only small intestine.
4. *Egressive zone* - includes large intestine

1. Ingressive Zone

(a) Mouth

The mouth is relatively small, transverse slit-like terminal aperture situated at the snout. It is bounded by two muscular mobile lips, the *upper lip* and *lower lip*. The lips are covered with skin on the out side and lined with mucous membrane on the inside. The upper lip is called *hare lip.* It has a median vertical cleft, which connects the mouth with external nares above and exposes the front teeth. The vestibule is a narrow space enclosed between the lips and cheeks externally and gums and teeth internally. It is lined with mucous glands. The mouth leads into buccal cavity.

(b) Buccal cavity

It is a space roofed with the *palate*, sides are formed by *jaws* and the floor by *throat*. The anterier part of palate is formed by three bones-premaxillae, maxillae and palatines, that is why it is a hard part hence called *hard palate*. The posterior part of palate is formed of connective tissue and is without any bone, hence this part is called *soft palate*. The posterior free end of the soft palate hangs down as a small flap, the *uvula*. The mucous membrane of hard palate is raised into many transverse ridges called *palatine ridges* or *rugae* and only a few mucous glands are present. A large number of mucous glands are present in the mucous membrane of soft plate, hence it is slippery and moist, therefore, help in swallowing of food. At about 3 mm. from the anterior end, hard palate has a pair of apertures called *nasopalatine ducts* open into buccal cavity. A *Jacobson's*

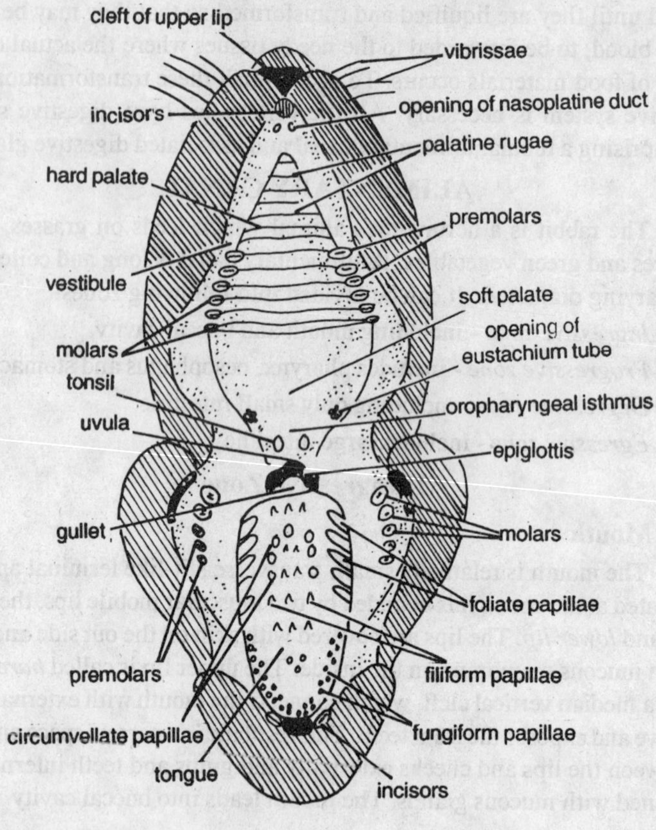

Fig. 6.1. Buccopharyngeal cavity of rabbit.

organ opens into each nasopalatine duct whose function is probably to recognize different kinds of food.

Tongue

A muscular tongue is formed on the floor of buccal cavity. Its anterior end is free and capable of slight protrusion while the posterior end is attached to the floor of buccal cavity along the greater part of its length. The surface of tongue is rough due to presence of many small projections called *taste papillae*. Following types of papillae are present - (a) *Fungiform* which are numerous and situated at the margins of tongue; (b) *Filiform* - which are filamentous, situated at the upper surface of the tongue; (c) *Foliate* which are broad leaf-like situated at the sides of base of tongue and (d) *Circumvallate* which are few in number and large sized situated at the base of tongue. The *taste buds* are situated in these papillae.

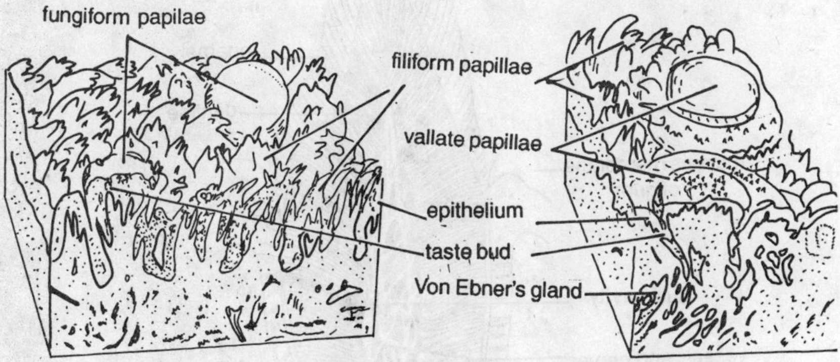

Fig. 6.2. Showing taste buds.

The tongue is made up of connective tissue with numerous interlocking bundle of striated muscles. It is covered by stratified epithelium, smooth on the lower surface, but raised on the above surface to form the taste papillae described above.

Teeth

The teeth are present on both the jaws. They are situated in the sockets, or alveoli of the jaws i.e. *thecodont*. They are of different shapes i.e. *heterodont*. Their number is fixed and they are present in two sets-the *milkteeth* and *permanent teeth*. The milk teeth are deciduous in young condition, and are replaced by permanent teeth in adult. This type of dentition is called *diphyodont*. In rabbit three types of teeth are present, namely *incisors, premolars* and *molars*. The *canines* are absent. As there are no canines, a large gap is formed between the incisors and premolars called *diastema*. The incisors have sharp cutting edges and occur at the anterior tips of the jaws. They are also called *cutting teeth*. The premolars and molars are called the *grinding teeth*. In structure they are similar. The dentition is expressed by *dental formula*. For rabbit this is i 2/1, c 0/0, pm 3/2, m 3/3 x 2 = 28 or simply 2033/1023 x 2 = 28. Here i, c, pm and m refer to incisors, canines, premolars and molars respectively. The numbers above and below the lines indicate the number of teeth in one half of upper and lower jaws. This formula gives half of the total number of teeth to determine the true number, it is doubled.

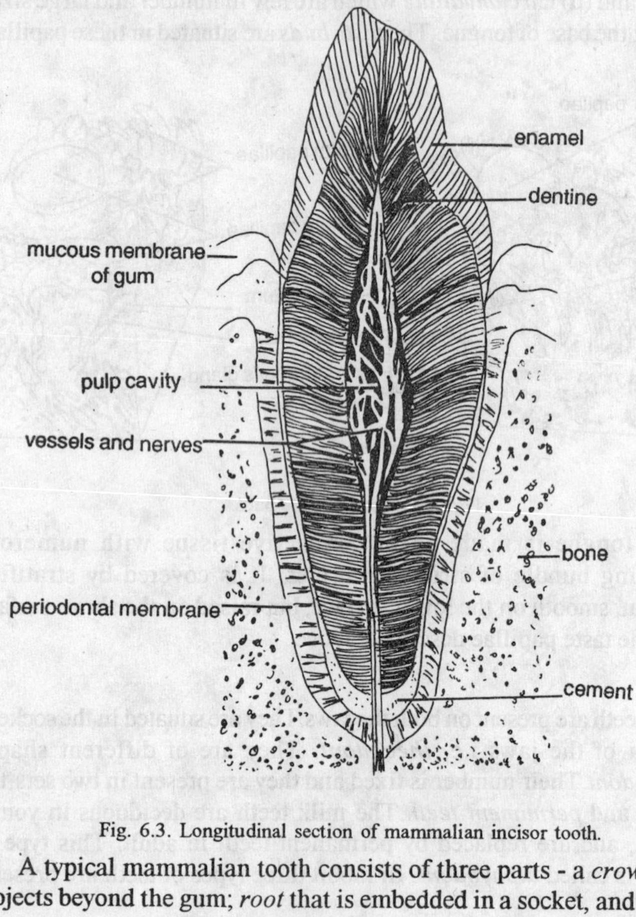

Fig. 6.3. Longitudinal section of mammalian incisor tooth.

A typical mammalian tooth consists of three parts - a *crown* which projects beyond the gum; *root* that is embedded in a socket, and the *neck* which is a transitional region between root and crown. Inside the hollow tooth there is a cavity called *pulp cavity* having blood vessels and nerves passing inside through a passage present at base. The tooth can continue to grow, if this passage remains open. This type of teeth is called *rootless* tooth and its cavity is called *persistent pulp cavity*. Example is the incisors of rabbit. Usually in most of the cases this opening becomes narrow and small, reducing the number of blood capillaries. Thus only that much nutritive substance reaches the tooth by which it can remain alive and its growth is stopped.

The greater part of tooth is composed of a bone-like substance called *dentine* or *ivory*. It is harder than bone and lacks Haversian canals, lacunae and cells. Dentine is permeated by tiny radiating canals called *canaliculi* occupied by protoplasmic processes of dentine secreting cells *odontoblasts* which line the pulp cavity. Dentine varies in composition from animal to animal but in general it has 67% inorganic, 13% water and 20% organic materials. The crown is covered by a white, shining material, the *enamel*. It is hardest substance of the body. Enamel is secreted by cells of ectodermal origin, the *ameloblasts*, are lost after the growing tooth erupts into position in the mouth, so that enamel, once fully formed,cannot grow or be replaced. Enamel consist of 96% of salts chiefly in crystaline form and is seen in clearly prismatic arreys

The root is fixed in bony socket by *cementum* and *periodontal membrane*. In periodontal membrane a network of blood capillaries is present. Collagen fibres form periodontal membrane pass both into the cementum and jaw bone as *Sharpey's fibres* to fit the tooth firmly in the socket.

2. Progressive Zone

Pharynx

It is a short, conical region behind the soft palate. It can be divided into *nasopharynx, oropharynx* and *laryngopharynx*.

The nasopharynx has a common internal nares in the roof and a pair of *openings of Eustachian tubes* on the sides. The Eustachian tubes connect pharynx to the air chamber of middle ear.

The oropharynx receives the buccal cavity and leads posteriorly into the *oesophagus* or food pipe dorsally.

The laryngopharynx is continuous with the oropharynx and leads into *larynx* or *sound box* ventrally. Opening of larynx is called *glottis* bearing a leaf like bilobed, cartilaginous flap, the *epiglottis* at its anterior border. When the animal swallows the food, the soft palate closes the internal nares and the epiglottis closes the glottis, so that the food passes into the oesophagus and never into the trachea.

On the sides of oropharynx are two masses of glandular or lymphoid tissue, the *palatine tonsils.*

Oesophagus

The oesophagus is a short comparatively unmodified part of the alimentary canal between the pharynx and the stomach. The length of oesophagus depend largely upon the length of neck. When not in use it collapses to modest dimensions, but at the time of swallowing, it is capable

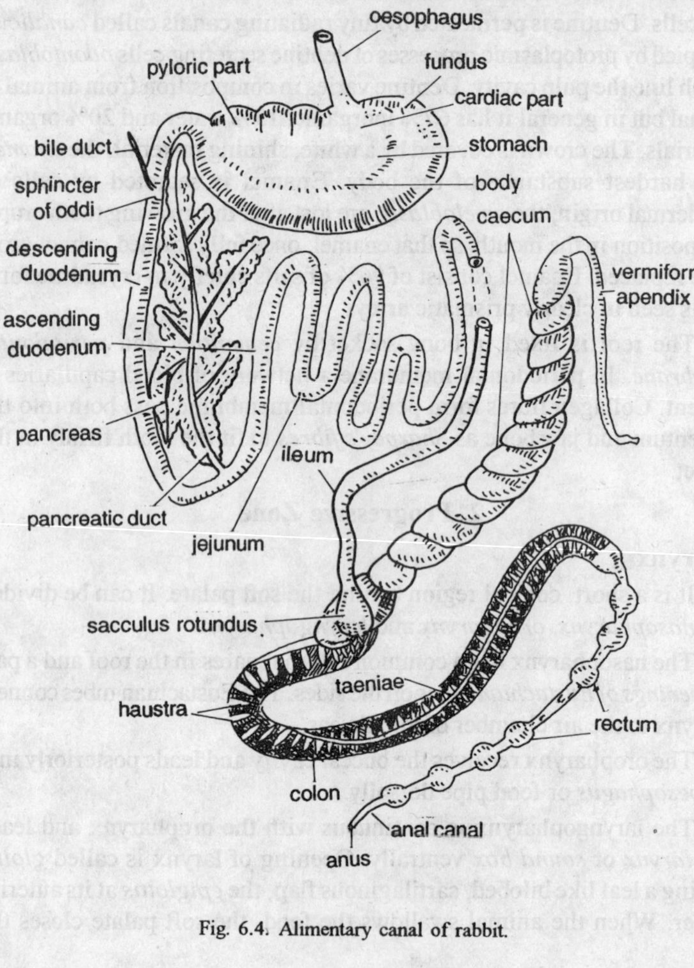

Fig. 6.4. Alimentary canal of rabbit.

of great temporary distension. There are well developed muscles in its wall to help in swallowing.

Histology

The structure of oesophagus shows following layers

The outer layer is thin known as *fibrous layer*. The thick *muscularis layer* follows fibrous layer. It comprises outer layer of longitudinal muscle fibres and inner layer of circular muscle fibres. Muscularis layer is followed by sub-mucosa layer which is followed by a mucosa formed of stratified epithelium. Stratified epithelium has mucous glands, secreting mucous to lubricate the food particles to pass down easily.

Stomach

It is a large, curved sac-like structure situated behind the diaphragm slightly towards the left side in the abdominal cavity. The part of stomach which receives the oesophagus is *cardiac part,* where as the part that joins intestine is the *pyloric part.* The portion of stomach between the

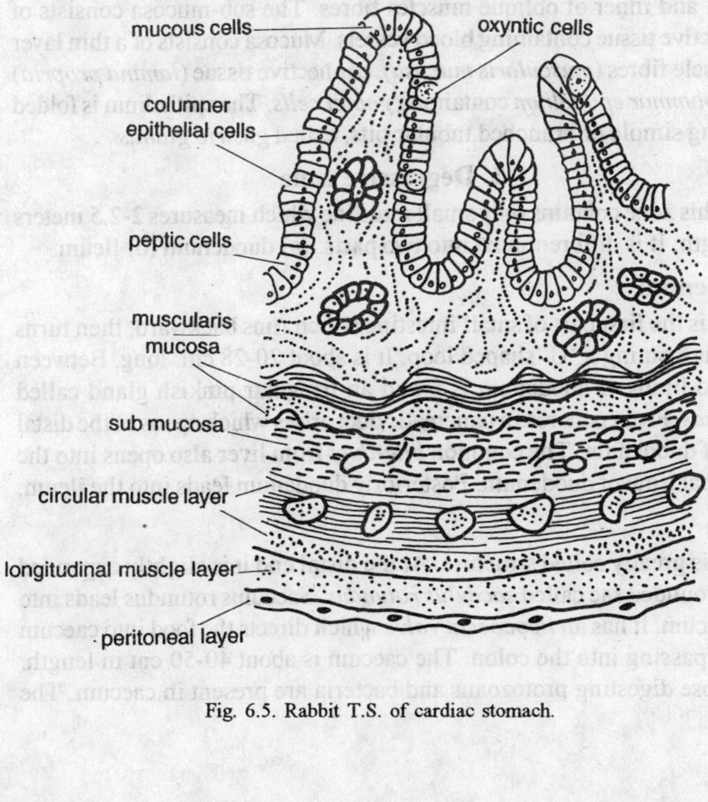

Fig. 6.5. Rabbit T.S. of cardiac stomach.

cardiac and pyloric parts, is largest and known as *fundic part.* The posterior convex and the anterior concave faces of the stomach are known as *greater* and *lesser curvatures* respectively. The opening of oesophagus into cardiac stomach is called *cardiac aperture* guarded by a valve *cardiac sphincter.* The pyloric part of stomach leads into intestine by an aperture, the *pyloric aperture* guarded by a thick ring like valve called *pyloric sphincter.*

In stomach, according to their location, there are three types of gastric glands - (i) cardiac, (ii) fundic and (iii) pyloric glands.The fundic glands secrete gastric juice.These glands contain zymogen cells, oxyntic cells and mucous secreting cells whereas cardiac and pyloric secrete mucous because they are lined with mucous secreting cells.

Histology

As usual the wall of stomach consists of four coats, beginning from out side, are peritoneum, muscular coat, sub-mucous and mucous.

Peritoneum consists of a layer of flat cells joined to the muscular coat by a thin sheet of connective tissue. The muscular coat consists of three layers, outer of longitudinal muscles fibres, middle of circular muscle fibres, and inner of oblique muscles fibres. The sub-mucosa consists of connective tissue containing blood vessels. Mucosa consists of a thin layer of muscle fibres (*muscularis mucosa*), connective tissue (*lamina propria*) and *columnar epithelium* containing *goblet cells*. The epithelium is folded forming simple or branched tubular pits, called *gastric glands.*

3. Degressive zone

This zone contains only small intestine which measures 2-2.5 meters in length. It is differentiated into two parts: (a) duodenum (b) Ileum.

Duodenum

It is the first part of small intestine which runs backward, then turns in front forming a 'U' shaped loop. It is about 20-28 cm. long. Between the two limbs of duodenum is found an irregular pinkish gland called *pancreas*. From pancreas a pancreatic duct arises which opens in the distal limb of duodenum. The common *bile-duct* from liver also opens into the proximal limb of duodenum. Posteriorly duodenum leads into the ileum.

Ileum

It is greatly coiled structure. At the distal end it is slightly expanded into a rounded sac called *sacculus rotundus.* Sacculus rotundus leads into the caecum. It has an *ileocaecal valve* which directs the food into caecum before passing into the colon. The caecum is about 40-50 cm in length. Cellulose digesting protozoans and bacteria are present in caecum. The caecum terminates in a narrow, smooth, thick-walled, blind tube, the *vermiform appendix*. It is about 13 cm long.

Histology

The wall of intestine is thiner than stomach. As usual four coats are present. The outermost layer is of peritoneum. The muscular coat is differentiated into two layers, outer longitudinal muscle fibres and inner circular muscles fibres. The oblique muscles being absent. Submucosa is well developed and consists of connective tissue having blood vessels, nerve fibres and numerous racemose glands called *Brunner's glands* that open into the crypts of mucosa. Muscularis mucosa is a thin layer of outer longitudinal and inner circular muscles. The inner most layer is the mucosa. It is produced into finger like projections called *villi*. The depressions between the villi are called *crypts of Lieberkuhn*.

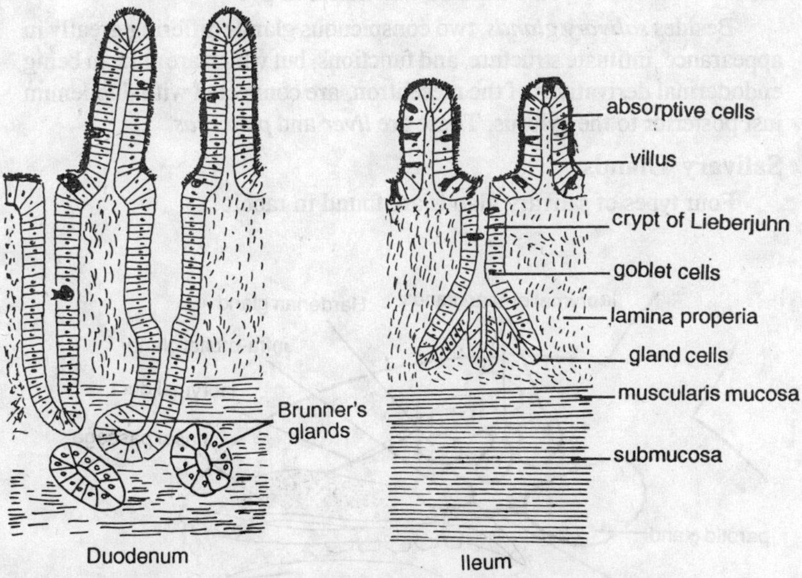

Fig. 6.6. A segment of each of two portions of mammalian small intestine showing similarities and differences in the villi, glands, and goblet cells.

Brunner's gland secrete mucous and crypts of Liberkuhn secrete *intestinal juice* or *succus entericus*. Along with blood vessels, lymph-vessels called *lacteal* extend into each villus from the sub mucosa.

In the ileum particularly, microscopic villi are frequently interrupted by irregular bare patches, called *Peyer's patches* or *intestinal tonsils*, which are areas of lymphoidal tissue.

4. Egressive zone

It includes *large intestine*. Large intestine measures about one metre in length. It has two regions (a) *colon*, and (b) *rectum*.

Colon

It is about 45 cm. in length. It bears a longitudinal muscle bands, the *taeniae*. The cavity of colon forms several small swollen structures called *haustra* on either side of this band.

Rectum

It is about 75 cm long. It gives beaded appearance due to presence of faecal pallets in it. It opens outside through the anus.

The inner wall of large intestine is devoid of villi but there are small folds containing *crypts of Lieberkuhn* and many mucous secreting cells.

DIGESTIVE GLANDS

Besides *salivary glands*, two conspicuous glands differing greatly in appearance, intimate structure, and functions, but which are alike in being endodermal derivatives of the mesentron, are connected with duodenum just posterior to the pylorus. These are *liver* and *pancreas*.

Salivary Glands

Four types of salivary glands are found in rabbit :

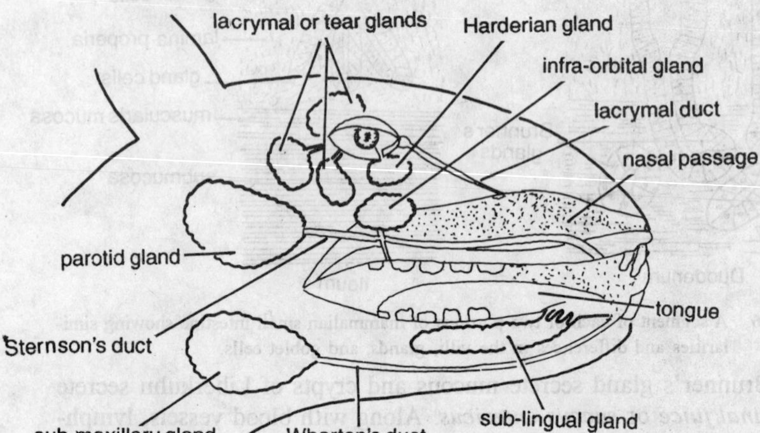

Fig. 6.7. Salivary glands.

(a) ***Parotid glands.*** These are larger glands located below and somewhat anterior to the pinnae. Each *parotid duct* or *Stenson's duct* opens into the vestibule opposite to the upper molar teeth.

(b) ***Sublingual.*** These are smaller glands, which lie under the tongue. Their ducts, *Wharton's ducts* open between tongue and lower jaw.

(c) ***Submaxillary or submandibular glands.*** They are found in the angle between the upper and lower jaws in their muscle.

(d) ***Infra-orbital*** or ***Zygomatic glands.*** These glands are found on the dorsal surface of each eye orbit. Their ducts open in the roof of buccal cavity near the molar teeth. This gland is absent in man and rat.

According to *Weichert C.K.* only parotid and sublingual glands are present in rabbit, the remaining two i.e. sub maxillary and infraorbital are absent.

The salivary glands are multicellular, branched structure. It is typically *compound tubular* or *racemose gland*. The secreting unit called the *acinus* which is made up of a single row of glandular cells arranged around a central cavity into which the secretion is poured. The glandular cells of the acinus are of two types: *serous cells* and *mucous cells*. The serous cells secrete *enzyme* rich in watery juice.

Pancreas

It is the second large gland after liver in the vertebrates. It is compound alveolar gland of irregular shape lying in the fold between the stomach and duodenum. Histologically, it has two kinds of functional cells *exocrine* or *acinar cells* and *endocrine* or *islets of Langerhans.* In pig (guinea) there may be 25000 islets of Langerhans in pancreas. The acinar cells secrete three digestive engymes namely *amylopsin, trypsin* and *steapsin*.

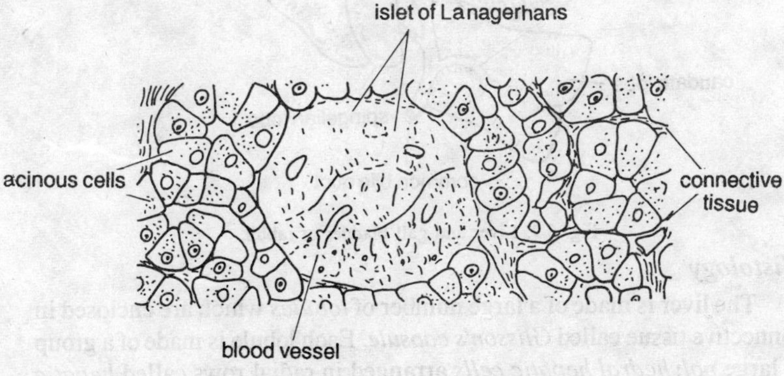

Fig. 6.8. Section of the pancreas of a mammal.

The islets of Langerhans secrete two principle hormones *insulin* and *glucagon*.

Liver

Situated just behind the diaphragm. The liver is the largest gland in vertebrate body. It is reddish-brown in colour and is covered over by a connective tissue capsule. It remains attached to diaphragm by suspensory ligament. It has two surfaces (parietal and visceral), and four borders, (dorsal, ventral, left and right) and five lobes in rabbit. Out of five lobes the lower three are present on left side and remaining two on right side. The three left lobes are known *left lateral, left central* and *spigelian lobes*. The two right lobes are known as *right central* and *caudate lobes.* From each of the five lobes, the hepatic ducts arise.The *gall bladder* is a saccular structure situated more or less between the right and left lobes. A large *cystic duct* arises from the gall bladder and unites with the hepatic ducts to form a *common bile duct* or *ductus choledochus* which opens in the proximal limb of duodenum. The opening of common bile duct is guarded by a sphincter muscle, the *sphincter of Oddi.*

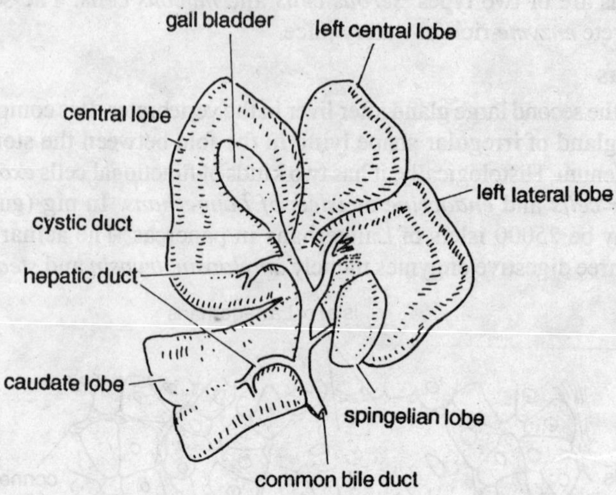

Fig. 6.9. Liver and gall bladder of rabbit.

Histology

The liver is made of a large number of *lobules* which are enclosed in connective tissue called *Glisson's capsule.* Each lobule is made of a group of large *polyhedral hepatic cells* arranged in radial rows called *hepatic cords.* An *intralobular vein* or central vein is present in centre of each

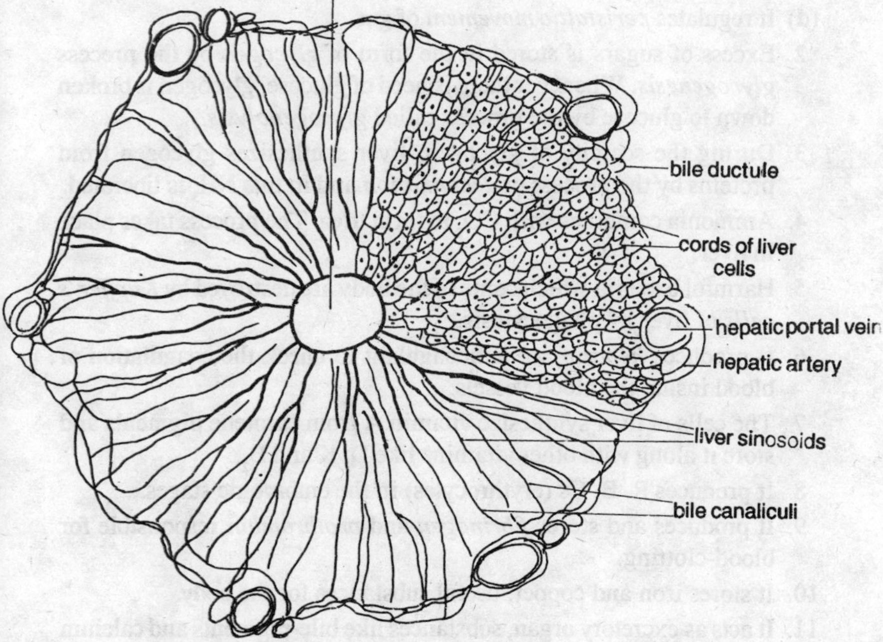

Fig. 6.10. Sectional view of Liver.

lobule. Where as between the lobules lie the *portal vein* or *inter lobular vein*. A network of blood capillaries is formed by the interlobular and intralabular blood vessels called *sinusoids*. Few *bile canaliculi* or capillaries are also present among the hepatic cells. Some specialized *Kupffer's cells* are also found in the liver cells which generally help in the destruction of many germs and also help in digestion of fats.

Functions of liver

1. One of the important function of liver is to secrete *bile*, which is an alkaline, dark greenish coloured fluid having a number of organic and inorganic salts as well as waste substances. Bile performs following functions :

(a) It makes the chyme alkaline for the proper action of pancreatic juice.

(b) It emulsifies fats for their complete hydrolysis.

(c) Some bile salts are necessary for the absorption of fat soluble vitamins like vitamin A, E, D, K etc. It is antiseptic in nature, therefore, it does not allow the growth and multiplication of bacteria.

(d) It regulates *peristaltic movement* of gut.

2. Excess of sugars is stored in the form of *glycogen* by the process *glycogenesis*. Whenever there is need of glucose, glycogen is broken down to glucose by the process called *glycogenolysis*.
3. During the scarcity of glycogen, liver synthesizes glycogen from proteins by the process of *deamination* and in this NH_3 is liberated.
4. Ammonia combines with CO_2 to form urea. The process takes place in liver.
5. Harmful bacteria which come in the body are destroyed by *Kupffer's cells* of liver by phagocytosis.
6. It produces *heparin*, an anticoagulant to check the coagulation of blood inside the blood vessels.
7. The cells of liver synthesize vitamin A from carotene pigments and store it along with other vitamins like D, K and B_2.
8. It produces R. B. Cs (erythrocytes) in the embryonic stages.
9. It produces and stores *fibrinogen* and *prothrombin* responsible for blood-clotting.
10. It stores iron and copper, useful substances for the body.
11. It acts as excretory organ, substances like bile-pigments and calcium phosphate go into duodenum along with bile juice and from here they are sent out of the body alongwith undigested food.
12. It helps in changing amino-acids into albumin which regulates the salt-water balance in body.
13. A toxic substance prussic acid is formed in body which is converted into a less toxic substance, the potassium sulphocyanide in the liver.
14. It helps in the destruction of old erythrocytes to manufacture bile from these erythrocytes.
15. Liver forms *lymph*.
16. It is the heat producing centre of the body. The heat is well maintained in the body.

7

Respiratory System

To perform various activities of life i.e., locomotion, digestion, reproduction etc. energy is necessary. The energy is obtained from the food materials by their physiological burning or oxidation. Oxidation of food is only possible in the presence of oxygen. The food is taken in and digested by the digestive enzymes. For its oxidation, oxygen is necessary and, during this process energy and carbon dioxide are produced. Energy is utilized by the body where as carbon dioxide must be eliminated out because it is harmful to the body. Thus intaking of oxygen and giving out of carbon dioxide is only possible by respiration. Respiration is carried by respiratory system. Thus this system is very essential for the animal.

MAMMALIAN RESPIRATORY SYSTEM

The respiratory system can be studied under two headings. *Respiratory tract* and *Respiratary organs*.

Respiratory tract

It includes external nares, nasal passages or chambers, internal nares, pharynx, larynx, trachea, bronchi and bronchioles.

(a) External nares

These are a pair of oval slits obliquely placed under the fleshy tip of snout. They lead intó the nasal passages.

(b) Nasal passages

They lie infront of cranium in olfactory capsules of skull. They are covered above by the nasal bones, laterally by premaxillae and maxillae and the floor is formed by the palatine process of premaxilla and maxilla bones infront, and palatine bones behind. Between two passages there is a median vertical partition. Each passage is divided into three regions: anterior *vestibular*, middle *respiratory* and posterior *olfactory*. The vestibular region is lined with stratified epithelium bearing hairs and sebaceous glands. The respiratory and olfactory regions form greater part of the each nasal chamber. There are thin and twisted bony plates called *turbinals* or conchae derived from nasal, maxilla and ethmoid bones in nasal chamber. These are of three types - *naso turbinals* present in the dorso-anterior part of nasal chamber. The *maxillo-turbinals* present on the ventro-anterior part of nasal chamber, and *ethmo-turbinals* present in the dorso-posterior part of nasal chamber. The respiratory region is lined with respiratory epithelium and the olfactory region with olfactory epithelium richly supplied with blood vessels. Three types of cells are seen in the epithelium are *olfactory receptor cells, supporting cells* and *olfactory gland cells.*

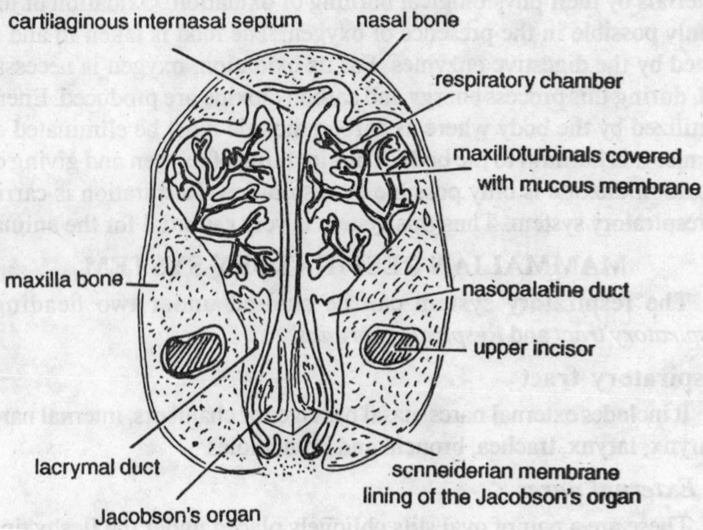

Fig. 7.1. V.S. of head of rabbit through respiratory part of nasal passage.

The nasal passage is very useful because:

1. It holds up dust particles in the vestibule.
2. The temperature of the outside air becomes equal to that of body when it passes through nasal passage.
3. The air is moistened due to presence of mucous secreting cells in them.
4. Due to presence of olfactory receptor cells, sense of smell is established.
5. It helps in holding up and sweeping minute particles such as bacteria coming into mouth cavity with air and get stuck to the mucous and are thus prevented from going into trachea.

(c) Internal nares

The nasal passages open behind into the pharynx by a common aperture the internal nares. The nares are bounded ventrally by the free semicircular edge of soft palate called *uvula*.

(d) Pharynx

It is a common passage for food and air. Its upper part, which receives the internal nares is called *nasopharynx* and its lower part lying directly behind the buccal cavity is *oropharynx*. Pharynx is lined with ciliated epithelium.

Glottis which is a slit-like aperture, lies at the hind end of pharynx. At its anterior end is a cartilaginous flap called *epiglottis*. The epiglottis closes the glottis during swallowing of food. Glottis leads into larynx.

(e) Larynx

Larynx or voice box is a modified anterior part of *trachea* or *respiratory tube*. It is supported by four cartilages. The largest and anterior most is the *thyroid cartilage*. It is formed of two pieces which are fused in the mid- dorsal line but remain free dorsally. In man, it forms a characteristic protubrance in the neck, called *Adam's apple*. A single ring like cartilage is *cricoid* which is broad on dorsal side but narrow ventrally. Two *arytenoid cartilages* are attached to the cricoid and make up the antero-dorsal part of larynx. The arytenoids are tipped with a pair of small nodules, the *cartilage of Santorini*.

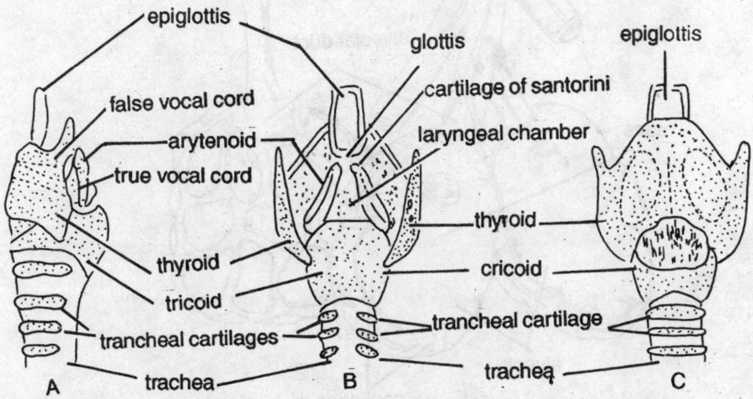

Fig. 7.2. Different views of larynx. A—Lateral, B—Dorsal, C—Ventral.

Two pairs of small *vocal cords* are stretched dorso-ventrally across the cavity of the larynx. The vocal cords are formed of yellow elastic tissue covered by mucous membrane of stratified squamous epithelium. A pair of these cords is found between the anterior part of thyroid and posterior part of arytenoids, these are *true vocal cords*. Another pair of cords found between anterior end of arytenoids and anterior part of thyroid cartilages called *false vocal cords*. Glottis lies between these two pairs of vocal cords. In elephants the false vocal cords are absent where as in hippopotamus true vocal cords are absent. There are muscles in larynx to alter the pitch of voice. In the resting condition the vocal cords lie at an acute angel to one another but when used to produce sound they are brought into a parallel position as arytenoids are drawn together by the action of certain muscles. When these cords are parallel, the aperture between them is simply a narrow slit, the forceful expulsion of air from lungs is responsible for causing the edges of vocal cords to vibrate and thus sound is produced.

The larynx is followed by trachea.

(f) Trachea

Trachea or wind pipe is a long tube running through the neck just ventral to oesophagus. Its size depends upon the length of neck. As usual,

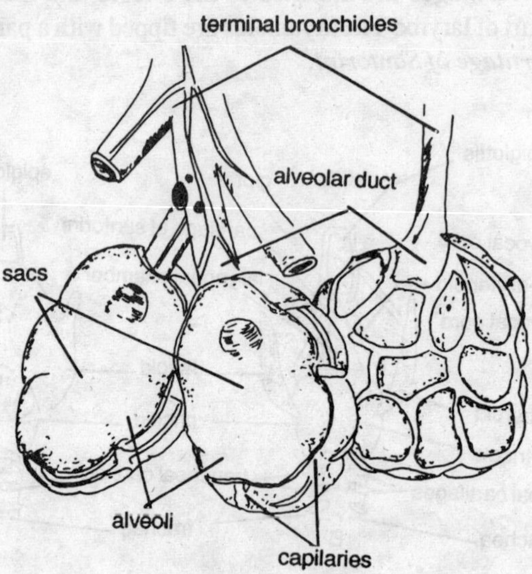

Fig. 7.3. Showing alveoli.

it is supported by C-shaped incomplete tracheal rings of elastic cartilage. Internally it is lined with ciliated epithelium, interrupted by the ducts of numerous mucous glands present in the underlying connective tissue. On entering the thorax it is divided into two branches, the *primary bronchii* which enter the corresponding lungs. Within the lung, the primary bronchus divides and sub-divide into thinner *secondary* and *tertiary bronchii*. Tertiary broanchii divide into still thinner tubes called *bronchioles*, which are further divided into *respiratory bronchioles* whose diameter is about 1-1.5 mm. Each respiratory bronchii divides again into many finer branches called *alveolar ducts* which end in small air sacs known as *alveolar sacs* or *atria*. Each atrium is formed of 6-8 air cells, the *alveoli* (formed by the outfold of atrium). Each alveolus is richly supplied with blood capillaries. This blood capillary bed is formed by the branches of pulmonary artery and pulmonary vein.

There are about 700 millions of alveoli in both the lungs of man. The alveoli are the actual sites of exchange of gases which are never fully emptied, always there remains some *residual air* in them. The alveoli form a total surface area of about 100 sq. meters, which is 50 times that of the skin surface. The bronchii and bronchioles are also lined by ciliated columnar epithelium containing numerous mucous secreting cells. The mucous helps in holding the dust and bacteria, which are swept towards the pharynx by cilia.

Respiratory Organ

The respiratory organs are a pair of lungs situated on the sides of the heart in thoracic cavity. They are hollow, pinkish, spongy structures. Each

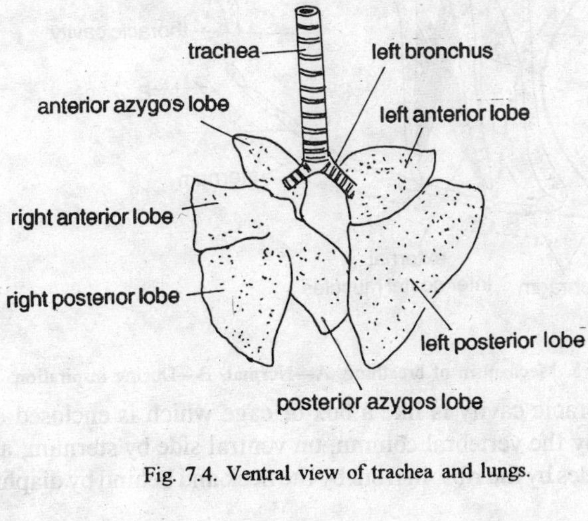

Fig. 7.4. Ventral view of trachea and lungs.

lung is enclosed in two membranes, the *pleura*, which are the layers of peritoneum of the thorax. The *inner* or *visceral pleural membrane* covers the lung surface while the outer or *parietal pleural membrane* lines the thoracic cavity. Between the two pleural membranes on each side is *pleural cavity,* contains a watery fluid, *pleural fluid,* for lubrication.

Lungs of rabbit, rat and squirrel are externally divided into lobes, always more on the right than the left. The left lung consists of two lobes, a *left anterior* and a *left posterior lobe* while the right lung consists of four lobes - viz. *anterior azygos* or *superior, right anterior, right posterior* and *posterior azygos* or *inferior lobes.*

Inside each lung the bronchioles divide and redivide and finally terminating into alveoli. Due to presence of innumerable alveoli, the lungs are spongy. All the components of lungs, namely alveoli, atria, alveolar ducts, bronchioles are held together by elastic connective tissue with some smooth muscles, which allows their expansion.

Mechanism of breathing

The mechanism of breathing involves alternate expansion and contraction of thorax. During expansion fresh air is taken into lungs called *inspiration* and during contraction, foul air from lungs is expelled out, called *expiration*.

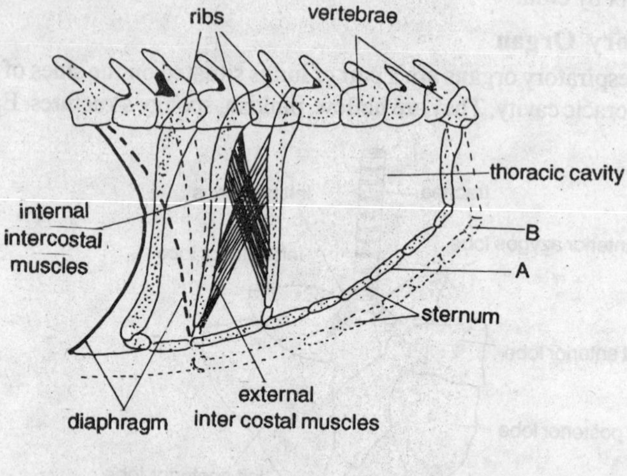

Fig. 7.5. Mechanism of breathing. A—Normal, B—During inspiration.

The thoracic cavity is like a box or cage which is enclosed on the dorsal side by the vertebral column, on ventral side by sternum, and on the lateral sides by the ribs, in front by the neck and behind by diaphragm.

Between two ribs, two types of muscles are present. (i) *internal intercostal muscles*, and (ii) *external intercostal muscles.*

The ribs are attached dorsally to the vertebrae and ventrally to the sternum. The external intercostal muscles extend in a downwards and forwards direction from the lower border of the ribs, above to the upper border of the ribs below. Their action is to raise the ribs upwards and outwards thus increasing the size of thoracic cavity laterally and dorsoventrally.

The internal intercostal muscles in a downward and backward direction from the lower border of the ribs above to the upper border of the ribs below crossing external intercostal muscles at right angles.

Inspiration

It is an active process because it is the result of muscular contraction. During inspiration, the external intercostal muscles and diaphragm contract due to which the ribs are dragged forwards and downwards and the sternum is moved downward resulting in the increase in volume of thoracic cavity. Thus, the enlargement of thoracic cavity causes the gases to pass through external nares → nasal passages → internal nares → glottis → trachea → bronchii → bronchioles → alveoli. Gaseous exchange takes place in the alveoli where inspired air comes in contact with the blood capillaries. Oxygen from the air diffuses in the blood and CO_2 diffuses out in the lung through alveoli.

Expiration

This is a passive process. When the external intercostal muscles and diaphragm relax, the ribs fall back into place, the diaphragm ascends and again becomes dome-shaped. This is aided by the elastic recoil of lungs and thoracic wall. With all this, the thoracic cavity decreases in dimensions, permitting the lungs to return to their original size. As they do so, air is forced out of the lungs through bronchioles → bronchii → trachea → nasal passages → external nares → outside the body.

Physiology of respiration

The respiration involves the two steps

1. External respiration.
2. Internal or tissue respiration

In the *external respiration* the oxygen is taken in and carbon dioxide is eliminated out through the respiratory system. The oxygen which is taken in the body is utilized for the oxidation of food stuff for liberating energy and other metabolic wastes, constitute the *internal* or *tissue respiration.*

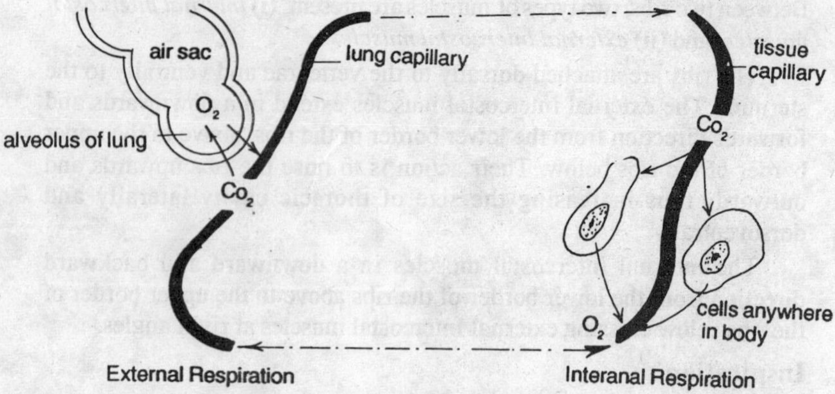

Fig. 7.6. Exchange of gases.

The oxygen which is taken in diffuses into the blood (due to its low concentration in blood) combines with haemoglobin, the red coloured respiratory pigment present on the surface of erythrocytes and forms oxyhaemoglobin. The oxygenated blood first goes into heart by the pulmonary veins. From heart via the arterial system, this blood reaches the tissues of the organs. Where there is low oxygen concentration, oxyhaemoglobin breaks into oxygen and haemoglobin. This oxygen is diffused in the tissue where it is utilized for oxidation of food in the presence of certain enzymes. As a result of oxidation, energy and carbon dioxide are formed as by products. Concentration of carbon dioxide increases in tissue and as the concentration of carbon dioxide is less in blood, carbon dioxide from tissue diffuses out. It is carried partly into the erythrocytes and partly in the plasma. This carbon dioxide reaches the lungs and due to low concentration, of carbon dioxide in alveoli, carbon dioxide from blood is diffused out in the alveoli.

8

Circulatory System

The circulatory system is the mechanism that attends to transportation within the organism of various substances needed for its sustenance. Thus, substances such as food, gases, hormones and wastes are transported by the circulatory system. Moreover, it is also responsible for protecting the body from germs, getting rid off dead cells and maintaining body temperature.

The circulatory system of rabbit is *closed type* i.e. the liquid media or *blood* flows through closed channels, the *blood vessels* and a pumping organ, the *heart* to all the parts of body. The circulatory system can be studied under following headings.

I. Heart, II. Blood Vessels, III. Blood and IV. Lymphatic system.

I. HEART

The heart is a pear-shaped or conical, muscular structure situated in the thoracic cavity a little to the left of middle line and lies in a space the *mediastinum* between the two *pleural sacs* enclosing lungs. Its anterior broad end is called *base* which is turned forward to the right side, the pointed end is called *apex* which is directed backward, downwards and slightly to the left side. The heart is enclosed in a thin walled, transparent, two-layered sac, called *pericardium*. The outer pericardium is called *parietal pericardium* while inner is called *visceral pericardium*. There lies a narrow space between two membranes, the *pericardial cavity* which is filled with *pericardial fluid* secreted by pericardium. The pericardial fluid protects the heart from external injuries and allows its free movement. The pericardium is attached to the ventral thoracic wall and diaphragm to keep the heart in position.

External Structure

The heart of rabbit is four chambered with two *auricles* and two *ventricles*. The *sinus-venosus* and *truncus arteriosus* are absent. The surface of heart is marked by two faint grooves, a transverse groove called *auriculo-ventricular groove* distinctly separates the heart into an anterior auricular part and posterior ventricular part. Similarly the other groove, called *inter ventricular groove* runs from the base obliquely backwards and to the right divides the ventricular part into *right* and *left ventricles.* The auricular part is divided into right and left auricles. The posterior part of each auricle is some what swollen flap-like called *auricular appendix* which covers the top of corresponding ventricle.

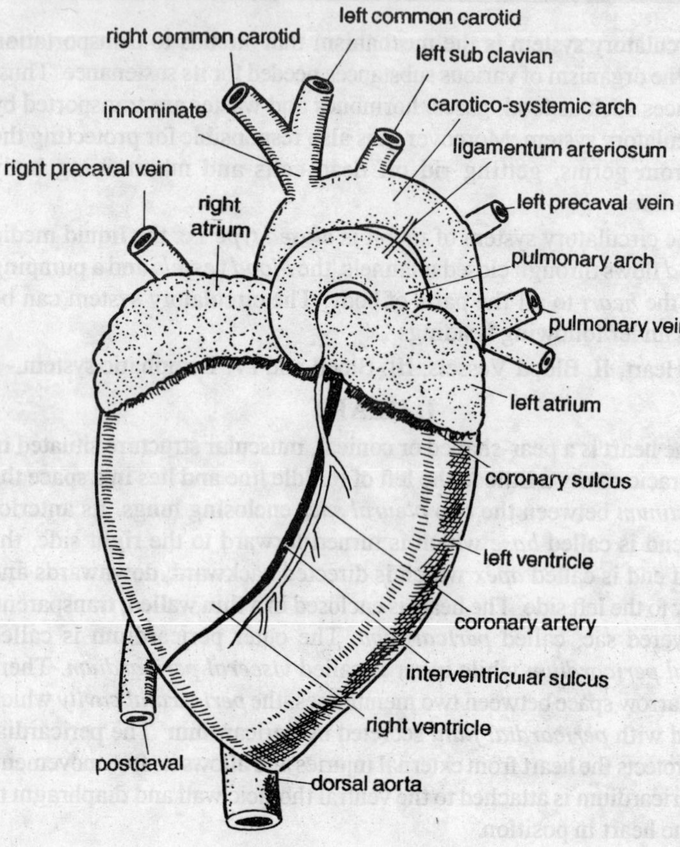

Fig. 8.1. Morphology of heart.

Internal structure

Internally also the heart is divided into four chambers two auricles and two ventricles. The auricles are thin walled structures their inner wall is smooth, except a network of low ridges, the *musculi pectinati*. Both the auricles i.e right and left are separated by a thin partition called *inter-auricular septum*. A small oval area called *fossa ovalis* is found on the septum, which has an opening the foramen ovalis in the embryo that connects the two auricles, but in adult foramen ovalis is fully closed when lungs become functional. The right auricle receives three vessels - a single *postcaval vein* or *inferior vena cava* and two *precaval veins* or *superior venae-cavae*. In man only one superior vena cava is there. Opening of postcaval into the right auricle is guarded by the membranous fold, the *Eustachian valve*. Near this valve remnant of sinus venosus called *sinu auricular node* is situated. The right auricle also receives the *coronary sinus*. The opening of coronary sinus lies just within that of the left anterior vena cava (precaval) and is guarded by the *valve* of *Thebesius*. The left auricle receives two blood vessels, the right and left *pulmonary veins*. These open by a common aperture.

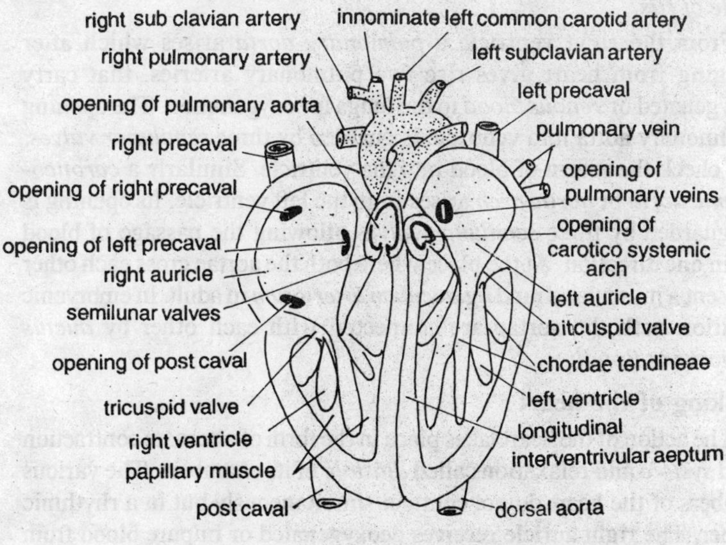

Fig. 8.2. Internal structure of heart.

The right auricle and left auricle both open into the right and left ventricles by *right auriculo-ventricular* and *left auriculo-ventricular apertures* respectively. The right auriculo-ventricular aperture is guarded by a one-way valve called *Tricuspid valve*. This valve consists of three membranous flaps, which are attached around the margin of right auriculo-ventricular aperture anteriorly but posteriorly project into the ventricle.

The free posterior edges are attached to the papillary muscles of right ventricle by a number of tough white cords called *chordae tendineae*. It checks the pushing of flaps into auricle during ventricular contraction. The left auriculo-ventricular aperture is also guarded by a one-way valve, the *bicuspid* or *mitral valve*. It consists of only two flaps. The free edges of these flaps are attached to the papillary muscles of left ventricle by *chordae tendineae*.

The ventricle is thick walled and like auricles it is separated completely by an oblique *interventricular septum* into *right* and *left ventricles*. The left ventricle is more thicker than the right ventricle because left ventricle is required to pump the blood to the farthest end of the body. The inner surface of the ventricles is raised into a network of low ridges called *columnae carneae* and few large,conical elevations, *musculi papillaries* or *papillary muscles*. A special type of muscles are grouped together at the top of interventricular septum to form the structure called *bundle of His*.

From the right ventricle a *pulmonary aorta* arises which after emerging from heart gives rise two pulmonary arteries, that carry deoxygenated or *venous blood* to the lungs for oxygenation. The opening of pulmonary aorta into ventricle is guarded by three *semilunar valves*. They check the return of blood into the ventricle. Similarly a *carotico-systemic aorta* or *aortic arch* arises from the left ventricle. Its opening is also guarded by three *semilunar valves* allowing the passage of blood only in one direction. At the place where both the aortae cross each other is present a muscular strand *ligamentum arteriosum* in adult. In embryonic condition both the aortae are connected with each other by *ductus arteriosus* or *Botelli*.

Working of the heart

The action of the heart takes place in the form of alternate contraction called *systole* and relaxation called *diastole* of its chambers. The various chambers of the heart do not contract simultaneously but in a rhythmic manner. The right auricle receives deoxygenated or impure blood from different parts of the body through post caval and precavals. The left auricle receives pure blood from pulmonary veins. Due to contraction of auricles (first right auricle contracts due to sinuatrial - node which spreads to left auricle) the blood reaches right and left ventricles through right and left auriculoventricular apertures. Now follows the contraction of the ventricles, which creates a considerable pressure on the blood contained in them. Due to this pressure bicuspid and tricuspid valves close the auriculo - ventricular apertures. So that the blood cannot go back into auricles. At the same time, semilunar valves are pressed and opened results the deoxygenated blood flows into *pulmonary aorta* and reaches the lungs and the oxygenated blood flows into *carotic systemic aorta* and supplied to various parts of the body. Again non-oxygenated blood is collected in right auricle and oxygenated into left auricles and same sequence of events is repeated. The pulse rate is 123-204 per minute.

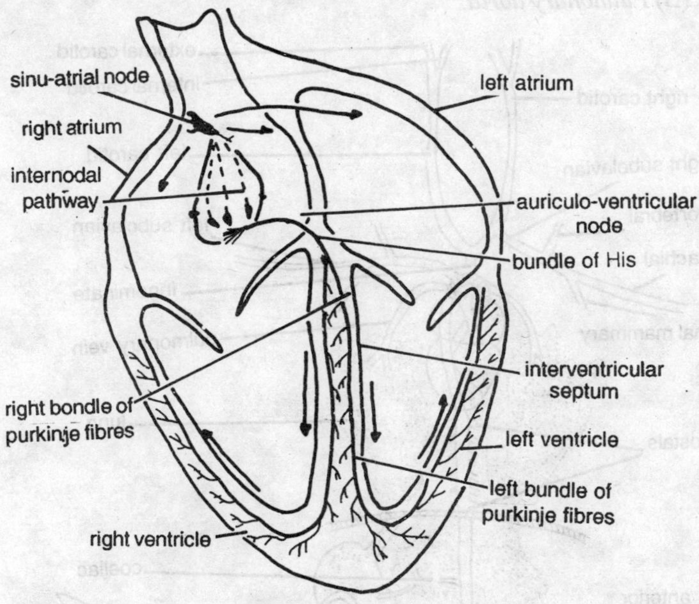

Fig. 8.3. Showing pace maker.

II. BLOOD VESSELS

In the mammalian heart the oxygenated and non-oxygenated or venous blood remain completely separate. Only the lungs are supplied with non-oxygenated blood. The right part of heart is concerned with venous blood where as left part is concerned with oxygenated blood. In one complete circuit in the body the blood has to pass once through the right side and then through the left side, such type of circulation is called *double circulation.*

There are two closed systems of blood vessels through which the blood flows, they are *arteries* and *veins*. The arteries carry pure blood from heart to various parts of the body while veins collect blood from all parts of body and carry towards the heart. All the arteries collectively forming the *arterial system.* Similarly the veins collectively form the *venous system*. Arteries supplying blood to particular organs ramify to form *arterioles* finally forming *arterial capillaries. Venous capillaries* unite together to form *venules* and finally to form veins.

Arterial system

The arterial system has two distinct vessels. (A) *Carotico-systemic aorta* (B) *Pulmonary aorta.*

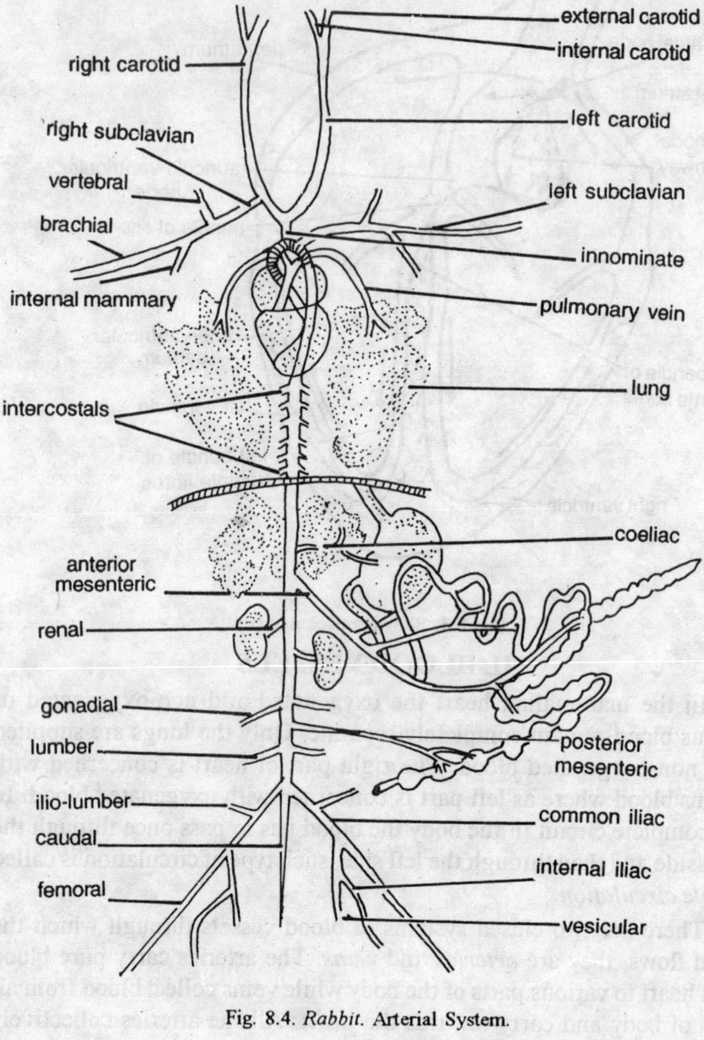

Fig. 8.4. *Rabbit.* Arterial System.

(A) Carotico-systemic aorta

Includes the aortic arch and its branches. The aortic arch arises from the left ventricle and turns towards the left. It loops round the left bronchus and reaches the dorsal side of heart, then it runs backward as dorsal aorta along the mid-dorsal line beneath the vertebral column in thorax and abdomen. The main arteries arise from aortic arch are as follows.

(i) ***Coronary arteries.*** A pair of small arteries, *left* and *right coronary arteries*, are given from the carotico-systemic aorta. These arteries supplying blood to heart itself.

(ii) ***Innominate artery.*** From the arching place of aortic arch an innominate artery is given out. It soon gives off a *left common carotid artery* and then divides into two arteries : the right *sub-clavian* and the right *common carotid.* The right and left common carotids run forward along the trachea and near the larynx divides into two branches - (a) *internal carotid* and (b) *external carotid.* The internal carotid supplies to the brain and external carotid to the tongue, jaws, pinnae and other parts of head region.

(iii) ***Left sub-clavian artery.*** It arises from the *carotico-systemic aorta* after it has given off innominate artery and is just curving backwards. Both the sub-clavians i.e. right and left run into the shoulder of their side and each is divided into following three branches.

(a) *Vertebral artery.* It enters the vertebrarterial canal of the cervical vertebrae and supplies blood to the brain and spinal cord, neck and shoulder muscles.

(b) *Internal mammary artery.* It gives off small branches to the pericardium, diaphragm and extends over the ventral surface of abdomen as *superior epigastric artery.*

(c) *Brachial artery.* It enters the fore limbs of its side and supplies it with several branches.

(iv) ***Intercostal arteries.*** *Dorsal aorta* travels into the thorax piercing the diaphragm called *thoracic aorta.* From thoracic aorta a series of small paired arteries are given out called *intercostal arteries* supplying blood to the intercostal muscles between the ribs.

(v) ***Phrenic arteries.*** These are a pair of fine arteries arising from the thoracic aorta behind intercostal arteries. They supply blood to diaphragm.

(vi) ***Coeliac artery.*** It is a median artery. It arises from the thoracic aorta about 12 mm. behind the diaphragm. It is bifurcated into:

(a) *Hepatic artery.* Supplies blood to liver.

(b) *Lieno-gastric artery.* Supplies blood to stomach by *gastric artery* and spleen by *splenic artery.*

(vii) ***Anterior mesenteric artery.*** Some distance after the coeliac artery, the thoracic aorta gives off *anterior mesenteric artery* on the left side. Branches of this artery supply pure blood to duodenum, pancreas, ileum, ceacum and colon.

(viii) ***Renal arteries.*** Behind mesenteric artery a pair of renal arteries arise from the aorta. The right renal artery arises a little above the left and these supply blood to kidneys.

(ix) ***Genital arteries.*** They arise after the renal arteries. In male they are called *spermatic arteries* supply blood to testis and in female they are termed as *ovarian arteries* supply blood to ovaries.

(x) ***Posterior Mesenteric artery.*** It is a small median artery that runs in mesentry. It supplies blood to hind part of colon and rectum.

(xi) ***Lumbar arteries.*** These are paired arteries supply blood to the dorsal body wall of the abdomen.

(xii) ***Common iliac arteries.*** These are a pair of arteries formed by the bifurcation of aorta. Each common iliac artery divides into :

(a) *Internal iliac artery*. It runs backwards, and supplies blood to the dorsal wall of pelvic cavity.

(b) *External iliac artery*. It gives off following arteries.

1. *Vesicular artery*. Supplies to the urinary bladder.

2. *Uterine artery*. It supplies blood to the uterus in female and may arise from vesicular artery.

3. *Posterior epigastric artery*. Distributes blood to the ventral wall of the abdomen.

(xv) ***Sacral artery or Caudal artery.*** The dorsal aorta continues backwards into the tail and supplies blood there.

(xiv) ***Ilio-lumbar artery.*** Near the origin of common iliacs, a small ilio-lumbar artery arises and supplies blood to the back muscles.

(B) Pulmonary Aorta

Gives rise pulmonary arteries to lungs

Venous system

The venous system of mammals is divided into four parts :

1. Pulmonary Venous System
2. Venae-cavae System
3. Portal System.
4. Coronary System.

1. Pulmonary Venous System

It includes a pair of *pulmonary veins* which bring oxygenated blood in the left atrium of heart. Both the veins open into left auricle of heart by a single aperture.

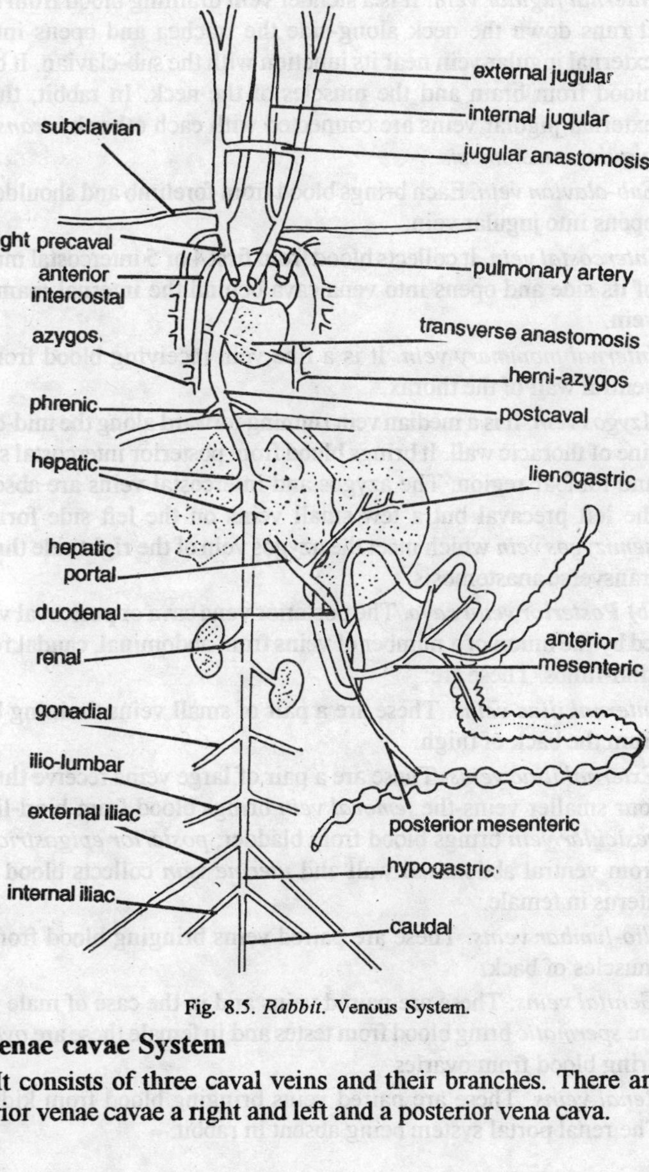

Fig. 8.5. *Rabbit.* Venous System.

2. Venae cavae System

It consists of three caval veins and their branches. There are two anterior venae cavae a right and left and a posterior vena cava.

(a) Anterior venae-cavae. They receive six veins:

(i) *External jugular vein*. It is large vein running through the neck outside the trachea. It is formed by the union of *anterior* and *posterior facial veins* that bring blood from the face and ears respectively.

(ii) *Internal jugular vein*. It is a slender vein draining blood from brain. It runs down the neck along-side the trachea and opens into the external jugular vein near its junction with the sub-clavian. It brings blood from brain and the muscles of the neck. In rabbit, the two external jugular veins are connected with each other by *transverse jugular anastomosis.*

(iii) *Sub-clavian vein*. Each brings blood from forelimb and shoulder and opens into jugular vein.

(iv) *Intercostal vein*. It collects blood from first 4 or 5 intercostal muscles of its side and opens into vena cava behind the internal mammary vein.

(v) *Internal mammary vein*. It is a fine vein receiving blood from the ventral wall of the thorax.

(vi) *Azygos vein*. It is a median vein running forward along the mid-dorsal line of thoracic wall. It brings blood from posterior intercostal spaces and lumbar region. The azygos and intercostal veins are absent in the left precaval but a few small veins on the left side form the *hemizygos vein* which meet the azygos vein of the right side through transverse anastomosis.

(b) Posterior vena cava. The posterior vena cava or postcaval vein is formed by the union of a number of veins from abdominal, caudal region and hind-limbs. These are:

(i) *Internal iliac veins*. These are a pair of small veins draining blood from the back of thigh.

(ii) *External iliac veins*. These are a pair of large veins receive three or four smaller veins-the *femoral vein* brings blood from hind-limbs; *vesicular vein* brings blood from bladder; *posterior epigastric vein* from ventral abdominal wall and *uterine vein* collects blood from uterus in female.

(iii) *Ilio-lumbar veins*. These are paired veins bringing blood from the muscles of back.

(iv) *Genital veins*. These are paired veins and in the case of male these are *spermatic* bring blood from testes and in female these are *ovarian* bring blood from ovaries.

(v) *Renal veins*. These are paired veins bringing blood from kidneys. The renal portal system being absent in rabbit.

(vi) *Hepatic veins.* These are two pairs of veins draining blood from liver lobes.

(vii) *Phrenic veins.* These are a pair of slender veins in the diaphragm.

3. Portal System

A vein which collects blood from one organ and distributes it to another organ instead of sending it directly to the heart is known as the *portal vein.* In rabbit only *hepatic portal system* is seen which collects blood from the alimentary canal. It includes a single large vein called *hepatic portal vein* which receives 4 main veins.

(i) *Lienogastric vein.* It collects blood from stomach by *gastric* and spleen by *splenic veins.*

(ii) *Duodenal veins.* Receive blood from duodenum and pancreas.

(iii) *Anterior mesenteric vein.* It collects blood from the ileum, caecum, colon and anterior part of rectum by several small branches.

(iv) *Posterior mesenteric.* From lower part of rectum.

The hepatic portal vein divides into capillaries and supplies blood to various lobes of liver. Here, excessive sugar and other nutrients are retained and stored for the future use. Blood from liver is drained into postcaval by the hepatic veins.

4. Coronary System

A number of *coronary veins* collect blood from heart and unite to form *coronary sinus.* The coronary sinus opens into the right auricle through an aperture guarded by the valve of Thebesius. Some veins independently open into the right auricle these are known as *venae cordis minimae* and their opening into right auricle is known as *foramina of Thebesius.*

III. BLOOD

Blood is a liquid connective tissue but it differs from the proper connective tissue in three respects (1) Its matrix is not fibrous but fluid (plasma) (2) Cells are free and (3) Its cells do not secrete matrix. Though it differs from connective tissue, in the nature of matrix, it is grouped with connective tissues, because of its mesodermal origin. At the same time blood is closely connected with the connective tissue since leucocytes of blood keep on passing into the connective tissue and come back by *diapedesis.*

Blood is a red vascular tissue forming 6-10% of body weight in mammals. It is opaque, somewhat sticky and slightly heavier than water. Its *pH* is about 7.4 i.e. slightly alkaline. Oxygenated blood is red while venous blood is purple.

The blood is composed of two parts :

1. Plasma - the liquid matrix
2. Corpuscles or cells

1. Plasma

It is a faint yellowish fluid, contains about 80-92% of water and a number of organic and inorganic substances dissolved and a few blood proteins as colloids in it. The salts forming only 1% of the plasma containing chlorides, bicarbonates and phosphates of sodium, potassium, calcium and magnesium. Blood proteins form 7-8%. In man, the chief proteins are *albumins, globulins* and *fibrinogens*. Albumins maintain the osmotic pressure of blood and it is formed in liver. Fibrinogen is also formed in liver and helps in coagulation of blood. Globulins are derived from leucocytes and are important in defence mechanism. In addition many other substances such as glucose, amino acids, urea, uric acid, CO_2, N_2, O_2, hormones, vitamins and enzymes are invariably found dissolved in plasma. They form about 1-2% of plasma.

2. Blood Corpuscles

Three main types of corpuscles are recognized in all the mammals.

(a) *Erythrocytes* or *red blood corpuscles*

(b) *Leucocytes* or *white blood corpuscles*

(c) *Bood platelets* in mammals & thrombocytes in lower vertebrates.

(a) *Erythrocytes* are most numerous floating elements of blood. These are biconcave, non-nucleated, circular discs. This shape favours flexibility and the absorbing and releasing of gases quickly. The erythrocytes of camel and lamas are oval nucleated (an exception). The average size of rabbit erythrocytes is 6.9 μ whereas in man it is 7.5 μ. The largest erythrocytes are 9.4 μ in elephant and smallest 2.5 μ in musk deer. The normal number of erythrocytes in man is 5.5 million per cubic millimetre of blood in female it is 4.5 -5 million per cubic millimetre of blood. In rabbit it is 7 million per cubic mm. The colour of single corpuscle is pale-yellow, but when seen in mass, the characteristic red colour. In resting and slow flowing blood, they forms piles called *rouleux*. The respiratory pigment which gives it red colour is *haemoglobin*. It is a complex protein having iron as one of the main constituents. Its molecular weight is 68000. It is present 14gm. per 100 ml blood in man and 12gm. per 100 ml. blood of female. In amphibians it is 6-10 gm., per 100 ml. blood. Due to absence of nucleus, the mammalian erythrocytes are short-lived. In man erythrocytes survive from 90-120 days, in dogs 90 to 135 days, in rabbit 50-70 days, after which they are destroyed in liver and spleen. Its iron part is stored for reuse and globin (protein part) is converted into *biliverdin* which is almost completely changed to *bilirubin* a yellow pigment. The process is called *haemolysis*.

Haemopoiesis

About 1.5 million erythrocytes are destroyed per second and to keep the normal number of erythrocytes new blood cells are being constantly manufactured. The process of formation of new cells is called

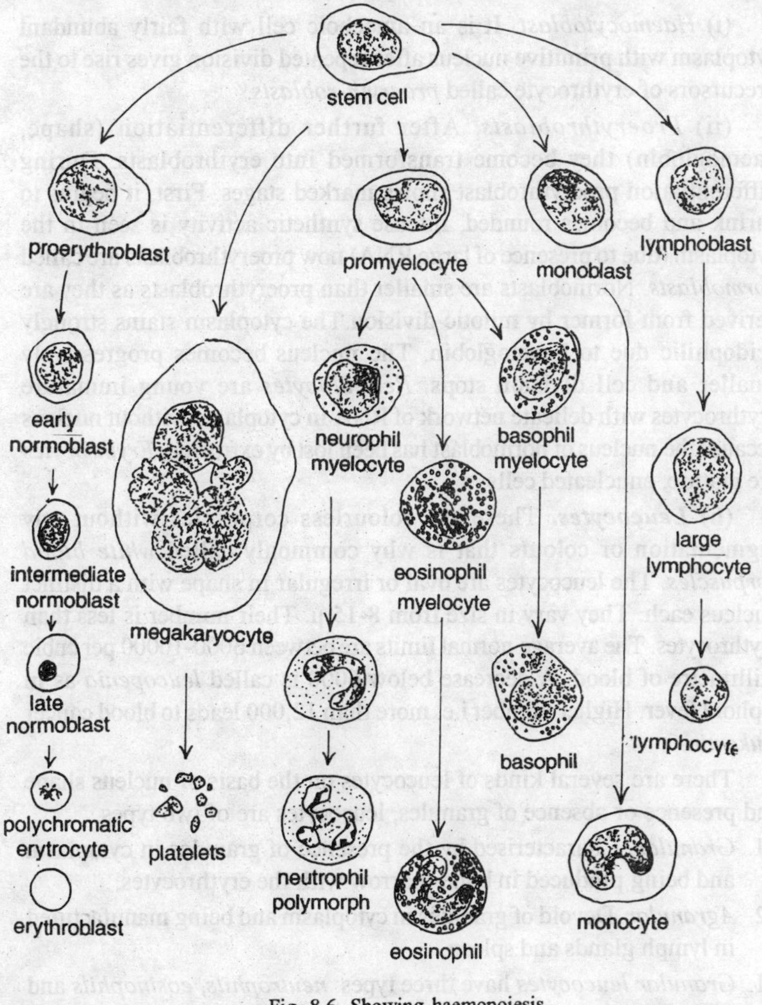

Fig. 8.6. Showing haemopoiesis.

erythropoiesis and the tissues involved are called *haemopoietic organs.* In adult the haemopoietic organ is the *red bone marrow* while liver, spleen and lymph nodes are haemopoietic organs in the embryo. The process of erythropoiesis is completed within 72 hrs.

The development of a mature erythrocyte takes about a week during which *endothelial cell* enlarges, divides, forms haemoglobin and finally loses its nucleus. This process is called *maturation* which takes following steps.

(i) *Haemocytoblast.* It is an amoeboic cell with fairly abundant cytoplasm with primitive nucleus after repeated division gives rise to the precursors of erythrocyte called *proeryth-roblasts.*

(ii) *Proerythroblasts.* After further differentiation (shape, haemoglobin) they become transformed into erythroblasts. During differentiation proerythroblast shows marked stages. First, it begins to shrink and becomes rounded, intense synthetic activity is seen in the cytoplasm (due to presence of large RNA) now proerythroblasts are called *normoblasts.* Normoblasts are smaller than proerythroblasts as they are derived from former by mitotic division.The cytoplasm stains strongly acidophilic due to haemoglobin. The nucleus becomes progressively smaller and cell division stops. *Reticulocytes* are young immature erythrocytes with delicate network of RNA in cytoplasm without nucleus because the nucleus of normoblast has been lost by extrusion. *Erythrocytes* are mature, enucleated cells.

(b) *Leucocytes.* These are colourless corpuscles without any pigmentation or colours that is why commonly called *white blood corpuscles.* The leucocytes are oval or irregular in shape with a distinct nucleus each. They vary in size from 8-15 μ. Their number is less than erythrocytes. The average normal limits are between 6000-10000 per cubic millimetre of blood. A decrease below 6000 is called *leucopenia* as in typhoid fever. Higher number i.e. more than 12,000 leads to blood cancer *leukemia.*

There are several kinds of leucocytes on the basis of nucleus shape and presence or absence of granules, leucocytes are of two types.

1. *Granular.* Characterised by the presence of granules in cytoplasm and being produced in bone-marrow with the erythrocytes.
2. *Agranular.* Devoid of granules in cytoplasm and being manufactured in lymph glands and spleen.

1. *Granular leucocytes* have three types: *neutrophils, eosinophils* and *basophils.*

Neutrophils : These are also known as *heterophils* or *microphages* forming 70% of total W.B.Cs. count. The cytoplasm is closely packed with fine, inconspicuous granules that pick up both acid and alkaline dyes. The nucleus has 3-5 lobes connected by thin chromatin strands. Neutrophils are phagocytic and appear in large number in and around the infected tissue. The pus which may exude from infected area consists of destroyed tissue, dead neutrophils and micro-organisms. Their life span is 30 hrs.

Eosinophils, also called *acidophils* were discovered by *Paul Ehrich.* They are non-phagocytic and from only 3% of total leucocytes count. The nucleus is usually bilobed with a connecting isthmus. The granules are fewer in cytoplasm and pick up an acid dye, *eosin* which is red. Their life span is 8-12 days. The function of eosinophils is not well known but their number increases in allergic conditions such as asthma and parasitic infections of the alimentary canal.

Basophils. These are non-phagocytic and form only 0.5-1 % of total leucocytes count. They are fairly large and have 1 to 3 lobed nucleus (usually bilobed) and coarse granules. Their significance is not known. Their life span is 12-15 days.

2. *Agranular Leucocytes.* The agranular leucocytes are of two types- *Lymphocytes* and *monocytes.*

Lymphocytes. These are non-phagocytic, more or less rounded in shape with a large nucleus. In size they are similar to erythrocytes. They form about 27% of the total leucocytes count. Their life span is 1-2 days. Latest researches have shown that they are of two types *B-type* and *T-type*. *B-type* have about 150 finger-like projections on their surface and produce the *antibodies*. *T-type* have few projections otherwise with smooth surface they reach the site of infection and attack micro-organisms directly and destroy them.

Lymphocytes are concerned with immunity, they produce beta and gamma globulins (plasma proteins that give rise to antibodies and anti-toxins). They also help in wound healing.

Monocytes. These are phagocytic, large-sized leucocytes. The nucleus varies from oval, rounded or kidney shaped and eccentric in position. They constitute 1-3% of total leucocytes. Their function is similar to that of neutrophils. Their life span is for several days.*Hankar. J. S.* (1980) reported a new type of leucocyte termed *medusa cell* because its tentacle like appendage resembles the tentacle of medusoid jelly fish. It is supposed to be a form of eosinophils. The tentacles are used for movement and to attack other cells but its function is yet to be confirmed.

The leucocytes (granular) originated in the bone marrow from the mother cell *haemocytoblasts* which divide repeatedly into myeloblasts. Myeloblasts are differentiated into three principal types of granulocytes known as *neutrophil myelocytes, eosinophil myelocytes* and *basophil myelocytes.* These myelocytes later distinguished into neutrophils, eosinophils and basophils by their staining property and differentiation in the shape of nucleus.

(c) ***Blood platelets***. Blood platelets were named by *Bizzozero*. These are protoplasmic discs that are formed in mammalian blood (in lower vertebrates it is spindle shaped cell and named as *thrombocytes*). These are colourless and non-nucleated structures. In man there are about 2,50,000 platelets per cubic mm in the blood. These are produced in the bone marrow by a giant cell *megakaryocyte* containing a large, many lobed nucleus. It undergoes fragmentation to form platelets.

These are the source of an enzyme *thrombokinase* required in the clotting of blood.

Functions of Blood

1. *Carrier of oxygen*. It carries oxygen to the tissue from lungs and brings carbon dioxide from tissue to the lungs.
2. *Transfer of materials*. It transports digested food materials, vitamins, hormones etc. to various parts of the body for their growth and normal functioning.
3. *In the removal of excretory products*. Urea, uric acids etc. which are produced in liver are transported to kidneys by blood, for their removal from the body.
4. *Clotting of blood*. It prevents loss of excess of blood from an injury by forming a clot from its fibrinogen protein.
5. *Regulation of body temperature*. It regulates and equalises body temperature by carrying heat away from region where it is produced.
6. Blood develops resistance and immunity against many kinds of infections and parasites.
7. *Healing of wounds*. It brings all the essential substances to the site of injury for healing wounds.
8. It maintains a physiological cooperation between parts of body by circulating from one to other part of the body.

IV. LYMPHATIC SYSTEM

Like blood, lymph travels through a system of vessels and capillaries that ramify in every part of the body within the tissues. This system helps in the exchange of materials between the blood and the tissue cells. It also maintains the volume of blood in the blood vessels by restoring to them the fluid that oozes out through the thin capillary walls.

This system comprises:

(i) *Lymph,* (ii) *lymphatic capillaries,* (iii) *lymph vessels* and (iv) *lymph nodes.*

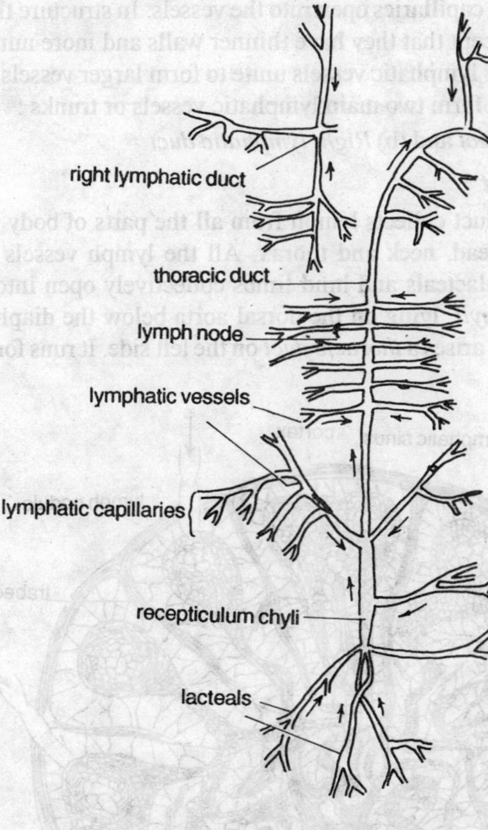

Fig. 8.7. The lymphatic system.

(i) Lymph

It comprises of two parts - a fluid matrix *plasma* and *white corpuscles* or amoeboid cells. Both are coming out from blood capillaries under pressure. The lymph is, thus, the blood without red blood corpuscles. It also lacks few proteins. The lymph surrounds the cells of the tissue filling up the intercellular space and is known as *tissue fluid.*

(ii) Lymphatic capillaries

These are wider capillaries than blood capillaries and are inter-woven but not connected to the blood capillaries. Their wall is extremely thin consist of a single layer of endothelium. They collect lymph from intercellular spaces.

(iii) Lymphatic vessels

The lymphatic capillaries open into the vessels. In structure they are similar to veins except that they have thinner walls and more numerous valves. The smaller lymphatic vessels unite to form larger vessels which in turn converge to form two main lymphatic vessels or trunks :

(a) *Thoracic duct* and (b) *Right lymphatic duct*

(a) Thoracic duct

The thoracic duct collects lymph from all the parts of body except the right side of head, neck and thorax. All the lymph vessels of the abdominal region, lacteals and hind limbs collectively open into large sac, the *cisterna chyli*, lying on the dorsal aorta below the diaphragm. From cisterna chyli arises a *thoracic duct* on the left side. It runs forwards

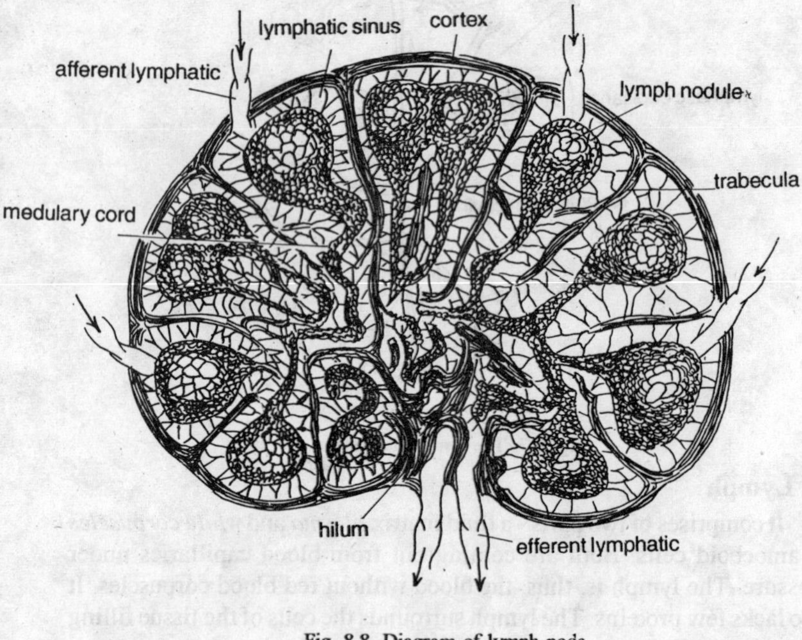

Fig. 8.8. Diagram of lymph node.

piercing the diaphragm enters the thoracic cavity, here it receives lymph vessels of the left side. It collects lymph from left side of head, neck and left arm and opens into the left external jugular vein where external jugular unite with the left sub-clavian vein.

(b) Right lymphatic duct

Lymph from right side of head, neck and right arm is collected in right lymphatic duct which empties into the right jugular vein where this vein connects with right sub clavian vein.

(iv) Lymph nodes

The lymph nodes or glands are present at short intervals throughout the lymphatic vessels. Nodes consist of connective tissue of collagenous and reticular tissues and masses of cells. Lymph hearts are absent in rabbit they contain abundant white corpuscles. Lymph passes through them that detect and destroy foreign bodies which invade the tissues, thus, serve as'check posts'. These are the characteristic of warm-blooded animals. They produce lymphocytes and macrophages.

Functions of Lymphatic System

1. Transport of materials from the tissue into the venous system, also transports fat from intestine.
2. In fighting the infections.
3. In production of lymphocytes.

9

Nervous System

Like other vertebrates, the nervous system of rabbit is also divided into three parts.

(I) *Central nervous system* including brain and spinal cord.

(II) *Peripheral nervous system* including cranial and spinal nerves which are coming out from brain and spinal cord respectively.

(III) *Autonomic nervous system* including a pair of ganglionated nerve cord and plexus associated with nerve cords.

I. CENTRAL NERVOUS SYSTEM

Central nervous system reaches the highest degree of complexicity, especially, in the placental mammals and much so in primates. It includes (1) *Brain* and (2) *Spinal Cord.*

1. Brain

Brain lies in the cranial cavity of skull. It is covered over by three membranes called *meninges.* The inner most meninx is the *piameter.* It is very thin and highly vascular and closely invests the brain. The outer most is *duramater.* It is thick and tough and lines the cranial cavity. The middle meninx is *arachnoid membrane.* It is also thin and vascular. Between the piameter and arachnoid membrane their is a thin space, the sub-arachnoid space similarly a *subdural space* lies between arachnoid membrane and duramater. These spaces contain *cerebrospinal fluid* to protect brain from external shocks and dessication.

The brain is divided into three region:

(a) Fore brain or *prosencephalon*, (b) Mid brain or *mesencephalon* and (c) Hind brain or *rhombencephalon*

(a) Fore brain or Prosencephalon

It is greatly developed in all the mammals. It comprises of (i) *Olfactory lobes,* (ii) *Cerebral hemispheres* and (iii) *Diencephalon*.

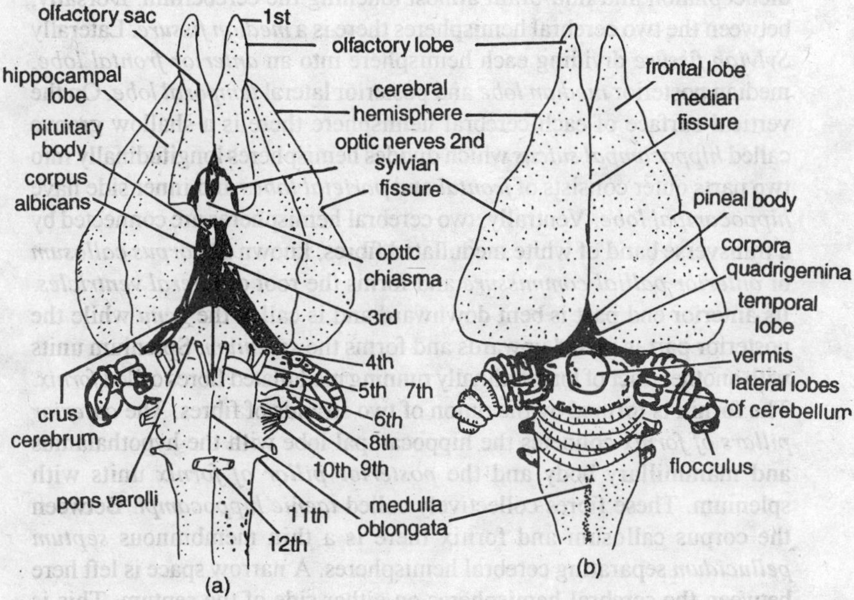

Fig. 9.1. Mammalian brain. A—Dorsal view, B—Ventral view.

(i) Olfactory lobes

These are a pair of club-shaped structures forming the anterior most part of brain. Both the lobes are separate i.e. not fused with each other. Each lobe consists of two parts an *olfactory bulb* and an *olfactory tract*. The olfactory tract can be observed from ventral side as they are concealed beneath cerebral hemispheres on the dorsal side. A groove on the outer side of this tract separates it from frontal lobes called *rhinal fissure*. At the anterior end of rhinal fissure are olfactory lobes while at the posterior end are hippocampal lobes. These two lobes together constitute *rhinencephalon*.

Each olfactory lobe encloses a cavity the *olfactory ventricle* or *rhinocoel* which is extremely narrow. It opens behind into the lateral ventricle of its side.

(ii) Cerebral hemispheres

These are well developed and form about 2/3 of the whole brain. These are a pair of very large triangular bodies, somewhat pointed in front and broad behind. Collectively they are called *cerebrum*. They partly cover the olfactory lobes in front and extend backward cover the diencephalon and mid-brain almost touching the cerebellum. Dorsally, between the two cerebral hemispheres there is a *median fissure*. Laterally *Sylvian fissure* dividing each hemisphere into an *anterior frontal lobe*, median posterior *median lobe* and posterior lateral *temporal lobe*. On the vertical surface of each cerebral hemisphere there is a shallow groove called *hippocampal sulcus* which divides hemispheres longitudinally into two parts outer consists of *frontal* and *parietal lobes* and inner side have *hippocampal lobe*. Ventrally, two cerebral hemispheres are connected by a transverse band of white medullated fibres, known as *corpus callosum* or *anterior pallial commissure* and forms the roof of *lateral ventricles.* Its anterior end part is bent downward and is called the *genu* while the posterior part is raised upwards and forms the *splenium.* Splenium units with another tract of longitudinally running medullated fibres called *fornix.* The fornix is formed by the union of two strands of fibres. The *anterior pillars of fornix* connetcs the hippocampal lobe with the hypothalamus and mammillary body and the *posterior pillar of fornix* units with splenium. These fibres collectively called *taenie hippocampi.* Between the corpus callosum and fornix there is a thin membranous *septum pellucidum* separating cerebral hemispheres. A narrow space is left here between the cerebral hemispheres on either side of the septum. This is called 5th or *zero ventricle* or *pseudocoel* because it is not a true ventricle.

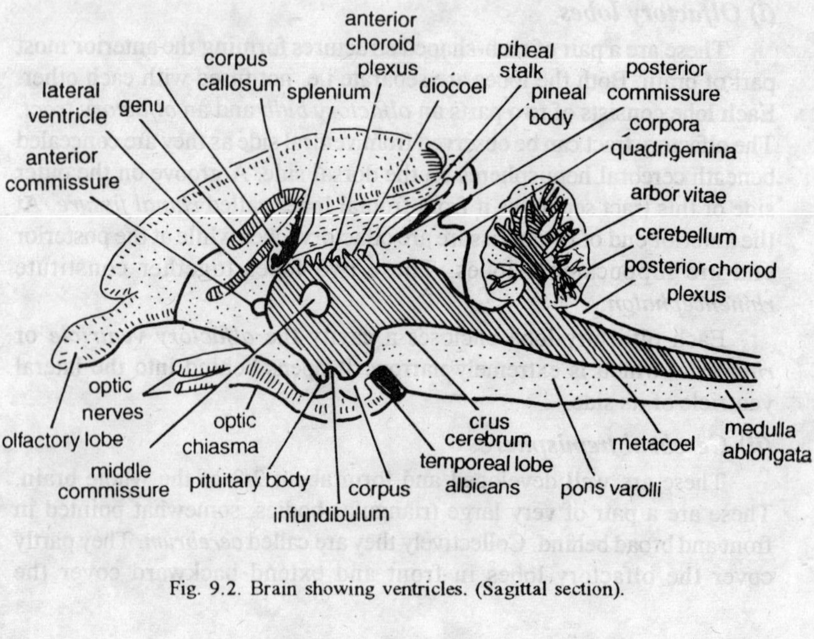

Fig. 9.2. Brain showing ventricles. (Sagittal section).

Each cerebral hemisphere contains a ventricle called *paracoel* or *lateral ventricle*. Paracoel have paired *anterior* and *posterior cornua* or prolongations. The anterior cornu is continued into olfactory bulb to form the *rhinocoel*. The roof and lateral walls of paracoel are thin and are called *pallium*. The floor and ventrolateral walls are thickened to form *corpora striata* joined by the *anterior commissure*. The inner vertical wall of the lateral ventricle is thin and termed as *septum lucidum*. The two lateral ventricles communicate with each other and also with third ventricle by *foramen of Monro*.

(iii) Diencephalon

It is comparatively small and is completely shadowed dorsally by the backward growth of cerebrum. Its dorsal surface is raised into a *pineal stalk* bearing a small rounded body, the *pineal body*. On the ventral side of diencephalon there is a funnel shaped depression, the *infundibulum* bearing *hypophysis* or *Rathke's pouch* at its free end. Hypophysis and infundibulum constitute together the *pituitary body*. The pituitary body is provided with a swelling on the posterior side called *corpus albicans* or *corpus mammilare*. Two optic nerves cross each other infront of the infundibulum to form the *optic chiasma*. The cavity of diencephalon is called *diacoel* which remains connected to *paracoel* by foramen of Monro. The roof of diacoel is formed of epithelium and is called *epithalamus*. It is covered by vascular piamater. The two layers are fused together are collectively called *tela choroidea*. Vascular folds of tela choroides project into diacoel to form the *anterior choroid plexus*, which extend into paracoel through the foramen of Monro. Anterior choroid plexus form the cerebrospinal fluid. The thick lateral walls of diacoel are called *optic thalami* forming *middle commissure* or *massa commissure*. The floor of diacoel is called *hypothalamus* bearing infundibulum and hypophysis.

(b) Mid brain

It consists of (i) *optic lobes* and (ii) *crura cerebri*

(i) Optic lobes

Four optic lobes are situated on the dorsal surface of mid-brain although most of the part of mid- brain remains covered by cerebral hemispheres. Out of 4 lobes anterior two are larger called *superior coliculi* than the posterior ones called *inferior coliculi*. The anterior and posterior lobes are connected by means of *posterior commissure*. The four optic lobes together form *corpora quadrigemina*. The optic lobes are solid devoid of *optocoel* but between them there is a narrow passage, the iter to connect the 3rd and 4th ventricles together.

(ii) Crura cerebri

On the ventral side of mid-brain below the optic lobes are two thick long bands of nerve fibres called crura cerebri. They are composed of white matter.

(c) Hind brain

It consists of (i) *cerebellum* or *metencephalon* and (ii) *medulla oblongata* or *myelencephalon*.

(i) Cerebellum

It is well developed in rabbit. It consists of a large median central lobe called *vermis, lateral lobes* situated on the sides of vermis and two *floccular lobes* situated on the outer sides of lateral lobes. The vermis is further divided into anterior, middle and posterior parts. The surface of cerebellum is not smooth, it is thrown into numerous folds, the *gyri*, separated by grooves, the *sulci*. The cerebellum is solid like optic lobes but in a section it shows a tree-like pattern of branching, the *arbor vitae*. *Metacoel* is hardly developed.

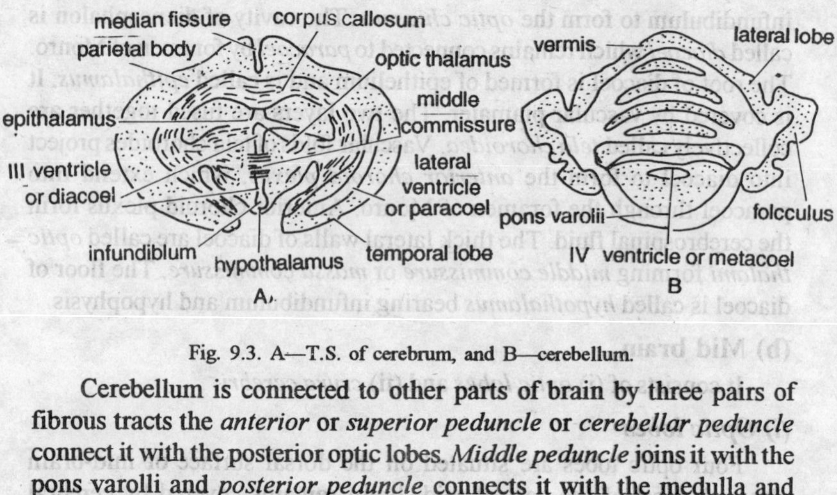

Fig. 9.3. A—T.S. of cerebrum, and B—cerebellum.

Cerebellum is connected to other parts of brain by three pairs of fibrous tracts the *anterior* or *superior peduncle* or *cerebellar peduncle* connect it with the posterior optic lobes. *Middle peduncle* joins it with the pons varolli and *posterior peduncle* connects it with the medulla and indirectly to the spinal cord.

(ii) Medulla oblongata

It is the posterior most part of brain and located underneath the cerebellum. It is broader in front but tapers posteriorly so as to form the spinal cord. The junction of medulla and spinal cord, forming a pointed depression called *calamus scriptorius*. On the ventral side of the anterior end of medulla oblongata there is a flat band of transverse nerve fibres called *pons varolli* which connect the two halves of cerebellum.

The cavity of medulla is called *myelocoel*. Its roof is thin, vascular and non-nervous. It consists of epithelium fused with piamater. Vascular folds of roof project into 4th ventricle called *posterior chorid plexus*. It is perforated by a small median aperture, *foramen of Magendie* and two lateral *foramina of Luschka*. The floor and lateral walls of myelocoel are very thick. The amount of cerebrospinal fluid in an average man is about 135 ml and about 500 ml is filtered daily, the fluid must be circulated and be reabsorbed into blood through arachnoid villi. If this fluid accumulates in subdural space, results into *external hydrocephalus* and if in the ventricles, it is *internal hydrocephalus*.

Functions of Brain

The olfactory lobes are concerned with the sense of smell. The cerebral hemispheres receive sensory impulses from sense organs and initiate motor impulses for voluntary movements. They are the seat of intelligence, will, memory and emotions. The hippocampal lobes are concerned with apetite for food, activity of endocrine glands and regulation of blood pressure. Diencephalon acts as a relay station in conveying the impulses to the cerebrum and as an integrating centre of autonomic nervous system. The anterior optic lobes or superior colliculi are concerned with sight while posterior colliculi are concerned with auditory sense. Crura cerebri carry sensory impulses from medulla to the cerebral hemispheres. Cerebellum maintains equilibrium and coordinates the voluntary movements. Medulla controls involuntary movements of the organs.

2. Spinal Cord

It is a whitish, tubular structure situated in the neural canal of vertebral column. All the three meninges i.e. piamater, duramater and arachnoid membrane covering it. It extends from medulla oblongata to the posterior most region of the body where it narrows into a non-nervous, slender thread like structure called *filum terminale*. It is swollen opposite the fore- and hind-limbs so as to form *brachial* and *lumbar enlargements*.

A deep median groove is present all along the midventral line, it is known as *ventral fissure*. *Dorsal fissure* is also present in the mid-dorsal line but it is a very shallow depression. The spinal cord encloses in it a narrow longitudinal cavity the *central canal* lined by epithelium. Central canal opens anteriorly into the myelocoel but closed posteriorly.

Histology. In a transverse section, the central canal surrounded by two types of nervous tissue, *grey matter* and *white matter*. The grey matter is internal in position with nerve cells which seems to be butterfly like structure. It is provided with the dorsal, lateral and ventral horns. The grey matter is surrounded by the white matter containing medullated nerve fibres.

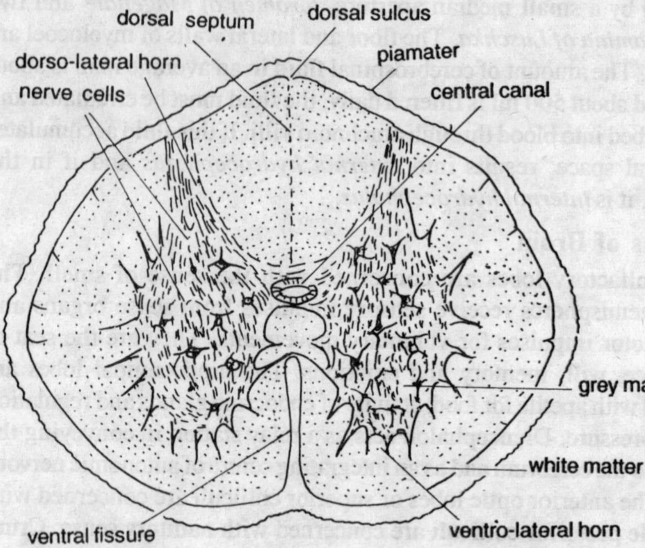

Fig. 9.4. T.S. of spinal cord of rabbit.

The whole matter is divided into two chambers by a *dorsal septum* and *ventral fissure*. In each chamber, grey matter divides white matter into three parts or funiculi, the *dorsal*, *lateral* and *ventral funiculi*.

The spinal cord conducts the sensory and motor impulses to and from the brain. It is also a centre for the reflex action.

II. PERIPHERAL NERVOUS SYSTEM

It includes - (1) *Cranial nerves* and (2) *Spinal nerves*

1. Cranial nerves

There are 12 pairs of cranial nerves in rabbit besides a pair of terminal nerve.

O. *Nervous Terminalis*. It is a fine nerve arising from the mucous membrane of nasal sac and joins the fore-brain. It is somatic sensory nerve of unknown function.

I. Olfactory nerve. It arises from the nasal sac as a number of bundles of non-medullated threads called *fila olfactoria.* The fibres passes through the olfactory foramina in the cribiform plate of the ethmoid bones on their way to the fore brain. A branch of olfactory nerve supplies to *Jacobson's organ.*

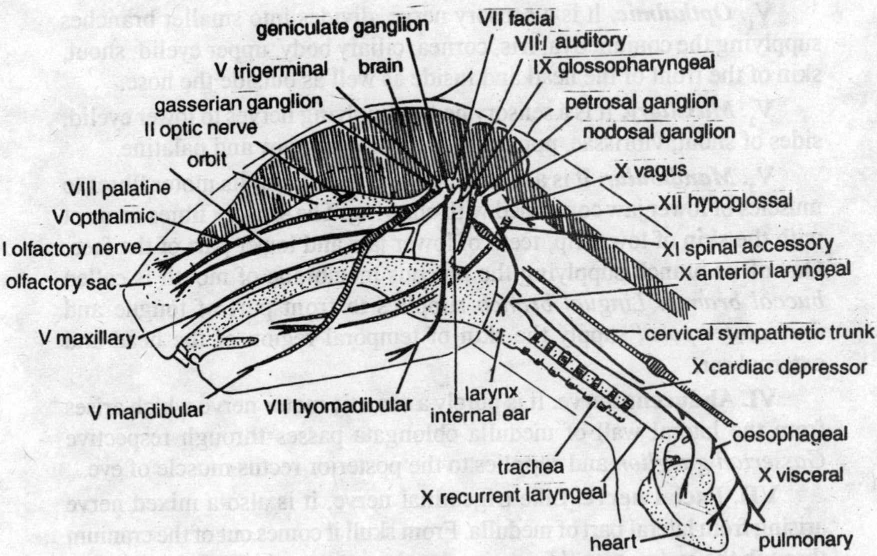

Fig. 9.5. Cranial nerves in lateral view.

The nerve is a somatic sensory and is responsible for the sense of smell.

II. Optic nerve. Starts from the retina of eye and form the characteristic *optic chiasma*. It is very thick and forms a part of brain rather than a cranial nerve. It enters the cranium through *optic foramen* in the middle of orbitosphenoid bone.

The optic nerve is a somatic sensory and is concerned with the sense of sight

III. Occulomotor nerve. It is a short nerve and through the *foramen lacerum anterius* (present between alisphenoid and besisphenoid bones) joins the crus cerebrum. It starts from 4 eye muscles, *inferior oblique, internal rectus, superior rectus* and *inferior rectus.*

It is mainly a somatic motor nerve. It controls the movement of eye ball, iris, ciliary body and lens.

IV. Pathetic or Trochlear nerve. It starts from the dorsal surface of the brain between optic lobes and cerebellum. From cranium it emerges alongwith occulomotor nerve through the foramen lacerum anterius. It is very small and fine nerve and is distributed to the *superior oblique muscles* of the eye balls.

It is mainly a somatic motor and causes rotation of eyeball.

V. Trigeminal nerve. Arising from the lateral sides of anterior end of medulla oblongata. It joins the *Gasserian ganglion* from which its three branches are given :

V_1. ***Opthalmic.*** It is a sensory nerve, divides into smaller branches supplying the conjunctiva, iris, cornea, ciliary body, upper eyelid, snout, skin of the front of the head and inside as well as outside the nose.

V_2. ***Maxillary.*** It is a sensory nerve supplying nerves to lower eyelid, sides of snout, vibrissae, upper lip, teeth of upper jaw and palatine.

V_3. ***Mandibular.*** It is a mixed nerve. It distributes its motor fibres to muscles of lower jaw concerned with chewing. The sensory fibres connect with the skin of lower lip, teeth of lower jaw and lower part of the face. One of its branch supplying the mucous membrane of mouth is called *buccal branch. Lingual branch* supplies to front part of tongue and *auriculotemporal* supply the skin of temporal region of the head and external ear.

VI. Abducens nerve. It is purely a somatic motor nerve which arises from the lateral wall of medulla oblongata passes through respective *Gasserian ganglion* and supplies to the posterior rectus muscle of eye.

VII. Facial nerve. Like trigeminal nerve, it is also a mixed nerve arising from lateral part of medulla. From skull it comes out of the cranium through the *stylomastoid foramen* near the tympanum. Each facial nerve enters into the *geniculate ganglion* of its side and gives rise three branches :

VII_1. ***Palatinus.*** It is purely a visceral sensory nerve formed by sensory fibres from mucous membrane of buccopharyngeal cavity, nasal passage and from taste buds.

VII_2. ***Chorda tympani nerve.*** It is also a visceral sensory nerve. Sensory fibres from taste buds, muscles of tongue and snout pass through the tympanic cavity to join other branches of facial nerve.

VII_3. ***Hyomandibular nerve.*** It is a mixed nerve with visceral motor and visceral sensory fibres. The visceral motor fibres supply the lower jaw muscles, dermal muscles of the face, pinna and skin and a few superficial neck muscles and salivary glands. The visceral sensory fibres emerge from the salivary glands.

VIII. Auditory or acoustic nerve. It is a somatic sensory nerve arising from the internal ear and joins the lateral side of medulla oblongata. It is formed by the union of *cochlear nerve* from cochlea and *vestibular nerve* from the utriculus, sacculus and semicircular canal. It enters the cranium through a foramen in the periotic bone and bears an *acoustic ganglion*.

IX. Glossopharyngeal nerve. It is a mixed nerve. It arises from the side of medulla oblongata. It bears the *pterosal ganglion* and leave the cranium through *foramen lacerum posterius*. Soon after its origin it divides into following branches:

IX_1. *Lingual nerve.* Its visceral sensory fibres supplying the back of tongue.

IX_2. *Pharyngeal nerve.* Its visceral motor fibres supplying the muscles of pharynx.

X. Vagus or pneumogastric nerve. It emerges from the side of medulla oblongata by many roots. It leaves the cranium through foramen lacerum posterius and bears two ganglia, *jugular ganglion* inside the cranium and *nodosal ganglion* outside the cranium. It gives rise 3 branches :

X_1. *Anterior laryngeal nerve*: also called superior *laryngeal* innervates the mucous membrane of the larynx and crico-thyroid muscles.

X_2. *Cardiac depressor.* Brings impulse from heart and aortic arches. A fine branch forms a plexus in the sinuatrial node.

X_3. *Main trunk.* It is a prominent branch, running straight backwards through the neck. It gives off the recurrent *laryngeal* or *posterior laryngeal* branch just before entering the thorax. It supplies to all the muscles of neck. The main trunk sends *oesophageal*, *cardiac* and *pulmonary branches* to the respective organs. It pierces the diaphragm and enters the abdomen supplying *gastric* and *intestinal* branches to stomach and intestine.

The vagus is mixed nerve.

XI. Spinal accessory nerve. It consists of a cranial and a spinal part. Cranial part is made up of visceral motor fibres derived from vagus nerve. The spinal part is made up of somatic motor fibres. The spinal fibres enter the cranium through foramen magnum to join the cranial fibres. It leaves the skull by jugular foramen. The cranial fibres innervate certain muscles of pharynx and larynx. The spinal fibres supply certain muscles of neck and shoulder.

XII. Hypoglossal nerve. It is a somatic motor nerve derived from posterior ventral spinal roots and supplies the muscles of the tongue and those below it. It leaves the cranium through the condylar foramen. Some fibres of XII together with certain spinal nerve form a plexus in the neck, called *ansa hypoglossi* from which nerves go to muscles that draw larynx backward.

2. Spinal Nerves

In rabbit there are 37 pairs of spinal nerves. They are classified into five categories on the basis of regions of back bone:

(i) *Cervical*. Comprising 8 pairs.

(ii) *Thoracic*. Comprising 12 pairs.

(iii) *Lumbar*. Comprising 7 pairs

(iv) *Sacral*. 4 pairs

(v) *Caudal or coccygeal* - 6 pairs.

Each spinal nerve arises from the spinal cord by the two roots: *dorsal* and *ventral*. The dorsal root is a prolongation of dorsal column of grey matter. It consists of sensory as well as viscerel fibres. It bears the *dorsal ganglion* adjacent to spinal cord. Like wise ventral root is a prolongation of ventral column of grey matter. It is composed of motor fibres. It has no ganglion like the dorsal ganglion. Two roots i.e. dorsal and ventral unite in the neural canal to form a spinal nerve. Thus spinal nerves are mixed in nature. Spinal nerve comes out through *intervertebral foramen* siuated laterally between two adjacent vertebrae.

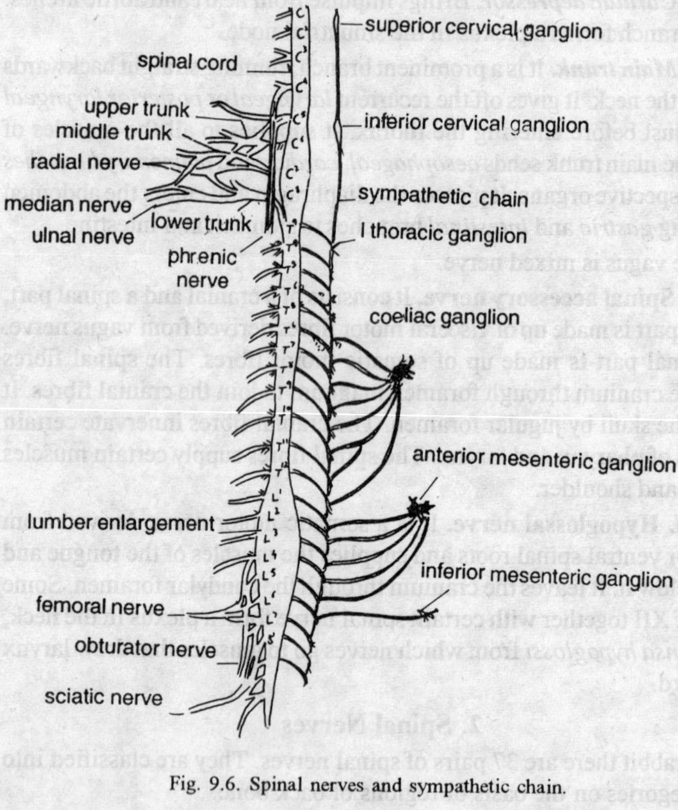

Fig. 9.6. Spinal nerves and sympathetic chain.

The first pair of cervical nerve emerge between skull and atlas vertebra. Similarly each thoracic, lumbar, sacral and caudal spinal nerve emerges via intervertebral foramen behind the corresponding thoracic, lumbar, sacral and caudal vertebra.

Outside the neural canal each spinal nerve is divided into 3 branches:

(a) *Dorsal branch* or *ramus dorsalis*

(b) *Ventral branch* or *ramus ventralis*

(c) *Central branch* or *ramus communicans.*

Ramus dorsalis branch innervates the skin, and muscles of dorsal part of the body; ramus ventralis to the muscles and skin of lateral parts of the body. The visceral branch joins a ganglion of autonomic nervous system.

The 1, 2 and 3 cervical spinal nerves supply the skin by their ramus dorsalis and to the muscles of neck by ramus ventralis. The ventral branch of 3rd cervical spinal nerve gives off *auricular nerve* which supplies the pinna of ear. The ramus ventralis of 4th, 5th and 6th unite to form *cervical plexus*. The cervical plexus gives off a nerve called *phrenic nerve*. Phrenic nerve innervates diaphragm, heart and lungs.

The ventral rami of 5th, 6th, 7th and 8th cervical spinal nerves and the Ist thoracic spinal nerve anastomose together to form the *brachial plexus*. Nerves that emerge out from this plexus innervate the skin and muscles of shoulder and the forelimbs *radial*, *ulnare* and *median* are main nerves. The ramus dorsalis of the cervical nerve supply skin of their own side.

The dorsal rami of the thoracic spinal nerves supply to the skin of the chest and the ventral rami form the *intercostal nerves* supplying intercostal muscles attached to the ribs. 1st, 2nd and 3rd lumbar spinal nerves supply to the abdominal muscles and skin. 4th, 5th, 6th and 7th lumbar spinal nerves and 1st, 3rd sacral spinal nerves unite to form *sacral plexus* or *lumbo-sacral plexus.* The main branches of this plexus are *femoral*, *obturator* and *sciatic nerves* supplying to the muscles and skin of hind limbs. 4th sacral spinal nerve supplies to the skin and muscles of sacral region. The caudal spinal nerve supply to the tail region.

III. AUTONOMIC NERVOUS SYSTEM

While the somatic portion of the nervous system operates to preserve the integrity of the organism with reference to the external environment, the *autonomic system* acts to help to maintain a steady state within the internal environment . For instance, it functions to maintain a constant body temperature and to regulate the rate of heart beat.

The autonomic system works automatically and without voluntary input. Its effectors are smooth and cardiac muscles and glands. Like the somatic system, it is functionally organized into reflex pathways. Receptors within viscera or internal organs relay information via afferent nerves to the central nervous system , the information is integrated at various levels, and the decision is transmitted along efferent nerves to the appropriate muscles or glands.

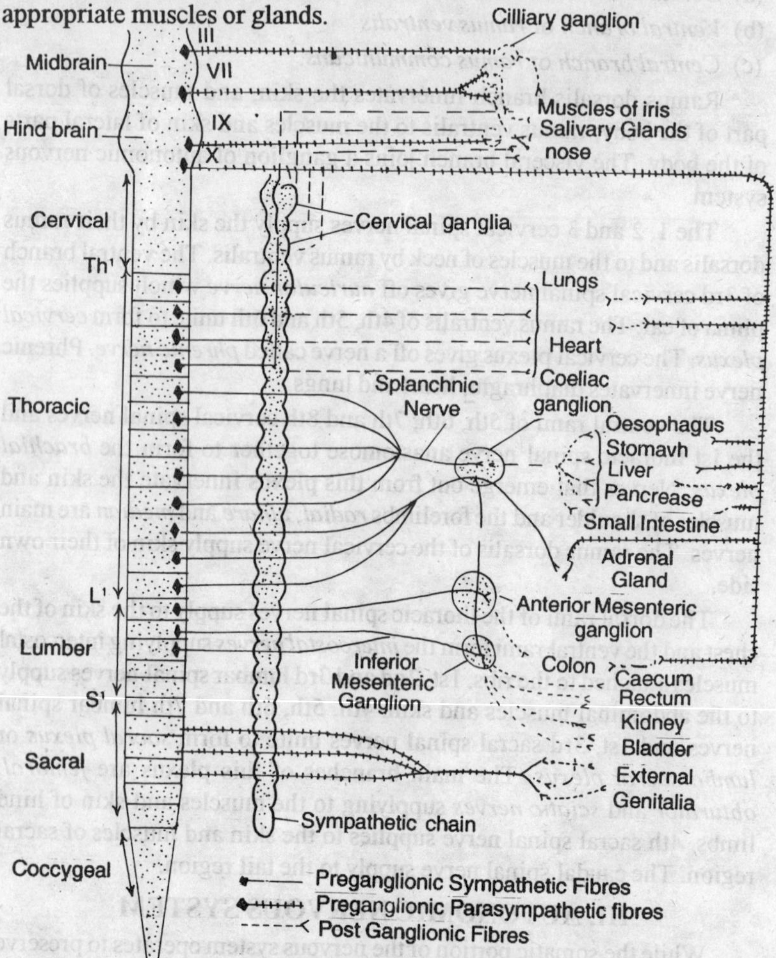

Fig. 9.7. The Autonomic Nervous system.

The autonomic nervous system is divisible into two systems.

(1) *Sympathetic nervous system* and (2) *Parasympathetic nervous system*

1. Sympathetic Nervous System

Sympathetic nervous system is said to be have a *thoracolumbar outflow* because this term indicates the level at which its fibres emerge from the central nervous system is spinal nerves. Preganglionic fibres are relatively short. They reach the sympathetic ganglia by way of the visceral rami of spinal nerves. Most of the small but tough ganglia are *chain ganglia* arranged like two parallel strings of beads on the *sympathetic trunks* which are just ventral to the vertebral column. There are also two pairs of *cervical ganglia*, the *anterior cervical ganglion* and the *posterior cervical ganglion* respectively. There are 12 pairs of thoracic, 6-7 pairs of lumbar and 3-4 sacral *sympathetic ganglia*. The thoracic and abdominal sympathetic ganglia are connected with the spinal nerves by short white rami communicants composed of medullated axons emanating from neurons situated in the spinal cord. These neurons are known as *preganglionic neurons* and their axons are *preganglionic fibres*. The fibres synapse with dendrons of other neurons which lie in *sympathetic ganglia* and send their non-medullated axons to supply the internal organs. These neurons are called *post ganglionic neurons* and their axons are *post ganlionic fibres*. Thus the sympathetic ganglia act as relay centre. The postganglionic fibres may reach the viscera directly or by way of the grey rami communicants and spinal nerves. Besides there are 3-large prevertebral ganglia (unpaired) located in abdominal region infront of lumbar vertebrae and constitute a *coeliac plexus*. From infront backwards these are *coeliac*, *superior mesenteric* and *inferior mesenteric ganglion*. These are obviously, additional sympathetic ganglia.

Long and non-medullated postganglonic fibres from cervical ganglia innervate ciliary muscles and sphincter muscles of the iris of eyes, mucous membrane of nose, palate and mouth, lacrymal glands and salivary glands. Postganglionic fibres arising from post cervical and first few thoracic ganglia innervate heart, larynx, trachea, bronchi and lungs. Fromc coeliac and superior mesenteric ganglia innervate various parts of gut, digestive glands and blood vessels of abdomen. Fibres arising from inferior mesenteric ganglion innervate posterior part of large intestine and urinogenital system.

The sympathetic nervous system is supplied to the viscera only. The postganglionic fibres are motor and chiefly control the movements of the viscera. As the movements of the viscera are involuntary, the sympathetic nervous system may be said to control involuntary action.

2. Parasympathetic Nervous System

This part of autonomic nervous system is said to have a *craniosacral flow* because it emerges from the central nervous system with cranial nerves, III (occulomotor), VII (facial), IX (glossopharyngeal) and X (vagus) with about 3 (2nd, 3rd and 4th) sacral spinal nerves. The preganglionic fibre of IIIrd terminates into *cililary gangila* located at the back of eye-orbit. Postganglionic fibres arising from a ciliary ganglia innervate the iris sphincter and ciliary muscles of eyes. Preganglionic emerging from the VII cranial nerve pass to the sub-mandibular or sphenopalatine ganglia situated in head. Postganglionic fibres from sphenopalatine ganglia innervate lacrymal glands, mucous membrane of nose, palatine and pharynx. The preganglionic fibres coming from IX cranial nerve ends in the *otic ganglion* that send postganglionic fibres to the parotid salivary gland and mucous membrane of buccal cavity. The preganglionic fibres of Xth cranial nerves terminate into very small ganglia located in the wall of heart, larynx, trachea, abdominal blood-vessel, liver, pancreas and adrenal.

The sacral part of parasympathetic system consists of preganglionic fibres located in white rami communicants of 2nd, 3rd and 4th pairs of sacral nerves. These firbes first converge to form a *pelvic-splanchnic* nerve, but then diverge again to terminate in small ganglia located close to or in kidneys, urinary bladder, genital organs and posterior parts of large intestine. From respective ganglia short postganglionic fibres emerge and innervate their respective organs.

Comparison of Sympathetic nervous system and Parasympathetic nervous system:

Sympathetic	*Parasympathetic*
1. Stimulates adrenal secretion.	1. Inhibits adrenal secretion
2. Accelerates heart beat.	2. Retards heart beat.
3. Dilates the trachea, bronchi and lungs.	3. Constricts these organs.
4. Dilation of pupils.	4. Contraction of pupil.
5. Inhibits secretion of salivary and digestive glands	5. Stimulates secretion of salivary and digestive glands.
6. Inhibit peristalsis of gut due to relaxation of gut muscles	6. Constriction of gut muscles causing peristalsis.
7. Closes anus by constricting anal sphincter.	7. Relaxes anal sphincter.

8. Relaxes urinary bladder but contracts its sphincter.	8. Contracts urinary bladder but relaxes its sphincter.
9. Contraction of blood vessels.	9. Dilation of all the blood vessels except coronary vessel of heart.
10. Stimulates secretion of lacrymal glands.	10. Inhibits its secretion.
11. Increases blood sugar by stimulating secretion of glucagon.	11. Decreases blood sugar stimulating secretion of insulin.
12. Contraction as well as relaxation of oviduct.	12. No. effect.
13. Secretion of Sweat glands (cold sweat).	13.
14. Stimulates ejaculation of semen.	14. Stimulates external genitalia and increase sex urge.
15. Increases R.B.C. counting and decreases blood clotting time.	15.

10

Sense Organs

Like frog and other vertebrates receptor organs are also present in rabbit. The varieties of information received by the body as input from environmental stimuli are sensed, appreciated and interpreted by the organisms in many ways. To codify the product of these stimuli several classifications have been proposed. Although none is wholly satisfactory. The senses and the sense organs may be named according to the organ system with which they are associated. *Somatic* refers to extremeties, body wall and portions of the head; *visceral* refers to the vital organs of the digestive, circulatory, excretory, respiratory and endocrine systems. The sense with a wide distribution in the body are called *general sense*, those limited to a restricted region are called *special sense*. The general senses include pain, temperature, appreciation, touch, visceral sense, body sense, position senses and unconscious sense associated with reflex activities. Those of special sense include hearing, smell, balance, sight and taste.

GENERAL SENSORY ORGANS

Tango Receptor (Mechano-receptor)

These are receptors for the sensation of touch, pressure (deep), pain, heat and cold and are present in the skin hence also called *cutaneous mechano receptor*. These are of three types:

1. Free nerve endings

They are present in the form of fine fibres endings. These are the primary pain receptors. They are located in many regions including the skin, pulp of tooth, corner of eye and the intestinal tract. Tissue damage may evoke pain sensations: damaged tissue release histamine that stimulates the pain receptors. Besides pain receptors, nerve endings are also thermal receptors.

2. Basket nerve endings

These are fine branching fibres of sensory neurons wrapped round the hair follicle forming a sort of basket. These are present only in hairy parts of body. These are tactile receptors.

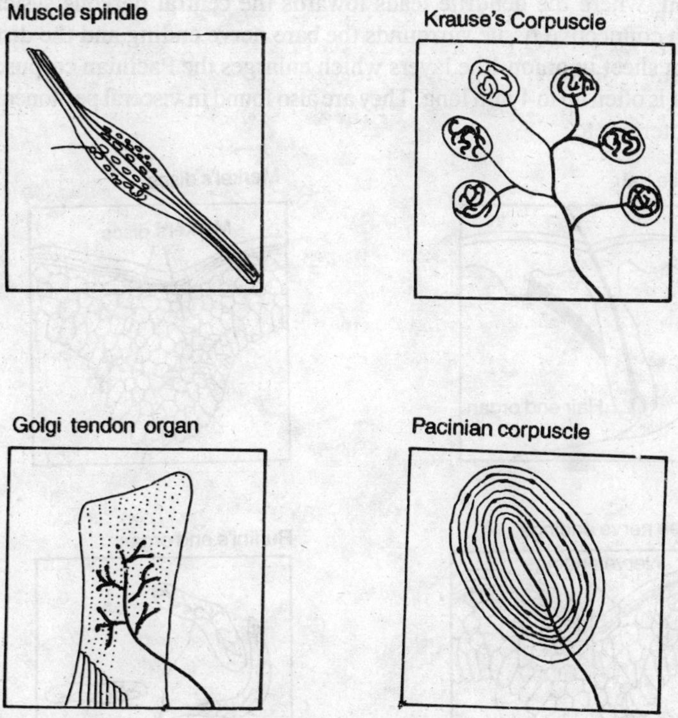

Fig. 10.1. Cutaneous receptors.

3. Encapsulated nerve endings

These comprise nerve fibres in the dermis surrounded by a sheath of connective tissue, the whole thing forming a *cutaneous* or *tactile corpuscles.* These include *Meissner's corpuscle* (touch), *Pacinian corpuscle* (pressure), *Merkel's corpuscle* (touch), *corpuscle of Ruffini* (warmth), *end bulb of Krause (*cold) etc.

Meissner's corpuscles are present in the skin of lips, nipples, penis, palm, sole, fingertips etc. It is composed of a thin connective tissue capsule enclosing epithelial cells on each of which rests a flattened, bare nerve ending.

The end bulb of Ruffini are flattened, bulb-like endings within a fine, connective tissue network. The end bulbs of Krause are similar but are more spherical bulb of connective tissue with knob-like nerve ending. These bulbs respond to decrease in temperature.

The central core of Pacinian corpuscle is single, slightly branched dendrite which terminates in a slight bulb. Myelin surrounds the proximal portion, where the dendrite leads towards the central nervous system. Tough connective tissue surrounds the bare nerve ending and the distal myelin sheet in onion-like layers which enlarges the Pacinian corpuscle until it is often up to 4 mm long. They are also found in visceral peritoneum, mesenteries etc.

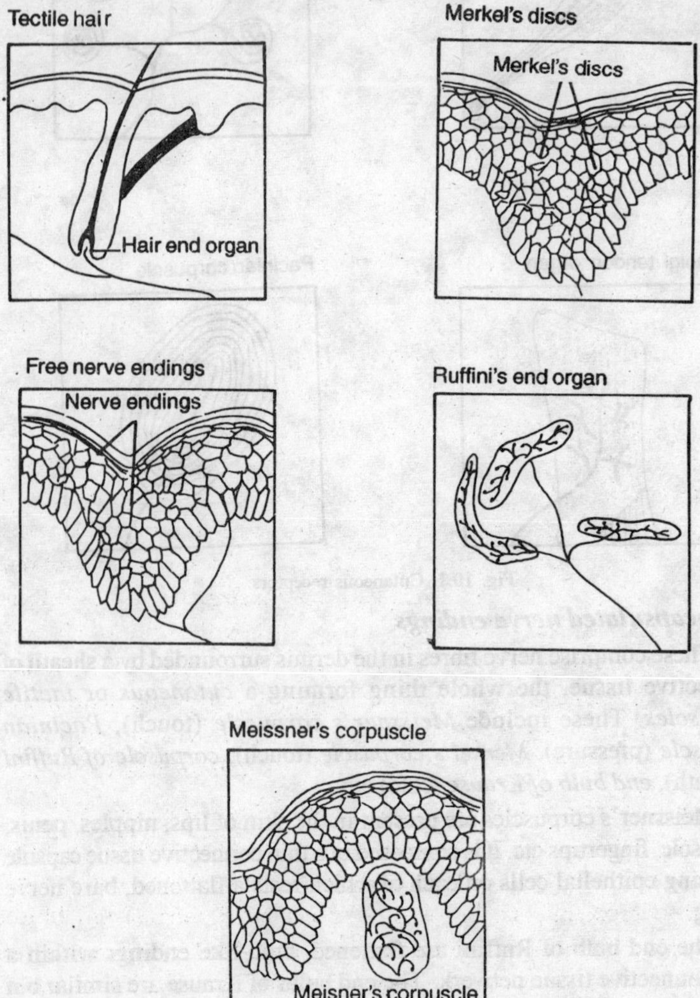

Fig. 10.2. Cutaneous receptors.

Mechano-receptors located in tendons, joints and skeletal muscles are called *proprioreceptors.* These report the movements of various parts of the body and are in the form of free nerve endings lying between individual muscle fibres. Complex mechano-receptors are neuromuscular spindles and neurotendinous endings of *Golgi* located at the junction of muscles and a tendon.

SPECIAL SENSE ORGANS

1. Chaemoreceptors

These receptors receive chemical stimuli from fluid medium. The stimulating chemicals probably form a weak bond with the receptor cell membrane, causing a temporary depolarisation of sensory cells. They are of two types:

1. Gustato-receptors (receptors for the sense of taste)
2. Olfacto-receptors (sense of smell)

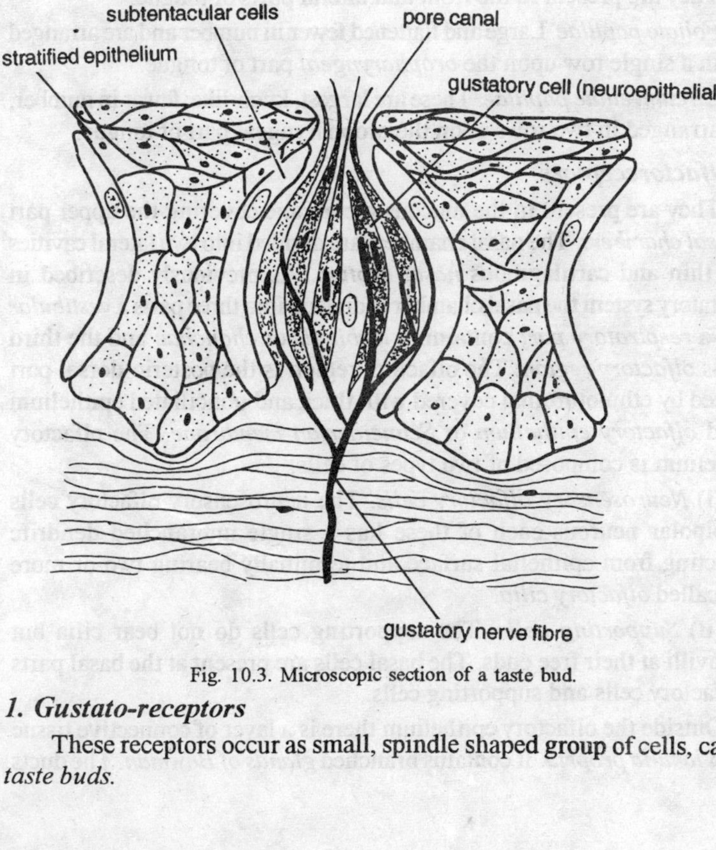

Fig. 10.3. Microscopic section of a taste bud.

1. Gustato-receptors

These receptors occur as small, spindle shaped group of cells, called *taste buds.*

These receptors occur in the mucous membrane of tongue, palate, pharynx and other parts of buccopharyngeal cavity. These taste buds are situated on papillae of the tongue. Each bud is made up of two types of cells *neurosensory cells* or *gustatory cells* and *supporting cells* or *sub-tentacular cells*. Each neurosensory cell bears a minute *sensory hair* or *taste hair* at its free end and its lower basal end is attached to fine nerve fibres which are joined to VII, IX and X cranial nerves. The sub-tentacular cells are immature taste cells. Each mature cell is replaced in about 10-12 days by unmature taste cell. The sensory hairs are not present in supporting cell. Each taste bud opens on the surface of tongue by a minute pore called *taste pore*.

There are four types of papillae in the tongue of rabbit.

(i) *Filiform papillae*. These are small, conical and present on 2/3 anterior part of tongue.

(ii) *Fungiform papillae*. These are rounded, knob-like fewer in number. They are present in the front and lateral parts of tongue.

(iii) *Foliate papillae*. Large and flattened fewer in number and are arranged in a single row upon the *oropharyngeal* part of tongue.

(iv) *Circumvellate papillae*. These are largest, knob-like, fewer in number, arranged in two rows upon the oropharyngeal part of tongue.

2. Olfactoreceptors

They are present in the mucous membrane covering the upper part of *nasal chambers*. The nasal chambers are divided into two lateral cavities by a thin and cartilaginous *nasal septum*. As previously described in respiratory system the nasal chamber is divided into three parts a *vestibular part*, a *respiratory part* containing *turbinals* or *chonchae* and the third part is *olfactory region*. The olfactory region is the posterio-dorsal part marked by ethmoturbinal covered with thick and nonciliated epithelium called *olfactory epithelium* or *Schneiderian membrane*. The olfactory epithelium is composed of two types of cells:

(i) *Neurosensory olfactory cells*. The neurosensory olfactory cells are bipolar neurous each of these has a single unbranched dendrite projecting from epithelial surface and terminally bearing two or more cilia called *olfactory cilia*.

(ii) *Supporting cells*. The supporting cells do not bear cilia but microvilli at their free ends. The basal cells are present at the basal parts of olfactory cells and supporting cells.

Outside the olfactory epithelium there is a layer of connective tissue called *lamina propria*. It contains branched *glands of Bowman*. The ducts of these glands open at the epithelial surface and secrete a watery mucous to protect the olfactory epithelium.

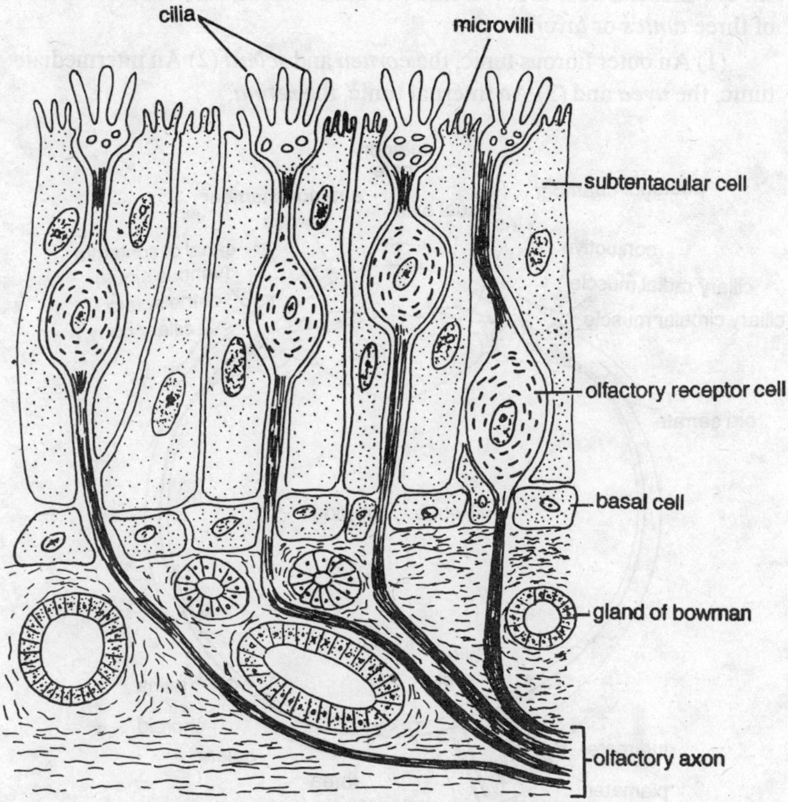

Fig. 10.4. Showing olfactory epithelium.

Vomeronasal organs of Jacobson. These are also olfactory receptor in frog and lower mammals. They are absent in rabbit and vestigeal in man. They are found in the nasal chamber.

3. Photoreceptors

Paired lateral eyes are the photoreceptors in the vertebrates. These are the sensitive detectors of light waves. The photoreceptor cells are stimulated by approximately radiomagnetic spectrum from 760-390 millimicrons. The complete structure of the photoreceptor comprises the eye proper and accessory parts such as eyelids, several glands and their ducts and the extraocular muscles. The optic nerve is made up of fibres projecting from the sensory retina of the eye to optic lobes in the brain.

Structure of Eye

The eye is roughly spherical and held within the orbit by means of six eye-muscles-four are *recti* and two are *obliques*. Its wall is composed of three *tunics* or *layers*.

(1) An outer fibrous tunic, the *cornea* and *sclera* (2) An intermediate tunic, the *uvea* and (3) An internal tunic, the *retina*.

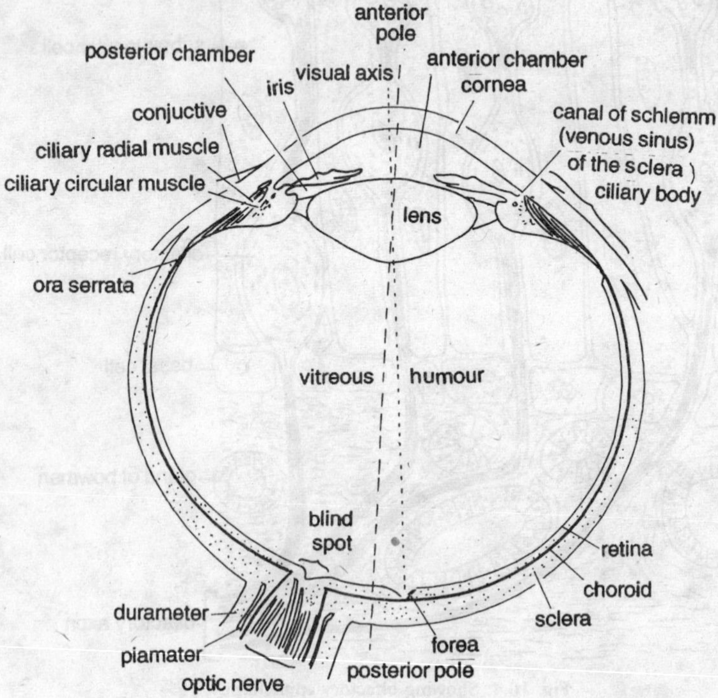

Fig. 10.5. Diagram of horizontal section of the eye.

1. Fibrous tunic

The fibrous tunic is a quite thick lamina consists of the larger, posterior opaque *sclera* and the smaller anterior transparent *cornea*. The sclerotic region composed of dense fibrous connective tissue and is largely hidden in the orbit. Only a small portion of it is visible externally. This is commonly called 'white' of the eye. All the six muscles described above are inserted over the sclerotic. The cornea is a transparent window that permits light to enter the eye. It is covered externally by a thin and transparent layer, *the conjunctiva*. Conjunctiva is composed of stratified epithelium and is continuous with the epidermal lining of eyelids. It is fused with the cornea. Conjunctiva is very sensitive to pain and irritating substances. The transparency of cornea is due to lack of any blood vessels and the state of hydration of its matrix. The avascular cornea is nourished by the *aqueous humour*, present in the anterior chamber, and by the lacrimal secretion i.e. tears in which it is bathed. Carotenoid pigments are responsible for the yellow tint of the cornea of some animals.

2. Uvea or Vascular tunic

It is comparatively thinner forming middle layer of the wall of an eye ball. It shows three regions (i) *Choroid,* (ii) *Iris* and (iii) *Ciliary body.*

(i) *Choroid.* It is a vascular, pigmented coat around the inner layer i.e. retina and just below the sclerotic. It is dark brown in colour and helps to darken the cavity of the eyeball so that the light rays are absorbed thus there is no internal reflection of rays that might blur the image. In many mammals, particularly *ungulates, cetaceans* and *carnivores*, there is light reflecting *tapetum lucidum* within the choroid layer. In the dark when flash of light fall into them so that, their eyes seem to glow like balls. At the junction of sclerotic and the cornea, the uvea abruptly bends into the cavity of the eye ball to form the anterior surface of a thin coloured partition, the *iris.*

(ii) *Iris.* It is perforated in the centre by the *pupil.* It contains two sets of muscles, the *sphincter* and *dilator muscles.* These muscles are involuntary. These muscles are innervated by postganglionic fibres of sympathetic and parasympathetic systems. These muscles regulate the amount of light entering the eye ball by varying the size of pupil. The degree of pigmentation in iris gives characteristic colour of the eye. In albino rabbits, there is no pigmentation in the iris, the pink colour of the eyes is due to its blood capillaries.

(iii) *Ciliary body.* On the inner side of the iris, choroid becomes thicker, less vascular and less pigmented muscular structure known as ciliary body. There are many folds on the inner layer of ciliary body forming ciliary *processes.* The ciliary body contains a number of *radial* and *circular muscle fibres.* It also has a rich autonomic nerve supply.

A space is left between the iris and cornea. It is called *anterior chamber* of the eye. Similar, but narrow chamber lies behind i.e. between iris and lens is called *posterior chamber.* Both the chambers communicate with each other around the margin of the pupil and are filled with aqueous humour containing 98% of water, some proteins and sodium chloride.

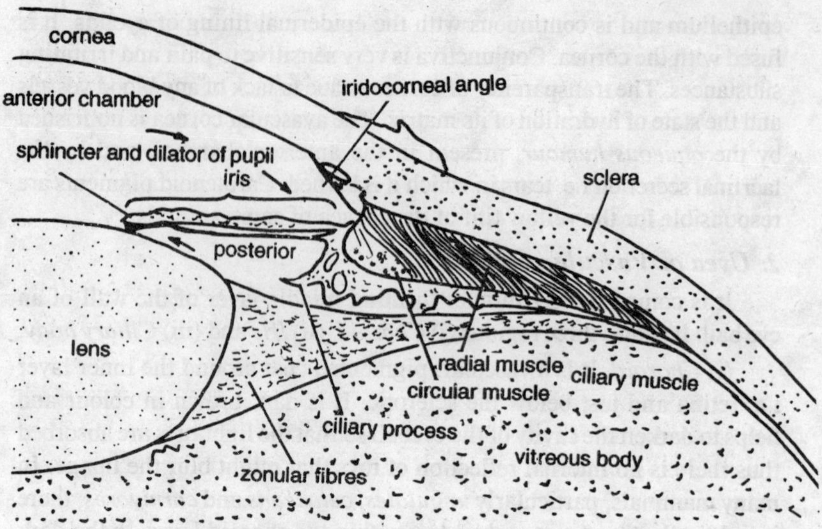

Fig. 10.6. Showing iris and ciliary body.

3. *Neurosensory tunic or Retina*

The innermost layer of the eye ball is called *retina*. Like uvea it also shows 3 distinct regions, *optic*, *ciliary* and *iridial regions*. The *iridial* and *ciliary regions* are pigmented, non sensory and thin. They contribute to the formation of iris and ciliary body respectively and terminate at the rim of pupil. The *optic region* is in contact with choroid. It is thick and sensitive to light. It terminates abruptly at ciliary body with an irregular and serrated area known as *ora serrata* or *ora terminalis*.

A small area of the optic part of the retina lying exactly upon the optical axis is called *area centralis* or *yellow spot* or *macula lutea*. There is a shallow depression in the area centralis called *fovea centralis*. This area has cone cells only and is the place of most distinct vision. The optic nerve leaves the eyeball from behind by piercing the eye coats. This point is known as *blind spot*, it lacks the rods and cones here amacrine and horizontal cells are present, their role is insignificant.

Retina is composed of four layers of cells pigmented epithelial cells, rods and cones, bipolar neurons and ganglionic neurons

(i) *Pigmented epithelial cells*. These are closely applied over the choroid. The pigmented cells extend and surround a part of the visual cells of second layer.

(ii) *Layer of rods and cones or photoreceptor cells*. These cells are sensitive to light and are also called *visual cells*. They are greatly elongated and are arranged with their axis perpendicular to the surface of retina. They are of two types (a) *Rods* and (b) *Cones.*

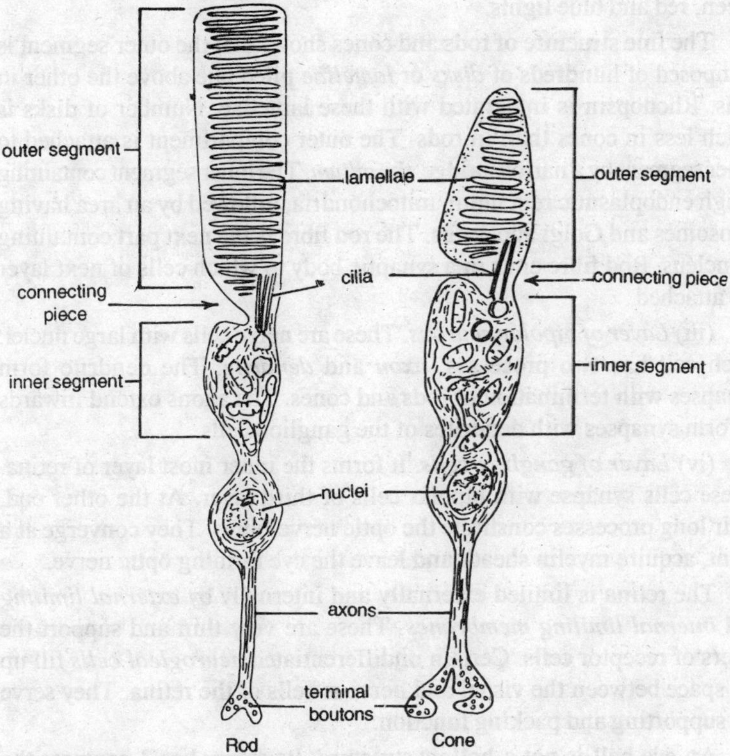

Fig. 10.7. A rod and a cone in section.

(a) *Rods.* These are long, slender and filamentous. A rod cell consists of outer rod like part, called *retinal rod* and an inner thread like part, the *rod-fibre*. The retinal rod shows two compartments outer cylindrical segment containing purplish red pigment, *rhodopsin* or *visual purple.* The inner segment is slightly bulged containing rod nucleus. These perceive variations in intensities of light and dark in dim light conditions. In the retina of owls only rods are there that is why owls prey during night and are called *night birds.*

(b) *Cones*. These are shorter and thicker as compared to the rods. A cone cell consists of two parts an outer broad and tapering part called *retinal cone* and an inner slender part, *cone fibre*. The retinal cone shows two compartments the outer conical segment and inner bulged segment containing a nucleus. The cones perceive objects and various colours in bright light. The retina of fowls contains only cones cells. The cones have more than one kind of pigment. In man there are 3 pigments for green, red and blue lights.

The fine structure of rods and cones shows that the outer segment is composed of hundreds of *disks* or *lamellae* piled one above the other in rods. Rhodopsin is integrated with these lamellae. Number of disks is much less in cones than in rods. The outer compartment is attached to inner segment by a narrow bridge, the *cilium*. The inner segment containing rough endoplasmic reticulum, mitochondria, followed by an area having ribosomes and Golgi apparatus. The rod fibre is the next part containing a nucleus. Rod fibre ends in a synaptic body to which cells of next layer are attached.

(iii) *Layer of bipolar neurons*. These are nerve cells with large nuclei. Each cell has two processes, *axon* and *dendrite*. The dendrite form synapses with termination of rods and cones. The axons extend inwards to form synapses with dendrites of the ganglion cells.

(iv) *Layer of ganglion cells*. It forms the inner most layer of retina. These cells synapse with bipolar cells of third layer. At the other end, their long processes constitute the optic nerve fibres. They converge at a point, acquire myelin sheath and leave the eye forming optic nerve.

The retina is limited externally and internally by *external limiting* and *internal limiting membranes*. These are very thin and support the layers of receptor cells. Certain undifferentiated *neurogleal cells* fill up the space between the visual and nervous cells of the retina. They serve the supporting and packing function.

An eye ball is not a hollow structure. Its cavity has 3 contents the *aqueous humour*, the *vitreous humour* and the *lens*. All these are transparent and play a part in refracting the light rays that enter the eye ball.

Lens. It is a transparent, biconvex somewhat flexible and fibrous crystalline body lying just behind the pupil and held in position by elastic *Zonular fibres* or *suspensory ligament* or *Fibres of Zinn* made up of radially arranged fibres. It is surrounded by a thin but tough and transparent *lens capsule*.

The *aqueous humour* is a clear watery fluid present in the *aqueous chamber* lying infront of lens. The *vitreous humour* is viscous, jelly like substance containing 99% of water, some salts, mucoprotein and hyaluronic acid. It is present in *vitreous chamber* lying behind the lens of eye ball. At its periphery the jelly is condensed to form *vitreous membrane* or *hyaloid membrane*. A narrow *hyaloid canal* runs through the vitreous humour obliquely from the region of blind spot upto the centre of posterior face of lens. Some rounded cells, hyalocytes and collagen fibres are found suspended in the vitreous humour.

Accessory structures associated with eyes

Eye lids. At dorsal and ventral edges of an orbit, the skin becomes transversely folded to form thin *upper* and *lower eyelids* infront of the eye. The two eyelids are united to each other at their ends. The upper eye lid is larger and both eyelids are movable. The free margin of each eyelid is provided with two rows of stiff edged hairs, called *eyelashes*. They protect the eye balls. The *nictitating membrane* is reduced. It is formed by folding of skin epidermis only from the inner angle of eye. A non-functional vestigieal nictitating membrane,called *plica semilunaris* occurs in human eye.

Fascial sheath of eyeball. A thin fascial membrane envelops an eye ball from optic nerve to sclerocorneal function separating it from orbital fat. It is, however, separated from the eyeball by a thin episcleral space traversed by delicate bands of connective tissue. It provides protection to the eyeball.

Glands of eyelids. At the median end of each eyelid is a small opening called, *punctum lacrimale* which leads into a slender canal, the *lacrimal duct*. The duct from the two eyelids leads into a *nasolacrimal canal*. Through this canal excess of tears produced by *lacrimal gland* is ordinarily drained into the nasal cavity. There are 3 lacrimal glands which form the *lacrimal apparatus* which is situated near the outer angle of each eye.

Between the outer skin and the inner conjunctiva each eyelid is reinforced by a stiffening fibromuscular layer, the *tarsal plate* containing numerous *Meibomian glands*. These glands pour out an oily secretion at the inner edge of the eyelid.

Glands of Moll are modified sweat glands pour out their secretion in the hair follices of eyelids.

Harderian-glands, modified sebaceous glands are absent in rabbit and man but present in frog, whale, mice and shrews.

Working of the eyes

The eye works more or less on the principle of a photographic camera. The light rays reflected from an object are refracted by the conjunctiva, cornea, aqueous humour and the rays are then focused by the lens on retina, so that sharp and inverted image is formed on retina. Maximum refraction is caused by cornea, which places the image approximately on the retina. The retina receive the inverted image is carried by optic nerve to the optic lobes, where real sensation of sight arises and the animal see the object upright.

The power of *accomodation* is well exhibited by the eyes for the objects situated at various distances i.e. the eye adjusts itself to distinctly see objects at varying distances. The accomodation is brought about by changing the convexity of the lens with the help of ciliary body and suspensory ligament because the distance between lens and retina is fixed and unchangable. In normal condition when the eyes are at rest, the lens is kept flattened by the suspensory ligament, and thus it is adjusted for seeing distant objects. For focusing the eye on near objects, the convexity of the lens is increased by reducing the tension in suspensory ligament. The tension is reduced by contraction of ciliary muscles of ciliary body. The lens becomes thickened which reduces its focal length and a clear image of the near objects are formed on the retina. Reverse occurs to see objects at greater distance.

Rhodopsin or visual purple is a visual pigment of rods. In light rhodopsin is resolved into *opsin* and *retinene*. In dark retinene and opsin combine to form rhodopsin. Vitamin A is an important constituent of retinene. Deficiency of vitamin A naturally causes deficiency of rhodopsin inducing night-blindness.

Iodopsin or *visual violet* is another photo-sensitive pigment sensitive to bright light and colour is found in cones. Its biochemistry is not well known. However, few workers are of the opinion that there are three types of cones for red, green and blue colours.

There are two types of visions, *monocular vision* and binocular vision. In rabbit both the eyes have divergent axes of vision because the fields of vision do not overlap each other. Therefore, animal sees all around by its two eyes, each eye covers a different field of vision, such type of vision is monocular vision.

In man and higher mammals the vision is binocular. In such a vision, the field of vision of the two eyes overlap or even coincide each other, thus both the eyes can see a single object and the animal can estimate the distance also.

4. Phonoreceptors

The function of ears is not only hearing but also to maintain equilibrium of the body. The auditory apparatus of a higher mammal consists not only of a sensory receiving apparatus, the *internal ear*, but also of a *middle* and *external ear*, whose supplimentary functions are primarily the collection and amplification of vibrations from the air.

(A) External ear

It is found only in mammals and absent in rest of the vertebrates. It consists of two parts.

(i) *Pinna or auricle*. It is a flap like structure found on either side of the head. It is made up of cartilage and striped muscles. In rabbit, it can be moved at the will of animal. In most animals they aid in catching the direction whence sound waves come.

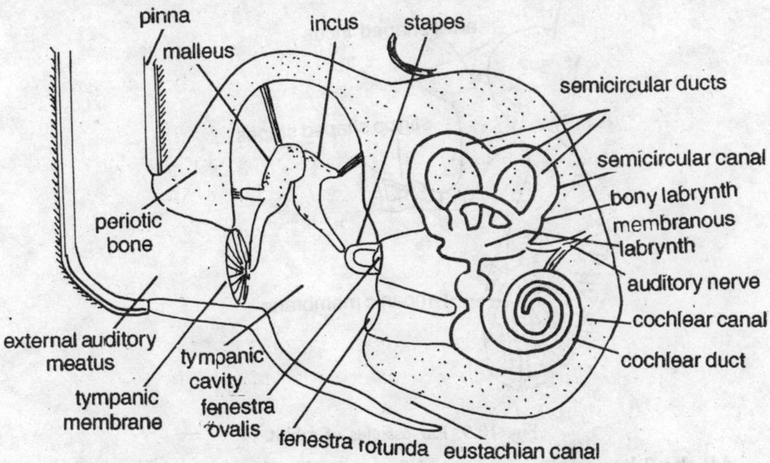

Fig. 10.8. The mammalian ear.

(ii) *External auditory meatus*. It is the passage way that leads to the middle ear. It is about 2.5 cm in length, slightly bent and larger at either end than in the middle. At the posterior end of the canal is attached a *tympanic membrane* or *ear drum*. The auditory meatus or canal is lined with skin, and is supplied with wax-glands and outward- projecting hairs.

(B) Middle ear

A middle ear or tympanum is in the form of an irregular air-filled chamber present between the tympanic membrane and internal ear in the tympanic bulla. The tympanum is connected with the pharynx by means of *Eustachian tube* or *pharyngo- tympanic tube*. The tympanic membrane or ear drum is made up of three layers. The central layer is made up of connective tissue core of mesodermal in origin, the outerlayer is skin of external ear which is ectodermal in origin and the inner layer is the pharyngeal epithelium of endodermal in origin. The inner wall of tympanic cavity is formed by bony auditory capsule and has two apertures, upper *fenestra ovalis* and lower *fenestra rotunda*. These put middle ear in communication with the internal ear. In the middle ear three small bones are present called *ear ossicles. Malleus* is the first bone which is club-shaped and attached on one side to the tympanic membrane on the other side to the other bone the *incus*. Incus is middle bone and is anvil shaped. The narrow end of incus is attached to 3rd ossicle, the *stapes*. The stapes is stirrup-shaped bone and is fixed to the membrane on the fenestra ovalis.

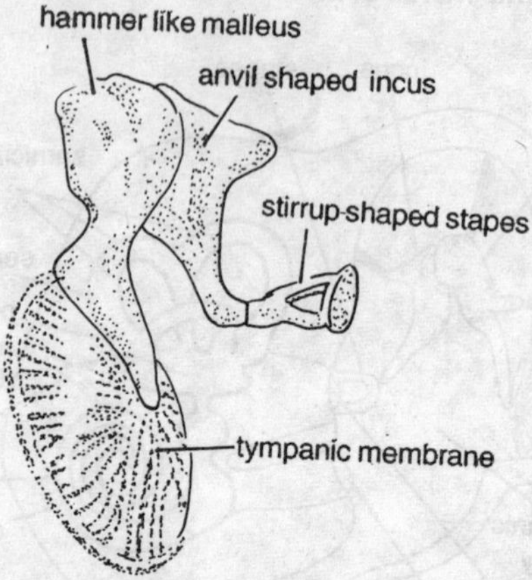

Fig. 10.9. Ear ossicles of rabbit.

All the 3 bones are originated from the jaw bones in mammals, the malleus from articular, incus from quadrate and stapes from hyomandibular.

(c) Internal ear

The internal ear also known as *membraneous labyrinth* consists of two chambers:

(a) *Utriculus* above and (b) *sacculus* below. Both are connected by the *sacculo-utricular duct.* A thin endolymphatic duct arises from the sacculo-utricular duct and terminates dorsally into an endolymphatic sac. Three *semicircular canals* arise from the utriculus. These are *anterior*, *posterior*, and *external* or *horizontal semicircular canals* according to their position. Each duct connects with utriculus at both the ends. The proximal parts of anterior and posterior ducts form a common duct, *crus commune.* Anterior and posterior semicircular canals arise together from an ampulla. Each ampulla contains sensory *crista* made up of ciliated cells and supporting cells. Crista resembles the *macula* in structure, except that the sensory hair of its receptor cells are much longer and there are no otolith. From the sacculus arises a long coiled duct known as *cochlear duct.* Utriculus, ampullae, semicircular canals, sacculus and cochlear duct all are filled with a thick fluid called *endoplymph* which contains minute particles of calcium carbonate known as *otoliths*.

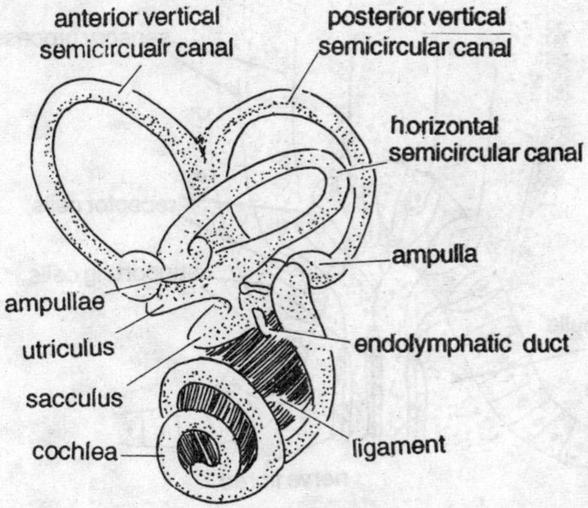

Fig. 10.10. The membranous labyrinth.

The internal ear is situated in the temporal region of the skull (periotic bone) which also takes the shape of internal ear. Thus entire internal structure is enclosed in a *bony labyrinth*. The space between two is filled with *perilymph*, a fluid very much like the cerebrospinal fluid.

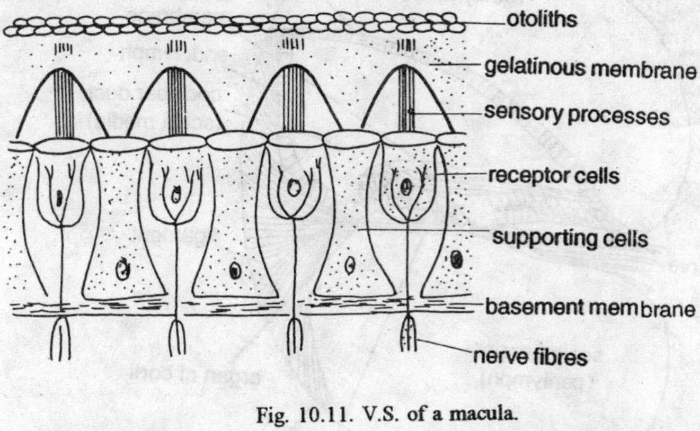

Fig. 10.11. V.S. of a macula.

In each internal ear there are six sensory areas: a *crista* present in the ampulla of each semicircular canal, *macula utriculi* in the wall of utriculus, *macula sacculi* in the wall of *sacculus*, *organ of Corti* in the cochlear duct. Each macula consists of a group of receptor cells and supporting cells.

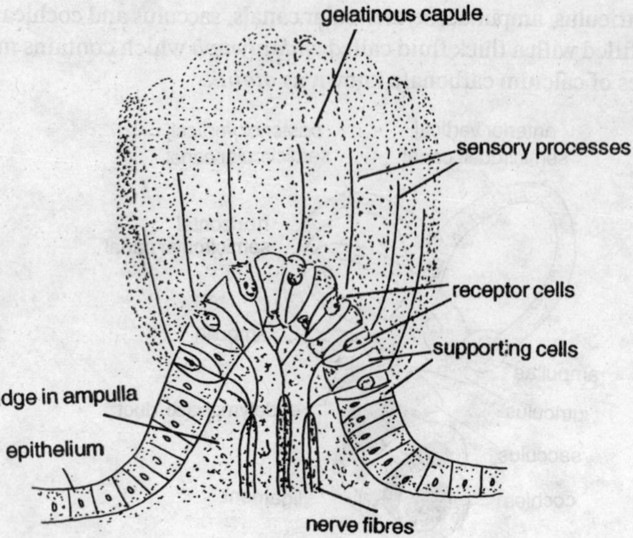

Fig. 10.12. V.S. of crista.

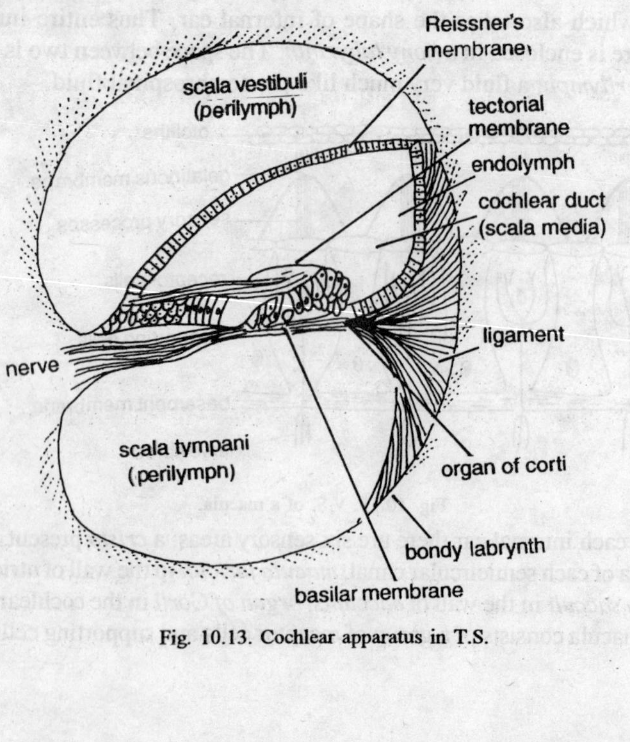

Fig. 10.13. Cochlear apparatus in T.S.

These receptor cells bear short hair like processes at the free ends and send fibres to the vestibular branch of Vlll cranial nerve. The sensory processes of the receptor cells are partly embedded in a gelatinous mass, the *cupula*.

Cochlea

The spirally coiled cochlear duct (2 turns) joins the bony labyrinth in such a manner that a chamber is formed above and below the duct called *scala*. A transverse section of bony labyrinth passing through the cochlea shows three chambers upper *scala vestibuli* filled with perilymph, middle *scale media* filled with endolymph and lower *scala tympani* filled with perilymph. The scala vestibuli and scala tympani communicate with each other at the tip of cochlea by a narrow passage called *helicotrema*. Scala media and scala tympani are separated from each other by *basilar membrane* and scala media is separated from scala vestibuli by *Reissner's membrane*. The basilar membrane bears on it the real receptor organ of hearing, the *organ of Corti*. Organ of Corti consists of cuboidal epithelium lining the scala media, some supporting cells and some sensory hair cells. The hairs of hair-cells are embedded in an overhanging gelatinous *tectorial membrane* resting very lightly over them. Axonic fibres from the other end of sensory cells pass into the basilar membrane and then into the

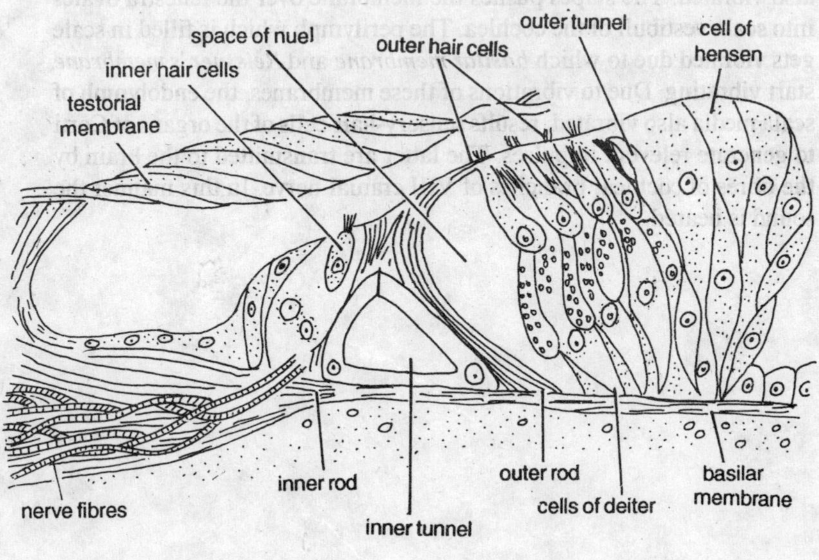

Fig. 10.14. Enlarged diagram of the organ of Corti.

cochlear branch of VIII cranial nerve. The supporting cells are without hairs and are called *pillar cells*.

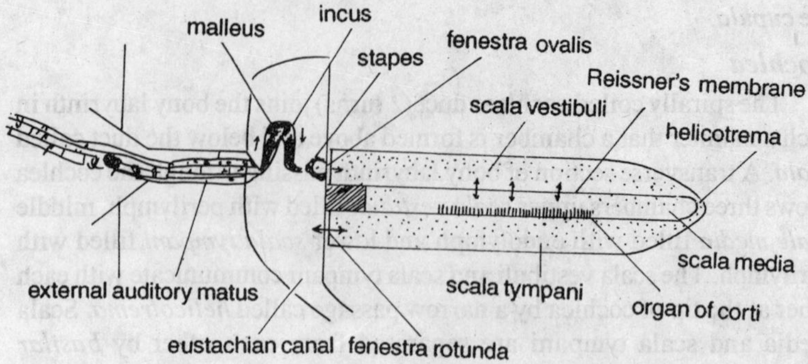

Fig. 10.15. Mechanism of hearing.

Working of ear

Rabbit move the air pinnae in all the directions to catch the sound waves. Passing through external auditory meatus and strike the tympanic membrane or ear drum which starts vibrating due to which the ear ossicles also vibrated. The stapes pushes the membrane over the fenestra ovales into scala vestibuli of the cochlea. The perilymph which is filled in scale gets vibrated due to which *basilar membrane* and *Reissner's membrane* start vibrating. Due to vibrations of these membranes, the endolymph of scala media also vibrated, results sensory-hair cells of the organs of Corti to generate relevent impulses. The latter are transmitted to the brain by the fibres of cochlear branches of VIII cranial nerve. In this manner the sound is heared.

11
Excretory System

In the living organism a number of chemical reactions are taking place, some reactions yield substances which are useful to the organism while other reactions yield various by-products that must be got rid off for the reason that they not only are useless to the organism but may become decidedly harmful if retained. One of such byproduct is carbon dioxide which is mostly eliminated by the process of respiration. The other byproducts are urea, uric acid, ammonia etc., which are called *nitrogenous waste products,* mostly these are eliminated outside the body along with water and ions in the form of urine by excretory system.

While most people tend to think of excretory system only as the system that disposes of the waste products of metabolism, its role is considerably broader. The excretory system also regulates salts, water contents and pH of blood, calcium contents, sodium contents and much else.

The excretory system consists of two *kidneys,* which produce the urine, paired *ureters,* which conduct urine to the bladder, *urinary bladder,* which stores urine, and the *urethra,* which conveys urine to outside.

KIDNEYS

The kidneys are closely associated with the dorsal body wall where they lie out side of peritoneum. They are not situated opposite but obliquely to one another. The right is situated at a somewhat higher level than the left. Each kidney measures 25 mm. in length but right one is slightly larger than left one.

The kidney is a dark red, bean-shaped organ. It is concave medially and convex laterally. The ureters and blood vessels are attached to the area of the concave edge called the *hilus.* The renal arteries and renal veins appear unproportionately large for the size of the organ, each artery being about the size of little finger, and the vein is even larger. Because the kidneys continuously regulate the fluid volume and composition of blood large amounts of blood must pass through them at all times. Each kidney is covered over by a thin renal capsule of fibrous connective tissue. If a kidney is cut in half (mid-sagitally) the cut surface shows that it is divided into two parts outer *cortex,* and inner *medulla.* A hollow structure called *pelvis* is continuous with the ureter. The kidney is subdivided by five connective tissue partitions into lobes. Each lobe is somewhat conical in shape and its apex is arranged to pass urine into the kidney pelvis. The apex of each lobe, called the *pyramid,* fits into cup shaped part of pelvis called, the *calyx*. The very tip of each pyramid is called *papilla.* Each papilla has a series of pores. Cortex is continued inside between the pyramids in the form of columns called *renal columns of Bertini.*

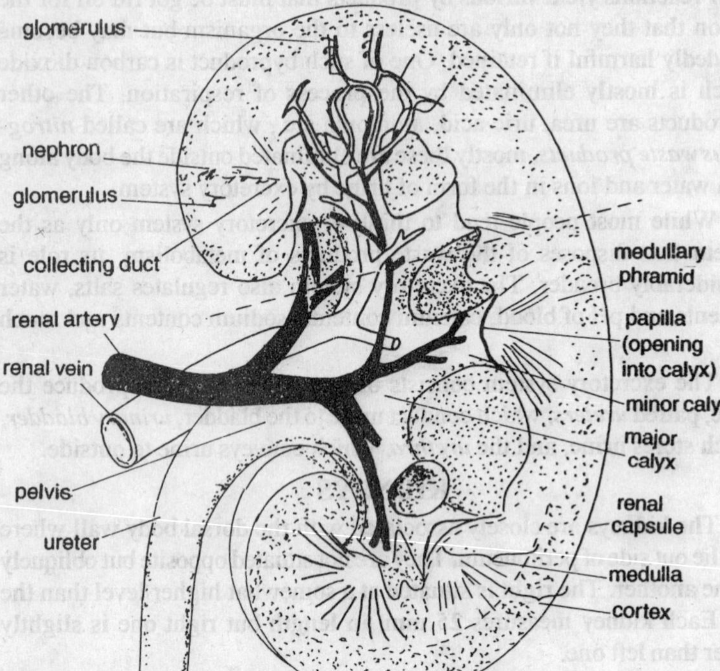

Fig. 11.1. The Mammalian kidney in section.

Microscopic examination of kidney reveals that it is composed of microscopic units called *nephrons* or *uriniferous tubules* about 2 lakh in rabbit, and 10 lakh in man which conduct the waste products to the papillae. Each nephron begins with a cup-shaped structure called *Bowman's capsule* situated in renal cortex. Each Bowman's capsule contains a network of blood capillaries called *glomerulus* connected with an afferent arteriole on one side and an efferent arteriole on other side. The Bowman's capsule and glomerulus are collectively known as *Malpighian capsule*. The outer wall of Bowman's capsule is made up of squamous cells while the inner wall that lines the concavity of capsule is composed of special types of less flattened cells, known as *podocytes*. These cells possess minute finger like processes which etwine around the capillaries of glomerulus. The Bowman's capsule is followed by a narrow and small neck, marked by ciliated cell.

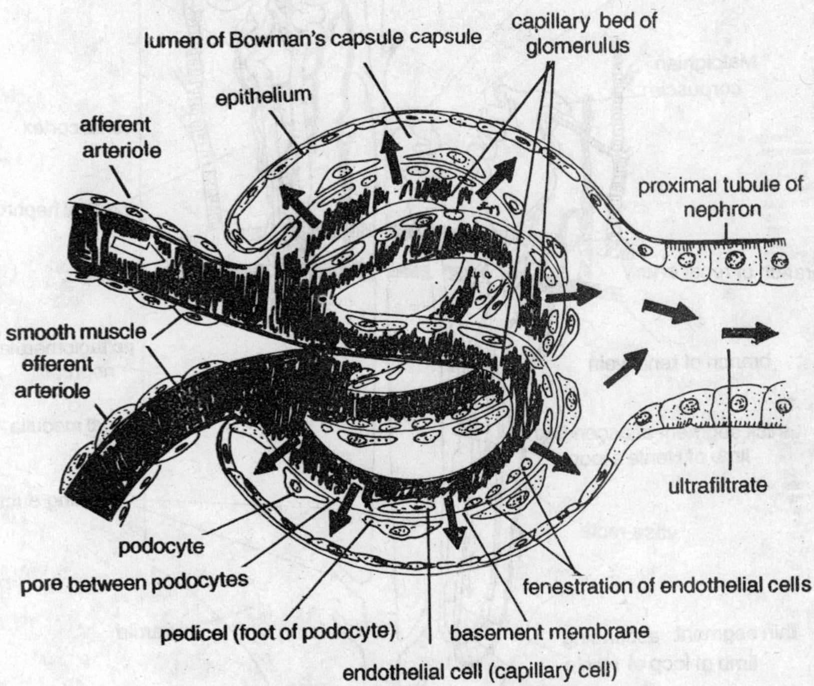

Fig. 11.2. Bowman's Capsule.

The remaining tube-like part of nephron is known as secretory tubule, which is very much coiled and divided into three parts :

(a) *Proximal convoluted portion*. It lies behind neck and marked by few coils. It is present in the cortical region.

(b) *Loop of Henle*. It is relatively narrow and'U'shaped tube. The part of this loop which comes down is called *descending limb* and the other part that goes up is known as *ascending limb*. Its some part lies in medulla and some part in cortex.

(c) *Distal convoluted tubule portion*. It is thicker and coiled and remains in the cortex.

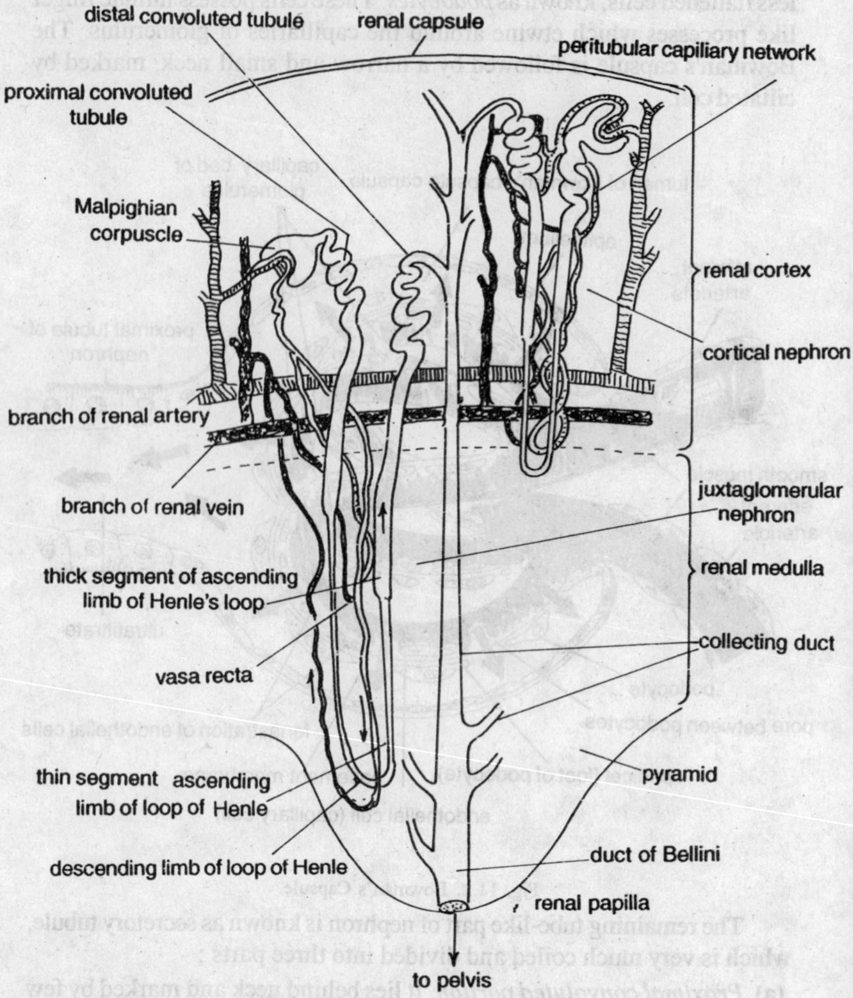

Fig. 11.3. Showing vascular supply.

The distal convulated tubule of neighbouring nephrons open into a *common collecting tubule.* These are long tubules which traverse through medulla in the pyramids. In the papilla of each pyramid, several adjacent common collecting tubules open into a common short and thick *duct of Bellini.* All the ducts of Bellini open at their tip into the pelvis.

On the basis of length, position and blood supply, there are two types of nephrons in the kidneys of rabbit:

(a) *Cortical nephrons.* The Malpighian capsules are located close to the kidney surface (cortex) and their loops of Henle are short. They form 15-35% of the total nephrons.

(b) *Juxta medullary nephrons.* The Malpighian capsules are present in the region where cortex and medulla meet. The loops of Henle are long, dipping down to the pyramids.

Blood supply to the kidneys

The renal artery enters the kidney and divides so as to form several arterioles. Each arteriole enters one Bowman's capsule as the *afferent arteriole* and divides into a number of capillaries forming the glomerulus. The blood from these capillaries is collected by the *efferent arterioles.* The efferent arteriole after leaving the capsule, divides into a network of capillaries called *peritubular network of capillaries* so as to distribute the blood in remaining parts of the tubule. In juxtamedullary nephron, the efferent arterioles breaks up in a network of capillaries in the form of hair pin loops called *vasa recta.* These capillaries unite to form the venuoles which unite to form the renal vein which leaves the kidney.

The ureters

From the *hilus* of each kidney arises a narrow, whitish duct called *ureter* which runs backwards along the dorsal abdominal wall and opens posteriorly into the urinary bladder.

Urinary bladder

It is a pear shaped body, having a transparent wall. It lies in the pelvic region ventral to the rectum and temporary stores the urine. The bladder opens into the *urinogenital canal* which is called *vestibule* in female and *urethra* in the case of male. In male urethra opens out at the tip of penis. In female the vestibules open out by vulva.

PHYSIOLOGY OF EXCRETION

Due to deamination of proteins or amino acids (metabolism) *ammonia* is produeed. It is a toxic substance as well as waste product. In liver it reaches in the form of *ammonium* and *carbonate* where it is converted into urea. This urea is then transported into kidneys through the blood, from where it is passed out with the urine.

The blood flows through the capillaries of glomerulus under pressure. As a result due to ultra-filteration, except blood corpuscles and some proteins, all the contents of blood come out in the Bowman's capsule through thin endothelium of blood capillaries. This is called filtrate and contains useful as well as useless substances. The useful being blood sugars, sodium ions etc. where as useless being urea, uric acid, hippuric acid etc. In the Bowman's capsule, some of the useful substances are reabsorbed and the filtrate passed into the lumen of the urinary tubule. All the useful substances and some water is reabsorbed. In the urinary tubules only concentrated urine remains. Excess of water and salts from the blood are eliminated by the kidneys and thus the composition of blood remains constant.

The urine is carried to the urinary bladder due to contraction of the walls of ureters. The urinary bladder collects the urine, which is passed outside at regular intervals at convenience. During passing out of the urine the sphincter muscles of bladder relax and muscles of the walls contract. Thus, urine is carried away to the urinogenital canal, from where it is passed out through the urinogenital aperture.

12

Reproductive System

The reproductive system is meant for the continuity of the race and production of young ones. The sexes are separate and sexual dimorphism is well marked.

MALE REPRODUCTIVE SYSTEM

It consists of a pair of *testes*, a pair of *vasa deferentia*, *uterus masculinus*, *urethra* and *penis* along with a number of *accessory glands* like *prostrate, Cowper's, perineal* and *rectal glands.*

Testes

These are paired oval, pinkish structures. They develop near the kidneys, on the dorsal wall of the abdomen but later shifted backwards and descend into two coelomic pouches, the *scrotal sacs*. Each testis measures about 25 mm. long. Each testis helds in its position within its scrotal sac by means of *spermatic cord* consisting of spermatic artery, vein, nerves and connective tissue. The cavity of the scrotal sacs are connected with the abdominal cavity by a narrow passage known as *inguinal canal*. Along the dorsal aspect of each testis there is a mass of twisted tubules, which is the part of kidney and is known as *epididymis*. This mass is differentiated into an anterior enlarged portion called *globus major* or *caput epididymis,* middle narrow called *corpus epididymis*, and posterior enlarged portion called *globus minor* or *cauda epididymis*. The whole epididymis measures upto 3 metres in rabbit and 6 metres in man. The cauda epididymis is connected with the scrotal sac by a cord of fibromuscular tissue known as *gubernaculum.* The testis communicates with its epididymis by fine ductules, the *vasa efferentia* which are lined with cilia. From the cauda epididymis a straight tube emerges out known as *vas deferens*. It enters the abdominal cavity through the inguinal canal. In abdominal cavity it curves round the ureter of its side and proceeds backwards to open into the *uterus masculinus*.

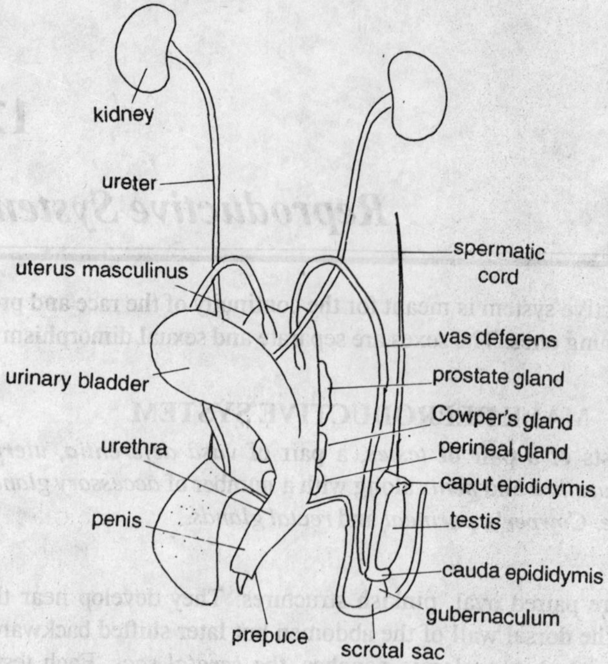

Fig. 12.1. Male urino-genital organs.

Uterus Masculinus

It is a dorso-median pouch like diverticulum opens into the urethra close to the opening of vasa deferentia. This is a remnant of embryonic *Mullerian duct.* It becomes glandular and secretes a thick and alkaline fluid.

Urethra

The urinary bladder and the uterus masculinus unite posteriorly to form a common passage the *urethra* or *urinogenital canal*. It is a long, narrow channel, which passes backwards through the muscular *penis*.

Penis

It is an erectile, cylindrical organ hanging in front of the anus from the ventral wall of abdomen, behind the pubic symphysis. It is covered by a loose sheeth of the skin. The distal portion of the penis is covered by loose fold of skin called *prepuce.* The tip of the penis covered by prepuce is called *glans penis*. Prepuce is attached to the glans at the base by means of a delicate fold of tissue *frenulum of the prepuce.* At the tip of penis

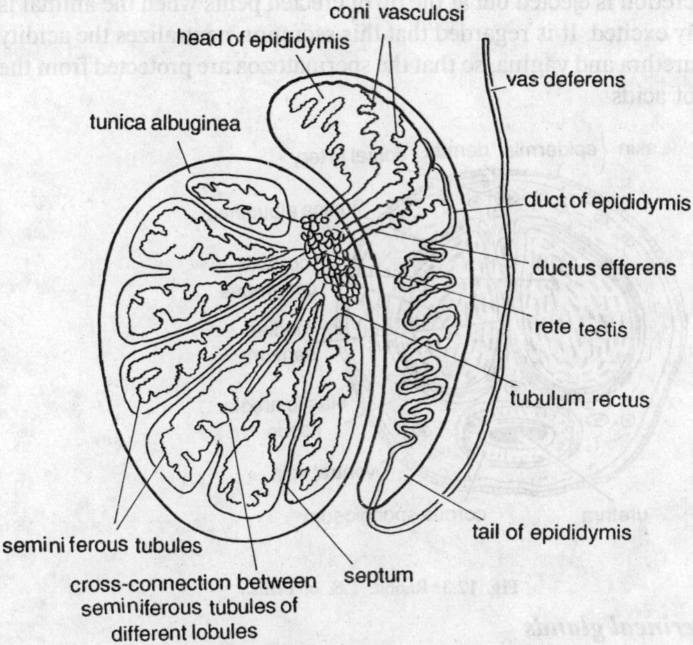

Fig. 12.2. Testis and epididymis. Showing general arrangement of seminiferous tubules and excretory ducts.

there is an aperture i.e. orifice or *urino-genital aperture*. The posterior wall of the penis is formed of a highly vascular, spongy tissue called *corpus spongiosum*. Its anterior wall is strengthened by a pair of hard ligamentous bodies, the *corpora cavernosa*.

Accessory glands

Three types of glands are associated with male reproductive system:

(i) Prostate glands

It is situated at dorso-lateral sides of uterus masculinus. It is composed of 4 or 5 lobes which open into the urethra by small prostatic ducts. It secretes a whitish fluid. The function of this fluid is to provide nourishment and activation of spermatozoa which are found in storage condition in epididymis.

(ii) Cowper's glands or Bulbo-urethral glands

These are situated on the dorsal wall of urethra behind the prostate gland. These are paired ovoid glands which open into urethra by short ducts. They secrete a transparent and alkaline viscous fluid. A drop of this secretion is ejected out at the tip of erected penis when the animal is sexually excited. It is regarded that this secretion neutralizes the acidity of the urethra and vagina, so that the spermatozoa are protected from the effect of acids.

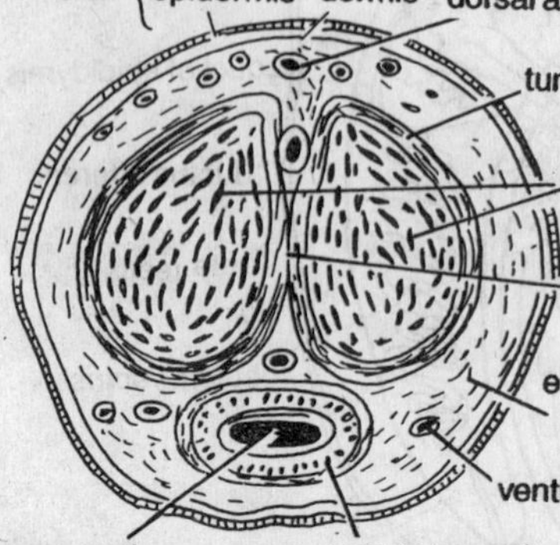

Fig. 12.3. Rabbit. T.S. of Penis.

(iii) Perineal glands

A pair of these glands are situated near the Cowper's glands. These glands open out by the ducts into the hairless perineal depression of the skin. These secrete odorous secretion whose smell attracts the opposite sex.

(iv) Rectal glands

These are situated on the sides of rectum in both the sexes. Probably they secrete odorous substance for the attraction of opposite sex during copulation.

Histology of Testis

Each testis is enclosed in a fibrous coat, the *tunica albuginea.* Out side tunica albuginea, there is a coat of serous membrane,called *tunica vaginalis* which continues over the gubernaculum and then lines the scrotal sac. Around the testis between two serous membranes there lies a coelomic space filled with coelomic fluid. A vertical partition, the *mediastinum* testis, extends inside from tunica albuginea and divides the mass of testis into a large ventral portion, and a small dorsal portion. In growths of the tunica albuginea, called *septula testis,* divide the testis into a number of lobules. These lobules contain one to three or more convulated *seminiferous tubules*, blood vessels, nerve fibres embedded in connective tissue mass. Numerous small groups of relatively large glandular cells called *Leydig's cells* or *interstitial cells* are present in connective tissue. These cells contain granules of a yellow pigment and secrete male sex hormones.

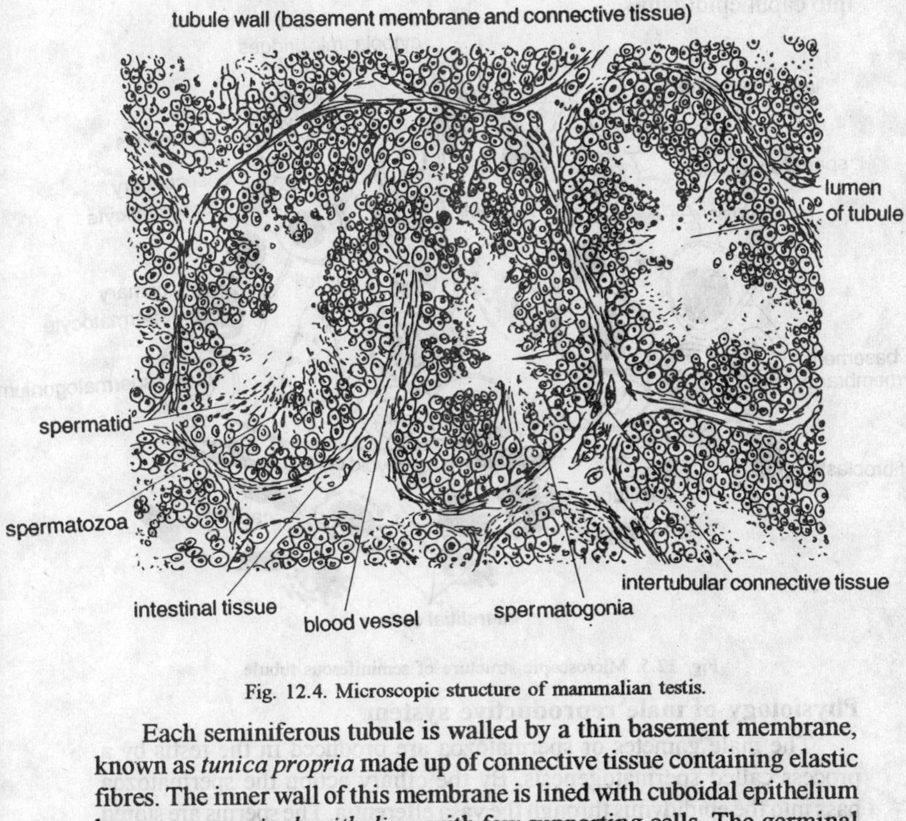

Fig. 12.4. Microscopic structure of mammalian testis.

Each seminiferous tubule is walled by a thin basement membrane, known as *tunica propria* made up of connective tissue containing elastic fibres. The inner wall of this membrane is lined with cuboidal epithelium known as *germinal epithelium* with few supporting cells. The germinal epithelium form *spermatogonia*, while supporting cells are large and are called the *cells of Sertoli* or *subtentacular cells.* The spermatogonia multiply by mitosis for sometime and then grow into primary *spermatocytes*. Each primary spermatocyte by first meiotic division gives rise to two haploid *secondary spermatocytes,* and each by the second meiotic division gives rise to two *spermatids*. Spermatids later get attached to Sertoli cells and change into spermatozoa by a process, the *spermiogenesis* or *spermateleosis*. Mature spermatozoa get free in the seminiferous tubules.

Seminiferous tubules are highly coiled proximally and gradually they become less coiled and finally straight before reaching the mediastinum testis. In the dorsal portion of testis, the seminiferous tubules form a network called *rete testis*. About 12-22 *efferent ductules* or *vasa efferentia* emerge out from rete testis, penetrate through tunica albuginea and open into caput epididymis.

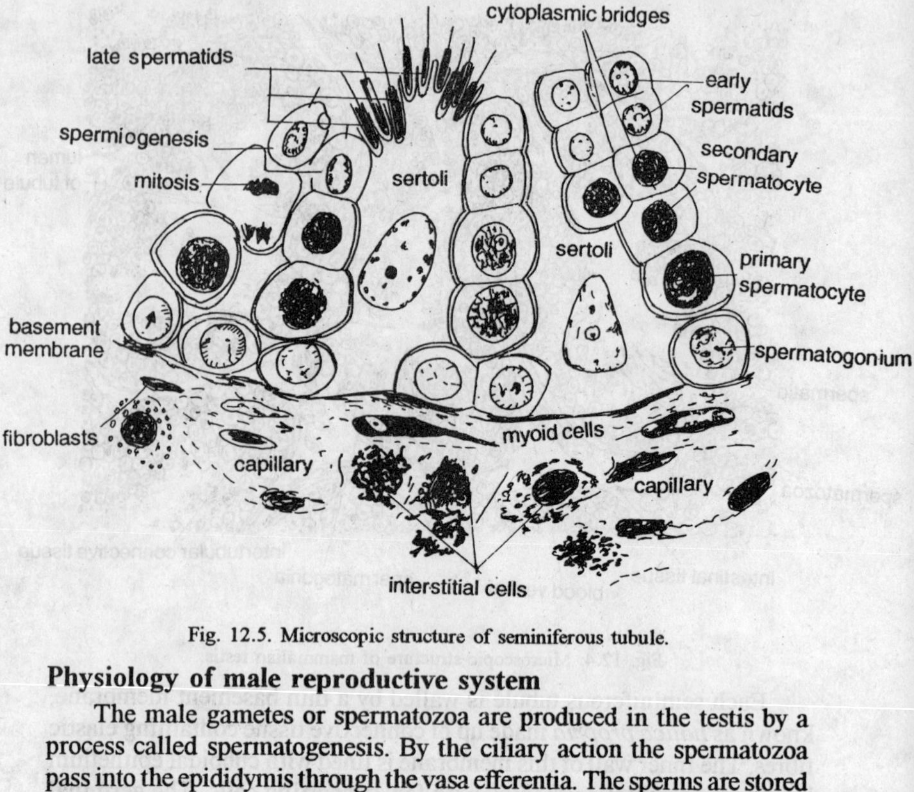

Fig. 12.5. Microscopic structure of seminiferous tubule.

Physiology of male reproductive system

The male gametes or spermatozoa are produced in the testis by a process called spermatogenesis. By the ciliary action the spermatozoa pass into the epididymis through the vasa efferentia. The sperms are stored in epididymis. From epididymis the spermatozoa are carried into uterus masculinus by the vasa deferentia. The movement of spermatozoa through epididymis and vasa deferentia takes place by peristaltic contraction of their muscular wall. From uterus masculinus the sperms are ejaculated partly by the contraction of muscular wall of urethra and partly by the muscles of *bulbo*-and *ischio-cavernosum*. Due to contraction of these muscles, the urethra is squeezed. The sperms are activated by the secretion of prostate glands. The Cowper's gland also helps in activation. The sperms mixed with prostate secretion form the semen. The semen is discharged into the vagina of female during copulation. The erection of penis is due to enormous blood supply to these muscles so that the whole penis becomes enlarged and stiff.

FEMALE REPRODUCTIVE SYSTEM

The female reproductive system consists of *ovaries*, *oviducts*, *vagina* and *accessory glands*.

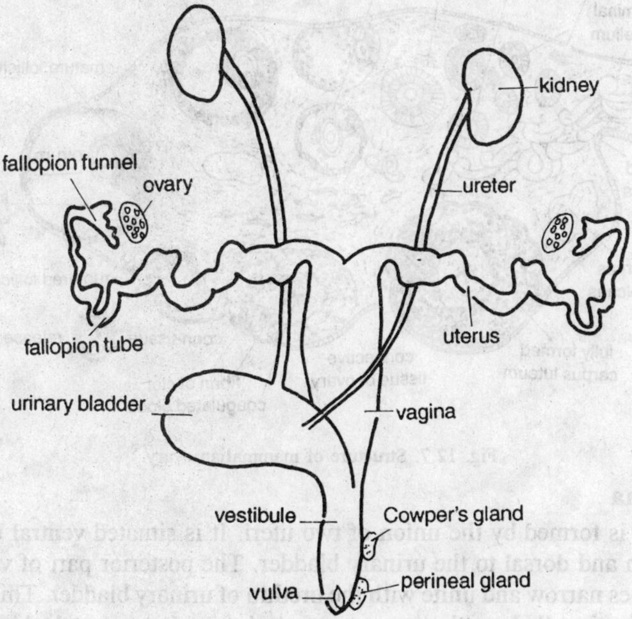

Fig. 12.6. Female urinogenital system.

Ovaries

A pair of ovaries, situated on either side of vertebral column behind the kidneys in the abdominal cavity, forms the main reproductive organs. Each ovary is about 20 mm. long and remains attached to the dorsal body wall by means of double fold of peritoneum, called *mesovarium*. Each ovary is formed of germinal epithelium and connective tissue.

Oviduct

The anterior end of each oviduct, which is placed close to the ovary of its side, is enlarged to form a structure called *funnel*. The mouth of funnel is wide and fimbriated. Its edges are beset with cilia. The funnel is held at its position by mesovarium. The part of oviduct behind the funnel is narrow and it is known as *fallopian* or *uterine tube*. Before reaching the median line, each tube becomes enlarged to form a thick walled *uterus*. The uteri of either side unite in median line so as to form a pouch like, wide *vagina*.

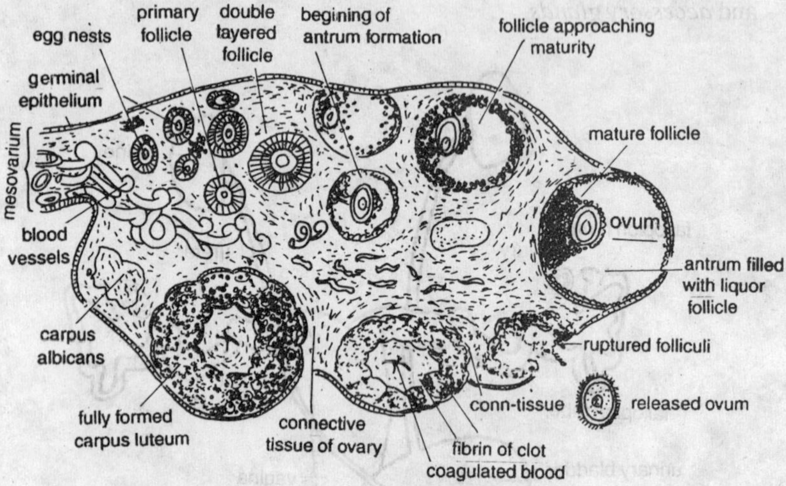

Fig. 12.7. Structure of mammalian ovary.

Vagina

It is formed by the union of two uteri. It is situated ventral to the rectum and dorsal to the urinary bladder. The posterior part of vagina becomes narrow and unite with the urethra of urinary bladder. This part of vagina is called *vestibule* or *urinogenital sinus*. It opens at the hind end of the body by a ventral slit-like aperture known as *vulva*. On the dorsal surface of the vestibule is found a small erectile muscular structure called *clitoris*, which is homologous with glans penis of male. Two prominent folds of skin behind the vulva form the two sides for protection. These are called *labia majora*.

Accessory glands

Female reproductive system possesses three types of accessory glands namely *Bartholin's glands*, *perineal glands* and *rectal glands*.

Bartholin's glands

These are present between rectum and vestibule. They are comparatively large, secreting a slimy, alkaline fluid into the vestibule to lubricate it for facilitating copulation.

Rectal and perineal glands

These are located near anus and they secrete odorous substance to attract opposite sex. The Cowper's glands are reduced or absent in female rabbit.

Histology of ovary

The ovaries are solid structures formed of a supporting connective tissue, called *stroma*. Each ovary is covered over by a covering made up of outer peritoneum, middle germinal epithelium and inner connective tissue membrane called *tunica albuginea.* The stroma is differentiated into two regions: a *cortical region* which is thick and compact; and a *medullary region,* small and loose. The cortical stroma contains a reticular fiber network and numerous spindle shaped cells. The medullary stroma consists of many elastic fibers, smooth muscle cells and numerous blood vessels.

A large number of small ovarian follicles are embedded in the cortical stroma of ovary. These follicles are formed during embryonic development by proliferation of primordial germ cells or germinal epithelium. In its initial form its follicle is known as *primordial follicle.* It contains a small *oogonium,* surrounded by single layered epithelium of flattened cells. Some of the primordial follicles are atretic, i.e. they eventually degenerate. In sexually mature animal during breeding season, the oogonia of some follicles grow to become *primary oocyte cells* by accumulating lipids and cytoplasm. At the same time the follicular epithelial cells become columnar. A membrane, *zona pellucida* begins to form between the oocyte and epithelium. Such follicles are called *primary follicles* at this stage. Gradually zona pellucida thickens due to deposition of carbohydrates and glycoproteins. The growth of oocyte and formation of zona pellucida are accompanied by transformation of single layered follicular epithelium into a thick multi-layered epithelium called *membrane granulosa.* The follicles, at this stage are called *secondary follicles.* Most of such secondary follicles are atretic and degenerate. However, in some secondary follicles a cavity called *follicular cavity* or *antrum folliculi* containing a fluid called *liquor folliculi,* appears between the layers of membrane granulosa. Such follicles are called *Graffian follicles* or *vesicular follicles.* These gradually enlarge due to a considerable expansion of follicular cavity. The oocyte along with a few layers of follicular cells, the *discus proligerus* or *cumulus oophorus* is left attached to the membrane granulosa on one side by a stalk of follicular cells, the *germ hill,* thus the cavity is not complete all around.

As a Graffian follicle further grows, some cells of stroma form a sheeth around it and called *theca folliculi.* It is composed of two layers : the *theca externa* which is fibrous; and the *theca interna* which is cellular and supplied with blood capillaries.

During growth and development of an ovarian follicle, its oocyte undergoes a meiotic division forming a large *secondary oocyte cell* and the minute *first polar body.*

After some time the discus proligerous breaks off and the secondary oocyte now floats freely in the liquor folliculi. The cells of discus proligerous, attached to the secondary oocyte forms a loose covering called *carona radiata.* Now the follicle is ready to ovulate or to release its secondary oocyte by rupturing at the surface of the ovary. In rabbit ovulation occurs during copulation.

The ruptured follicle later changes into a yellow body called *corpus luteum* which secretes *progesterone* hormone. The rupture is soon healed, blood collects and clot in its cavity. The follicular cells of membrane granulosa become large, spherical and glandular. These cells are now called *luteal cells*. They accumulate yellowish pigment called *lutein*. The entire process of corpus luteum formation is called luteinization.

PHYSIOLOGY

The female gametes called ova are produced in the ovaries by a process known as oogenesis. The eggs are released from the mature Graffian follicle at the time of copulation. The breeding season is from January to June in wild rabbit. The copulation takes place only when female is willing to receive male for sexual desire. The animals are said to be in heat and series of changes, which take place between successive periods of heat are known as *oestrous periods.* The eggs are released and are received by funnels of oviducts. Then the eggs are passed on to the fallopian tube by ciliary action. During copulation the spermatozoa are shed into the vagina. From here they pass on to the vestibule uteri, and finally to the fallopian tubes. Here fertilization takes place. After fertilization the eggs reach to the uteri for their complete development. The *gestation period* is about 23-28 days. Thus a young one is formed and called a minature adult.

13

Subclass Prototheria

This subclass includes most primitive egg-laying mammals. They diverged from the base of the main mammalian stock and present many features in common with the bird-like reptiles, *Sauropsida. Echidna* and *Ornithorhynchus* are the only living members of this group. They are confined to Australian region.

GENERAL CHARACTERS

1. *Distribution*: They are found only in Australia, Tasmania, New Guinea and neighbouring islands.
2. *Habits and Habitat*: Aquatic or terrestrial, burrowing (live in burrow during day time), noctural, insectivorous mammals.
3. *External features*: Their body is small and covered by hair and spines. The *external ears* or *pinnae* are absent. Muzzle or snout produced into a beak in *Echidna* or rostrum in *Ornithorhynchus*. Tail may he present or absent. Male with a horny, perforated spur projecting inwards from each hind leg. Spur is internally connected to a poison gland. The mammary glands are without nipples or teats.
4. *Body cavity*: Like other mammals a diaphragm divides body cavity into anterior thoracic cavity and posterior abdominal cavity.
5. *Skeleton*: Skull with two occipital condyles i.e. *dicondylic*. The sutures or joints between the skull bones are indistinct. Alisphenoid is absent but an ectopterygoid or pterygoid is present. Lacrymal and tympanic bulla are absent. Orbits are continuous with temporal fossae. Three ear ossicles *malleus, incus* and *stapes* are present. The malleus and incus are relatively large. Each ramus of mandible or lower jaw is made up of single bone called *dentary*. Two halves of mandible are not united firmly at the anterior symphysis. Moreover, the coracoid processes are small. There are seven cervical vertebrae without zygopophyses. Epiphysis is also absent. The ribs are single headed i.e. unicephalous. Pectoral girdle has coracoid, bearing spine of scapula

at its anterior border. Interclavicle is 'T' shaped. Ischium and pubis are fused with each other on the ventral symphysis. Acetabulum is perforated and epipubic or marsupial bones are present in pelvic girdle.

6. *Digestive system*: Teeth are absent in adult, they are present in embryonic stages and are replaced by horny plates. Teeth, when present, are arranged in a pattern of irregular tubercles. Stomach is globular, the intestine is distinguished into small and large intestine. Rectum opens into cloaca. Gall bladder is absent and spleen is capacious.
7. *Respiratory system*: Lungs are somewhat small in size as compared to the size of body. Well developed diaphragm is also present.
8. *Circulatory system*: Heart is completely four chambered. Right auriculo-ventricular valve is muscular and incomplete. Tricuspid valve guards the left auriculo-ventricular aperture. Chorda tendinae are absent. Single left aortic arch is present. R.B.Cs are small and non-nucleated. Body temperature ranges between 25° C to 28° C and partly homeothermous.
9. *Nervous system*: Brain is simple, corpus callosum joining the cerebral hemispheres is absent. There are four optic lobes (*corpora quadrigemina*). Cochlea of internal ear in less coiled with a lagena.
10. *Excretory system*: The kidneys are metanephric, ureters open into a urinogenital sinus which terminates into cloaca.
11. *Reproductive system*: Testes are abdominal in position i.e. scrotal sac is absent. The penis is retractile and is made up of *corpus spongiosum* and *corpus fibrosum*. It has a groove through which only sperms are passed out but not the urine. The right ovary is reduced in female. The oviducts open separately in cloaca. The vagina and uterus are absent. Temporary abdominal mammary pouch is formed during breeding season in female.
12. *Development*: Fertilization is internal. They are oviparous i.e. egg laying mammals. Eggs are large with plenty of yolk and whitish shell. Cleavage is *meroblastic*. The newly hatched young ones are immature, and are fed on milk produced by sweat glands on the ventral abdominal wall of female but the ducts of these glands do not open on nipples.

AFFINITIES

Both reptilian and mammalian characters are found in these animals, therefore, it is speculated that synapsid reptiles may have progressed towards homeothermy and lactation, and the speculation that the prototherians represent an independent warm blooded line derived from Triassic Cyonodont.

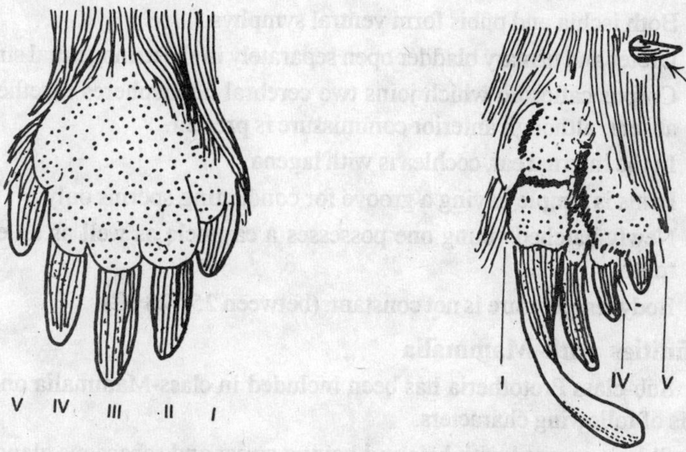

Fig. 45.1. Hand of female showing the spatulate claws adapted for rapid digging. Right foot of male.

Affinities with Reptilia

Although there is no definite connecting link known between mammals and reptiles, yet it is universally accepted that mammals had a reptilian ancestory. This view is supported by the following resemblances between prototherians and reptiles.

1. External ears or pinnae are absent.
2. A cloaca is present.
3. The testes are abdominal is position.
4. Oviparous animals.
5. Eggs are large, megalecithal with a leathery shell.
6. Cleavage is meroblastic.
7. The sutures of skull bones are indistinct.
8. Tympanic bone ring-like without forming tympanic bulla.
9. Prevomers are dumb-bell shaped.
10. Extra pterygoid bone is present in the form of epipterygoid which can be compared with reptilian ectopterygoid.
11. Alisphenoid bone is absent.
12. The ribs are single headed.
13. A median 'T' shaped interclavicle is present.
14. Vertebrae without epiphysis and symphysis.
15. Large coracoid and precoracoid are present.

16. Acetabulum of pelvic girdle is perforated.
17. Both ischia and pubis form ventral symphysis.
18. Ureter and urinary bladder open separately in the urinogential sinus.
19. Corpus callosum which joins two cerebral hemispheres together is absent, although anterior commissure is present.
20. In the internal ear, cochlea is with lagena.
21. Penis is simple having a groove for conducting sperms only.
22. Newly hatched young one possesses a caruncle as well as an egg-tooth.
23. Body temperature is not constant. (between 25°-28 °C).

Affinities with Mammalia

Sub-class Prototheria has been included in class-Mammalia on the basis of following characters.

1. Skin is covered with hair and having sweat and sebaceous glands.
2. Mammary glands are present.
3. Skull with two occipital condyles.
4. A well developed diaphragm divides body cavity into thoracic and abdominal cavities.
5. Three ear ossicles are present in middle ears.
6. Each ramus of mandible is made up of single bone, the dentary.
7. Seven cervical vertebrae are present.
8. Sternum is segmented.
9. A caecum is present between large and small intestine.
10. Liver is lobed.
11. Heart is completely four chambered.
12. R.B.Cs. are non-nucleated and a single left aortic arch is present.
13. Four optic lobes are present in brain.
14. Chondocranium is typically mammalian.

Besides reptilian and mammalian characters as mentioned above, there are few peculiar characters, which are :

1. Tarsal spurs are present in each hind limb of male.
2. Mammary glands are derived from the sweat glands and not by the sebaceous glands as in other mammals. Moreover, they are without nipples.
3. Teeth are replaced by horny plates in adults.
4. Marsupial or epipubic bones are present attached to the pelvis.

5. Temporary abdominal mammary pouch is formed in female during breeding season.
6. Right ovary is smaller and probably functionless.

Conclusion

Presence of above mammalian characters establishes prototherian to be a mammal but they also retain reptilian characters which separate them from true eutherian mammals. Thus it can be concluded that they are connecting link between reptiles and mammals and are very remote from other modern mammals. *Gregory* pointed out that monotrems were derived from archiac marsupials or premarsupial stock during *Triassic period*. Their peculiarties were due to degeneration, neoteny and specialisation plus retention of certain marsupial characters (presence of epipubic bones). There is almost no fossil record of prototherian. In view of these facts prototherians can never be regarded as ancestors of higher mammals, but as a side line of mammalian evolution.

Revision Questions

1. Give an account of distribution, general characters and affinities of Protoheria.
2. What are egg-lying mammals ? Describe their general characters and affinities.
3. Write short notes : (a) Egg-lying mammals, (b) Zoological names of prototherian.

14

Infra-Class Metatheria

Infra-class Metatheria is included in sub-class *Theria* along with *Eutheria*. Metatherians are primitive types of mammals. Their young ones are born in a rudimentary condition, and their further development takes place in the marsupium (integumentary pouch) of the female. Due to presence of this pouch they are called marsupials and the order is named as *Marsupialia*. Their complete evolution took place in *Cretaceous Period*. During *Eocene*, they were found all over the world but now confined to some areas.

GENERAL CHARACTERS

1. *Distribution*. At present they are confined to Australia, South America and North America. Majority to them are found in Australian regions. In America only american opposum is found.
2. *Habits and haitat*. Mainly terrestrial, burrowing or arboreal animals and rarely aquatic. Some are herbivorous, others are carnivorous or omnivorous. Diurnal or nocturnal. Viviparous and pouched mammals.
3. *External features*. Body is covered over by soft hairs. The external ears or pinnae are present. Mammary glands with nipples or teats are present in the abdominal pouch or marsupium of female. Tail is long, prehensile and generally, providing an additional support to the body and balancing the body during running. The hind-limbs are comparatively longer than the fore-limbs. These are used for running, burrowing or grasping.
4. *Body cavity*. Muscular diaphragm divides body cavity into anterior thoracic and posterior abdominal cavities.
5. *Skeleton*. Skull is dicondylic with a small cranium and flat top. In the cranium median and occipital crests are well developed. The sutures of bones are indistinct. Orbit and temporal fossa are confluent because post-orbital bar is absent. The palate is imperfectly ossified with large posterior vacuities. Jugal is large and extends backwards to reach the glenoid articulation of lower jaw. Tympanic bulla is absent. In some

cases the tympanic chamber may be covered by the alisphenoid forming the bulla. Mandible is made up of dentary, a single bone. Middle ear contains three ear ossieles. The inteclavicles and coracoids are absent, the clavicles are large. Vertebrae with epiphysis. Seven cervical vertebrae in neck region. Scapula bears a spine. A long bone epipubic or marsupial bone is present infront of the symphysis of pelvic girdle. The third trochanter is absent in the femur. The ribs are double headed.

6. *Digestive system*. Teeth are monophyodont, heterodont or homodont. Teeth exceed the typical mammalian numbr of 44 and the incisors are unequal in the two jaws. Anus and urinogenital aperture open into a shallow cloaca surrounded by a common sphincter.
7. *Circulatory system*. Heart is four chambered and auriculo-ventricular valve is membranous. An azygos vein opens into the superior venacava.
8. *Nervous system.* Brain is small and poorly developed. Olfactory lobes are large. Cerebral hemispheres are small and do not extend posteriorly over the cerebellum. Cerebellum is small and exposed. Corpus callosum is absent. Cochlea of internal ear is spirally coiled.
9. *Excretory system*. Kidneys are metanephric. Ureters pass between the genital ducts.
10. *Reproductive system*. In males penis is well developed and bifurcated at the tip. Testes are extra-abdominal in the scrotal sac which lies in front of penis. In females two oviducts open separately into urinogenital sinus hence there are two uteri and two vaginae.
11. *Development.* They are viviparous animals but their young ones are born in an immature condition. Development takes place in uterus but a true allantoic placenta (except *Perameles)* is absent. Gestation period small about two weeks in opposum and five weeks in kangaroo. Young ones when born are blind and kept in marsupium and nourished with milk until fully formed. The milk is produced by mammary glands.

AFFINITIES

Metatherian shows a mixture of primitive and advanced characters. Some of their characters are similar to those of prototherian and some characters are similar to those of eutherians.

Affinities with Prototheria

Similarities

1. The cloaca is present.

2. True allantoic placenta is absent except *Perameles*.
3. Large olfactory lobes are present in brain. The anterior commissure is simple. Corpus callosum is absent.
4. Tympanic bulla is present.
5. Clavicles are absent.
6. Pelvic girdle possesses epipubic or marsupial bones.

Dissimilarities.

1. Metatherians are viviparous while prototherians are oviparous.
2. Mammary glands are modified sebaceous glands having teats.
3. Ribs are double-headed in metatherians and single headed in prototherians.
4. Vertebrae without epiphysis.
5. Interclavicle is absent.
6. Cervical ribs are absent in metatherians.

Affinities with Eutheria

Similarities

1. They are viviparous animals.
2. Mammary glands possess teats.
3. External ears or pinnae are present.
4. Cochlea of internal ears are spirally coiled.
5. Teeth are heterodont.
6. Coracoids are reduced and interclavicle is absent.
7. Four optic lobes are present.
8. Vagina and uterus are present.
9. Testes are extra-abdominal in scrotal sac in front of penis.
10. Eggs are small and with small yolk. Cleavage is holoblastic.

Dissimilarities

1. Presence of marsupial pouch in all the forms of metatherians.
2. Two vagina and two uteri are present.
3. Penis is bifurcated at the tip in males.
4. Eggs are comparatively larger than eutherians.
5. The young ones are born in extremely immature condition.

Conclusion

The above mentioned facts lead to the conclusion that the metatherians are essentially very similar to eutherians, but they are primitive in several characters. Therefore, it is regarded that they diverged at some earlier stage from main mammalian stock. Hence they are placed between Prototheria and Eutheria.

Revision Questions

1. Describe the distribution, general characters, and affinities of Metatheria.
2. Write short notes in : (a) Zoological names of Metatheria, (b) Distribution of Metatheria, (c) Marsupium.

15

The Origin and Evolution of Mammals

The mammals evolved from reptiles during the *Triassic* and, probably avoiding direct conflict and competition with the ruling and mostly diurnal reptiles, occupied a different niche, the night. Several specific requirements were necessary to be dominant at night. Paramount among these was the regulation of a high body temperature. This is not a simple adaptation but affects every system in the body. The most readily apparent mammalian alteration is the hairy integument, of great importance to the efficient maintenance of a high internal body temperature. In addition to the evolution of mammalian hair, the integument has provided the morphological basis for unique features which contribute to homeostasis, communication and nourishment of the young.

The earliest mammals of the late *Triassic* and *Jurassic* periods, unfortunately known for the most part only from teeth and jaws, were very small and comparatively insignificant, and all through the remainder of the *Mesozoic era* the mammals continued as small and minor members of the *Jurassic* and *Cretaceous* faunas, completely overshadowed by the numerous reptiles that populated the lands and waters of the earth. It was during middle and late *Mesozoic* times that the small mammals were going through the initial stage of their development to establish the basic mammalian type from which arose the tremendous variety of mammals that lived during the *Cenozoic era*.

Establishment of Mammalian characters

There can now be little doubt that the mammals are an offshoot of the reptilian subclass Synapsida, and more particularly of some type or types of Triassic Therapsida, the true mammal like reptiles. The later were probably derived from primitive *Pelycosaurs*, and these in turn from the stem reptiles, *Cotylosaurs*.

Following characters were established during evolution of mammals.

1. Hairy skin
2. Double occipital condyle

3. Secondary hard palate
4. Squamosal and dentary joint
5. Three ear ossicles from single (stapes) reptilian ossicle
6. Large brain case
7. Increased intelligence
8. Differentiated dentition like incisor, canine, molar etc.
9. Double headed ribs
10. Fused bones of pelvic girdle
11. Reduced toe bones
12. Constant body temperature
13. Development of diaphragm
14. Limited growth
15. True copulatory organs with definite placentation except prototherians.

Fig. 15.1. A Cynodont, an advanced mammal-like reptile.

Mammal like Reptiles

In some therapsids, there are so many mammalian features in the skeleton that inspite of the complex lower jaw articulation with a fixed quadrate, the presence of *pre*-and *post frontals* etc., some have doubted whether they should be ranked reptiles at all. These therapsids lived for the most part in South Africa in *Triassic times*. Abundant fossil remains of many types of the mammalian precursors have been unearthed from Karoo rocks of South Africa, and a few have been found in North America, which represent a parallel line of evolution. All our evidences about them must of course be based upon the study of hard parts, which can become fossilized, and in particular on the skull. The shape of the brain, ofcourse, is known from the study of the cavity of the skull. The characteristic feature of the skull in the populations that led to the mammals is the development of a hole bounded by post-orbital and squamosal above and by jugal and squamosal below in the roof. It was supposed to be formed by the union of two, present in the diapsid skull, and that is why the term synapsid is used for such skull. Animals having this characteristic appear in the rocks at the same time as the Cotylosaurs, with no hole in the skull roof (Anapsida). Synapsid,skull of *Dimetrodon* (about 40 cm long) and of *Varanosaurus* (about 23 cm long) are well preserved from Carboniferous. *Captorhinus* and other similar anapsid fossils appeared from the lower Permian on which amphibian otic notch had disappeared.

The bones and teeth developed many mammalian characteristics. The teeth of all were heterodont and were well differentiated into incisors, canines, and molars, and in general these resembled the teeth of a dog. The dentary bone of lower jaw was greatly enlarged and the other reptilian jaw bones much reduced. In some types the quadrate bone was very small and loosely articulated to the other jaw bones. There was a large process on the posterior end of the dentary that nearly touched the squamosal, apparently almost ready to form the new mammalian type of jaw articulation.

Captorhinus and its allies were 30 cm or more in length and showed some development of the limb towards the mammalian condition, in that the bones were moderately elongated and slender and the limbs perhaps tended to be held vertically under the body. The position and shape of the limbs joints reveal that the backwardly directed elbow and forward knees had been tucked under the body, raising the latter high off the ground and favouring a mammalian running gait.

In adjustment to this position, the femur has a knob-like head on the side, as in mammals. In some forms the phalanges had been reduced to the mammalian formula of 2-3-3-3-3.

A secondary hard bony palate, separating the nasal passages from the mouth cavity, was present almost as in mammals. The stapes is already articulated with small, loose quadrate.

These features do not cast doubt on the theory that mammals were derived from some type or types of mammals like reptiles.

PRIMITIVE MAMMALS OF THE MESOZOIC

Five orders of mammals are known from sediments of late *Triassic* and *Jurassic* times, and are represented by fossils discovered in all of the continents except South America and Australia. These are the *Docodonta*, the *Triconodonta*, the *Symmetrodonta*, the *Pantotheria*, and the *Multituberculata*.

Docodont

The docodonts, known only from teeth, appeared in the upper Jurassic of North America. In these primitive mammals the upper molars were expanded so that they were broad, with two main cusps, that were transversely arranged in relation to one another. However, the lower molars, also broad, had a rather complex cusp pattern, with a main cusp on the outer side of the tooth.

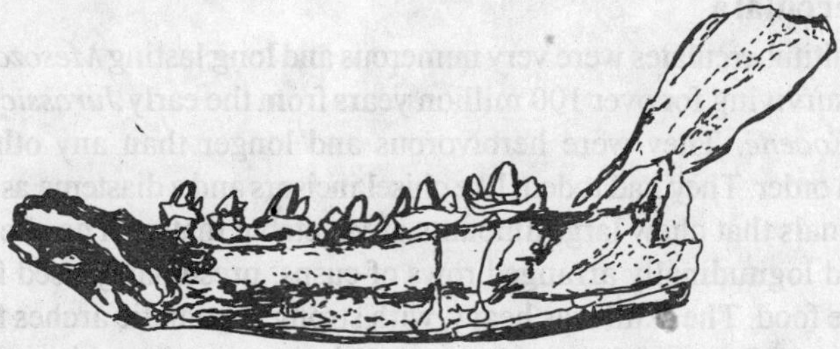

Fig. 15.2. Jaw of tricondont mammal, *Triconodon ferox*.

Tricodonts

The tricondonts are known from partial skulls, teeth, palates and jaws. They were probably mainly carnivores and, the molars carry three cusps all in one line. These animals ranged in size from tiny beasts, no larger than mice, to animals like *Triconodon* of late *Jurassic* age, that were as large as cats. The differentiation of the teeth into incisors, canines, premolars, and molars constitutes one of the very important characters of mammals that is first seen in the primitive *Triassic* and *Jurassic* forms. The jaw articulation included medial quadrate articular and lateral squamosal dentary facets, perhaps connected with shearing action of the teeth. The brain was probably larger than in reptiles. There was a division between thoracic and lumbar vertebrae, characteristics of mammals. This allows a dorso-ventral flexure, useful for tree life and for running.

Symmetrodonta

The symmetrodonts were *Jurassic* and *Cretaceous* animals with three cusped molars arranged in a rather symmetrical triangle, but the cusps arrangement was entirely different from that of the Tricondonta. They were also carnivorous, as judged by their teeth, and were of moderate size.

Pantotheria

They sometimes called *Trituberculata* on account of the three tubercles on the teeth. The jaws were long and slender, and there was a large array of cheek teeth. In *Amphitherium*, there were 4 incisors, 1 canine, 4 premolars and 7 molars. They include a relatively numerous series of small mammals about the size of rats or mice. They are regarded as either the ancestors of later mammals or as close to the stock from which the latter were derived. They were supposed to be the more successful early mammals. Fossil remains of Pantotheres are confined to the last half of the *Jurassic*, but they may have survived into the *Cretaceous*.

Multituberculata

The multituberculates were very numerous and long lasting *Mesozoic* mammals, surviving for over 100 million years from the early *Jurassic* to the lower *Eocene*. They were herbivorous and longer than any other mammalian order. They had rodent like chisel incisors and a diastema as in other mammals that chew large amounts of vegetable matter. The cheek teeth carried logitudinally arranged rows of cusps, presumably used for grinding the food. The skull was heavy, with strong zygomatic arches for the attachment of powerful muscles to move the massive lower jaws. In primitive multituberculates there were two parallel rows of longitudinal cusps in both upper and lower molars; in the latter forms there were three rows of cusps in the upper teeth. In general these adaptations of the skull and dentition in the multituberculates were broadly similar to those seen in the latter rodents.

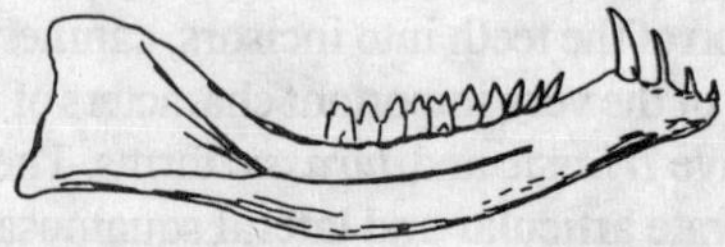

Fig. 15.3. Lower jaw of Dromatherium.

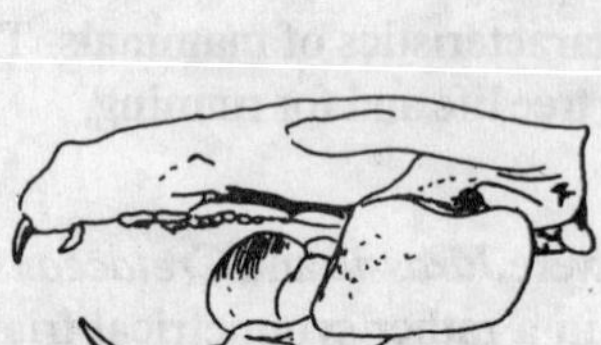

Fig. 15.4. Skull of multituberculate mammals.

Cenozoic Mammals

Cenozoic era is the era of mammals. At the beginning of this era, the mammals found the land cleared of the most formidable reptiles and wide open for exploitation. The birds apparently had an equal opportunity to take over the leadership, but went off upon a side line of specialization becoming denizens of air, leaving the land surface free for mammals. With the close of the Age of Reptiles came a most momentous change in mammalian evolution, when the sluggish stream of their existence was quickened into life and their remarkable radiation began that will be dealt under the seperate heading the "Adaptive radiations in Mammals".

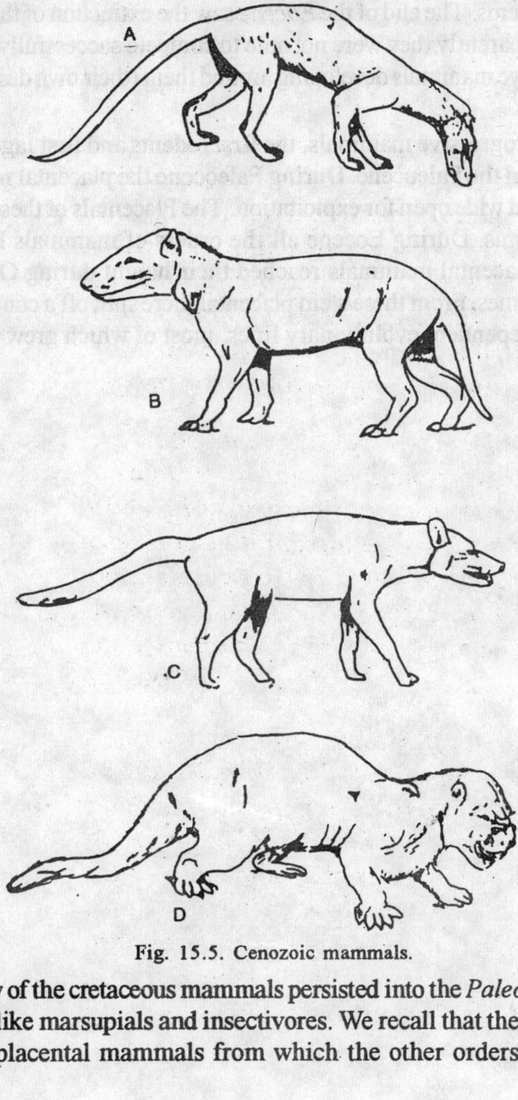

Fig. 15.5. Cenozoic mammals.

A few of the cretaceous mammals persisted into the *Paleocene* notably opposum like marsupials and insectivores. We recall that the latter are the group of placental mammals from which the other orders of placental mammals are believed to have arisen. The carnivores and ungulates living at this time were quite unlike their modern relatives, however, most of them belonged to groups that underwent a relatively rapid evolution during the *Paleocene* and *Eocene* and then disappeared. Thus they sometimes are called 'archaic mammals'. During the Paleocene and Eocene, the archaic mammals had their brief period of ascendancy. Some of the archaic ungulates became quite large. *Uintatherium* with its curious horns was as large as a modern rhinoceros. The end of the *Eocene* saw the extinction of the archaic mammals. Apparently they were not able to compete successfully with the more progressive mammals developing around them (their own descendants in some cases).

Among progressive mammals, the first rodents and first lagomorphs appeared late in the Paleocene. During Paleocene the placental mammals found the world wide open for exploitation. The Placentals of these periods were small forms. During Eocene all the orders of mammals had been established. Placental mammals reached their height during Oligocene and Miocene times. From these stem placental there split off a considerable number of independent evolutionary lines, most of which grew to larger size.

16

Aquatic Adaptations in Mammals

Adaptation to environment is one of the most obvious and at the same time remarkable qualities of living organisms; in fact, it sums up nearly the whole result of evolution and the real cause of it all lies in the germplasm itself, although it is manifested only in the somatoplasm of the animal. Adaptation can also be defined as 'any modification in a part or in whole organism that makes it better far its existence in its present environment or enable it to live in a different environment so that it can secure food, protect itself and rear its young ones'.

A striking feature among various animals is their adaptation to their environment which is of great importance, because this adaptation helps them to survive in the struggle for existence. In aquatic mammals these adaptations are exhibited in change of body, locomotion, limbs, external covering etc.

The aquatic adaptations can be distinguished into two types. The one, which includes primitive gill breathing vertebrates. Their adaptation to the watery medium is perfect. Second includes those animals, which are secondarily adapted to the water medium due to their inability to breath in water. Fishes are the primary aquatic forms which have never had a terresterial life, but have evolved from more primitive aquatic forms. On the other hand, secondary adaptations are studied in lung breathers which due to stressed circumstances including scarcity of food and great competitions for existence, returned once more to the primary home to their remote ancestors. As an effect of change in their life, they have some handicap in their life and the most important one is of the breathing. They breath by lungs but for other modifications they are well adapted for aquatic environment.

There are some examples leading amphibious life while some of them lead only aquatic life.

S.No.	*Order*	*Name of mammal*	*Ambhibious*	*Aquatic*
1.	Monotremeta	*Ornithorhynchus*	+	
2.	Marsupialia	*Chironectus* (aquatic opposum)	+	
3.	Insectivora	*Desmia* (aquatic-Shrews)	+	
4.	Rodentia	Musk rat, Water rat (Beaver)	+	
5.	Carnivora			
	(i) Fissipedia	*Latax* (Sea otter)	+	
		Lutra (Aq. otter)		
	(ii) Pinnipedia	Walrus, Sea lion (*Otonia*)	+	
6.	Cetacea	Whale, Dolphin		+
7.	Sirenia	Dugong (sea cow) Manatee.		+
8.	Ungulata	Hippopotamous	+	

MODIFICATIONS

Body Contour

The body contour becomes spindle shaped, the neck constriction disappears, the tail is enlarged, loss of external ears, external nostrils or nares move towards the apex of head are the other features. This assumption of the fish-like forms is best seen in the fully aquatic orders Cetacea, Sirenia, Pinnipedia and to a lesser extent in several other groups.

Skull

Shortening of craniun takes place which becomes proportionately higher and wider. The fascial portion of the skull tends to elongate. The zygomatic or temporal arch in Cetacca is reduced almost to a vestige.

Neck

Neck is reduced without affecting the number of cervical vertebrae. In whales the number of vertebrae is the standard mammalian seven, but they may be fused into a solid compressed mass of bone. In Manatee (Sirenia) there are six cervical vertebrae.

Vretebrae

Vertebrae tend to simplify secondarily because the body is equally supported throughout. Vertebrae are often completely fused into a continuous bony mass, or the atlas alone may be separated from the rest. Sometimes, however, all the vertebrae are complete and separate. Sacrum is more or less reduced because there is the loss of supporting or propelling functions on the part of appendages. Thus in cetaceans and sirenians the sacrum can not be distinguished from the other vertebrae. The zygapophyses are poorly developed, and are absent in the posterior portion of the trunk.

Chest

Chest tends to become cylindrical. It is also modified in such a way as to bring the internal cavity higher towards the back. This ensures greater stability of floatation and increases lung capacity, and is accompanied by the ribs tending to become highly arched dorsally and then to move upwards from their points of attachment. In the Pennipedia the position is transitional whereas in the whales the articulation of ribs and vertebrae is extremely loose probably to allow greater mobility of the chest for the rapid breathing necessary after prolonged submergence in water. In sirenians and cetaceans the diaphragm has become horizontal in position instead of being vertical as in most quadrupedal mammals.

Bones

Bones tend to become light and spongy. In whale the bones remain filled with oil. Sirenian is an exception to this because it feeds on submarine vegetation and hence remains at the bottom that is why the bones are comparatively heavy and massive as in manatee.

External Ears, Nostrils and Eyes

External pinna is absent in most of aquatic forms, however, it is present in Hippopotamus. The nostrils are shifted to the tip of snout and are often capable of being closed. Eyes tend to shift higher on the face as in Hippopotamus whose nostrils, eyes and ears can appear above the surface of water while the rest of head and body remain submerged.

Fig. 16.1. Killer whale, *Orcinu rectipinna.*

Limbs

Webbed feet are the first adaptation. Extreme aquatic adaptation employs the development of a paddle in which there is a loss of mobility of the various joints, the entire skeleton being enclosed by the skin as a single mass showing no external division into fingers and toes.

Locomotive Mechanism

Fleshy fins-like expansion of body wall occur in the whale. These fins may be dorsal and caudal. The dorsal fin is a triangular structure. It is very high and narrow in the killer whale and is absent in white whale whereas in sulphur whale, the fin is small and situated well upon the tail. The development of this fin must be entirely a response to mechanical needs correlated with a certain bodily form and peculiarity of locomotion. In the Sirenia, the same is true, the Manatee having a round tail while Dugong has notched tail like that of a whale.

Integument

The modification of integument include the reduction of armouring of hair, absence of skin glands, and external ears. The whales and sirenian have lost all traces of hair except perhaps a few bristles around the mouth but most of them are well covered with foetal hair before birth. In white whale even the foetus has lost its hair thus showing extreme specialization

As a compensation for the loss of hair, the aquatic mammals have developed layers of fat in the form of blubber beneath the skin and this serves admirely for the retention of the body heat which would otherwise radiate out very rapidly into the surrounding water.

Mouth Armourment

Except in the sea cow and Walrus, the jaws being no longer used for mastication but only for the prehensation of prey. Teeth modifications usually in the direction of simplification, the increased number or total loss of teeth from one jaw (Sperm whale), on both jaws (Beleen whale).

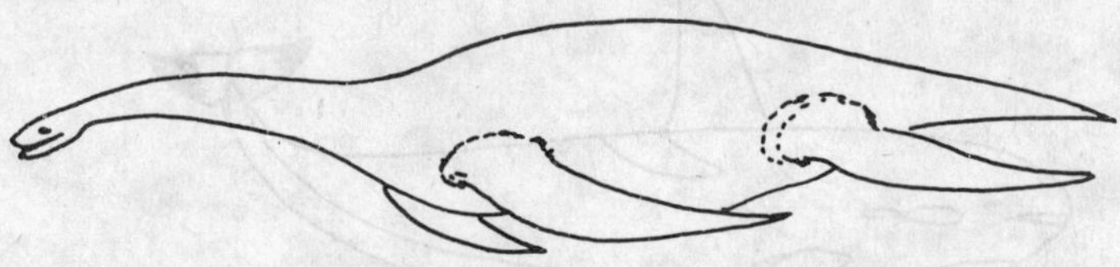

Fig. 16.2. Plesiosaur, *Cryptocleidus*.

ADAPTIVE PECULIARITIES IN CETACEANS

The group Cetacea includes whales and dolphin. This assemblage of large aquatic mammals is profoundly modified for marine life. They are unquestionably the most highly specialized structurally of all mammals, although certain of their characters are persistently primitive. Whales are the largest fish-like mammals and also largest in the animal kingdom. The return of whales to the sea is a fine example of convergence in evolution.

The cetaceans are widely distributed in almost all oceans of the world and also in large fresh water rivers. They show following peculiarities.

External characters

Whales are fish like vertebrates, highly streamlined for efficient swimming. The body is torpedo shaped, and there is no visible neck distinct from the trunk. The head is continuous with the body. There is no hair on the body of the modern whales. The smooth skin makes a sleek surface that offers little resistance to the water as the animal moves forward. Eyes are strikingly small and with immovable upper and lower lids. Nictitating membrane is absent. External nostrils are shifted to the top and the back of the skull. The nostrils can be closed by valves. The anterior limbs are very much modified and are represented by a short externally unjointed structure

Fig. 16.3. Cetaceans.

known as *flipper*. Numerous phalanges are present to support paddle. Pelvis and hind limbs are reduced to mere vestiges.

The whales are unique among marine vertebrates in that the tail terminates in a horizontal fin that moves up and down, rather than in a vertical fin that moves from side to side. The horizontal tail fin of the whale is generally called *flukes*. It is stiff and strong and contains no bones. There is a fleshy dorsal fin that acts as stabilizer and prevents the animal from rolling.

Peculiarities of Skeleton

Skull bones are spongy in texture. The weight of body is reduced due to the less specific gravity of the oil. Brain case is large though small as compared to large facial part of the head. Bones of cranium are separated by sutures and are loosely connected, this helps in the absorption of shocks. Temporal bones are hard and dense and loosely united with the squamosal. Maxilla is very large and extends as far as the anterior end of the snout. The premaxilla is devoid of teeth except in *Squalodon* and *Zeuglodon*. Snout is composed of maxilla, premaxilla, vomer and mesethmoid. Pterygoids meet one another to form hard palate and this helps in the formation of nasal passage. Mandibles have small coracoid processes. Hyoid is broad plate-like.

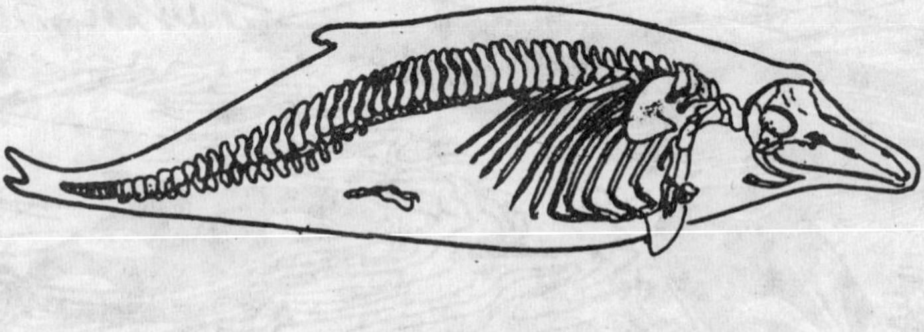

Fig. 16.4. Skeleton of Porpoise.

Dentition

Due to the restricted nature of the food available in the sea, the teeth except *Squalodon* and *Zeuglodon* are numerous and monophyodont. Their crowns are compressed conical in shape. The lower jaw of sperm whale is long and narrow and is armed with from 40 to 48 conical teeth which fit into the toothless groove of the upper jaw.

Vertebral Column

The usual vertebral formula is $C_7\ T_{12}\ L_{21}\ C_{32}$. The cervical vertebrae are shortened, compressed and fused together to a greater or lesser extent. (In

Balana, for example, there is complete fusion; in *Balanopleura*, complete separation). The thoracic vertebrae are well developed with normal features of the vertebrae like neural spine, neural canal, transverse processes etc. In addition to these parts the thoracic vertebrae have the metapophysis showing some changes in the lumbar vertebrae. The lumbar and caudal vertebrae are numerous. Thick fibrous intervertebral discs are present between the vertebrae.

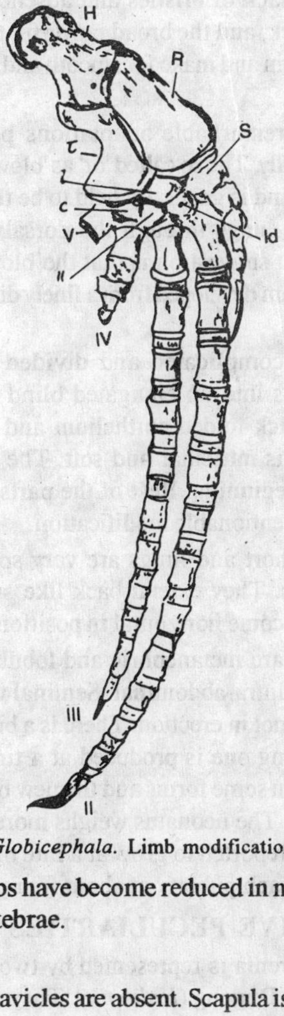

Fig. 16.5. *Globicephala.* Limb modification.

Sternum is short and ribs have become reduced in number and remain fused with the thoracic vertebrae.

Girdles

In pectoral girdle, the clavicles are absent. Scapula is large. In Dolphin, the scapula is very broad and flat and also fan shaped. The scapular fossa is extermely reduced. The acromian is long.

Pelvic girdle is greately reduced due to the absence of hind limbs. It is represented by ischium which is longitudinal cylindrical in structure and placed parallel to vertebral column.

Internal Anatomy

Cetacea have redeveloped piscine characteristics, e.g., in body form, the almost total lack of bristles and absence of external ears; the long snout, lack of neck, and the broad powerful tail. These characters mimic the typical fish form and make for smooth and unimpeded progress through water.

Even more remarkable adaptations peculiar to the group, have developed internally. The so called 'or' as 'blow' was traditionally explained as a jet of water, and is generally held to be the condensation of warm air expired from the lungs through the dorsal blow hole when the whale surfaces. A recent suggestion is that the'blow' is composed of nitrogen-charged foam. Foam developed from a finely divided emulsion of fat droplets and gas.

Stomach is complicated and divided into three chambers. The oesophagus opens into an elongated blind sac like structure which is provided with thick folded epithelium and serves as store house. The lining of the sac is muscular and soft. The duodenum is also a dilated structure at the beginning. Rest of the parts of alimentary canal do not show any other mentionable modification.

Trachea is short and lungs are very spacious and are not divided further into lobes. They extend back like swim bladder of fishes. The diaphragm has become horizontal in position instead of being vertical.

The kidneys are metanephric and lobulated. Whales lack scrotum, and the testes are intra-abdominal. Seminal vesicle absent. Penis is large and curved when not in erection. There is a bicornuate uterus, but usually only a single young one is produced at a time. The gestation period is more than a year in some forms and the new born caif may be one-third of the mother's size. The neonatus weighs more than two tons and in some 23 feet long. It is reported to grow at a rate of about 200 lb per day while suckling and to reach puberty at about four years of age.

ADAPTIVE PECULIARTIES IN SIRENIANS

The order Sirenia is represented by two living forms, the Manatee (*Tricheus*) and the Dugong (*Halicone)*. They are fully aquatic and present a number of structural features convergent with those of the Cetacea. The adaptive peculiarities of sirenians are given below:

External features

Body is fish-like in appearance. Thick and almost hairless skin with an underlying layer of blubber. Head as compared with the size of entire body is larger in both the animals. No external pinna. Eyes are small with nictitating membrane. Fore limbs paddle like and extremely movable to all sides. Digits are enclosed in a common cutaneous covering and the number of phalanges is normal. The dorsal fin absent. The tail is horizontally expanded forming the caudal fin.

Skeletal peculiarities

The skull is characterized by its extreme hardness. The cranial cavity is rather long and narrow as compared with that of the cetacea. The external nares are very wide, but they are situated relatively farther forwards. The nasals are vestigeal. The tympanic and periotic are readily separable from the other bones. The premaxillae are enormous in the Dugongs. The

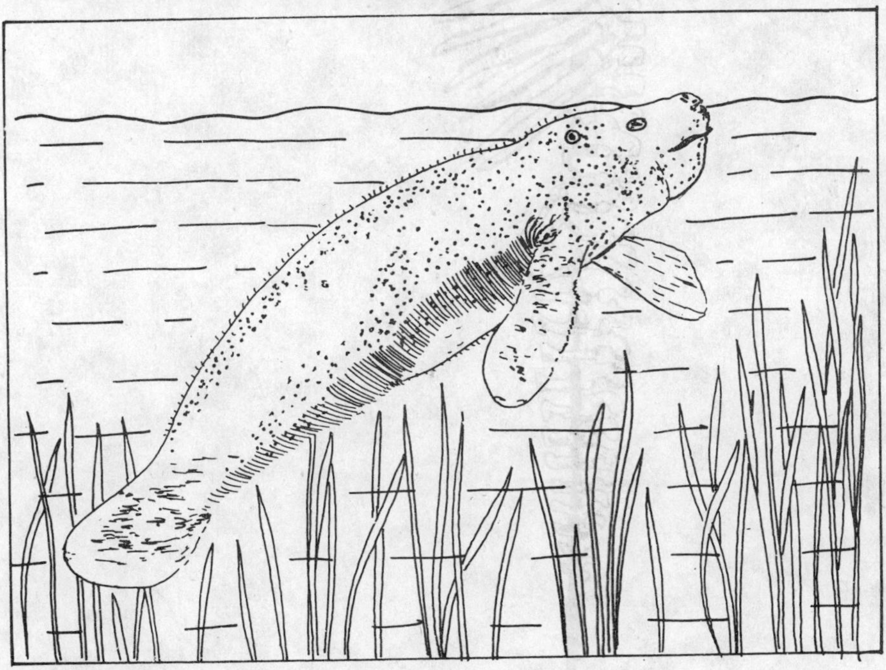

Fig. 16.6. The Sirenia.

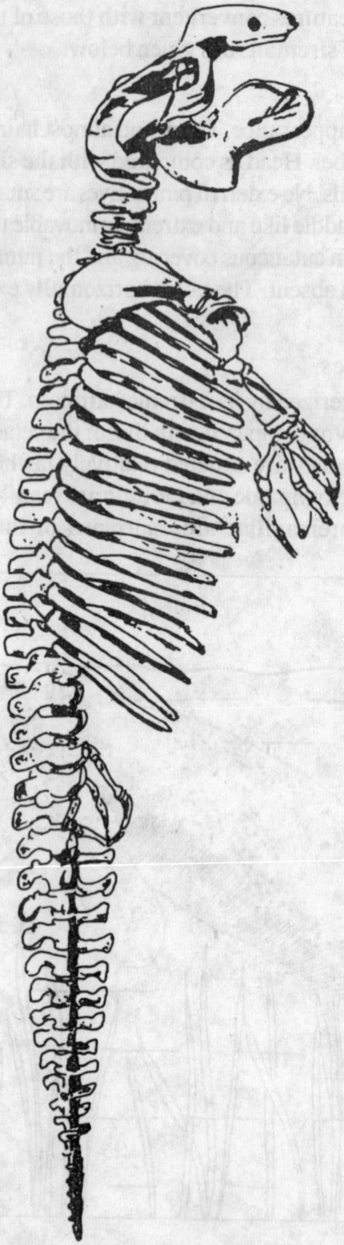

Fig. 16.7. Skeleton of Dugong.

mandible has a well developed ascending ramus and coronoid process. Dentition is variable. Dugong has 5-6 molars while in Manatee there are 11-12 molars.

Vertebrae

Cervical vertibrae are as a rule free except 2nd and 3rd which are fused in case of Manatee. The centra are thin. In Manatee the cervical vertebrae are six while in Dugong the number is seven. In trunk the thoracic vertebrae are numerous. All have well developed facets for the heads of the ribs, and well developed zygapophyses. Metapophyses are rudimentary. The caudal vertebrae are numerous and compressed dorsoventrally and are also provided with wide transverse processes. Sacrum is absent. Sternum is a broad bone. Ribs are numerous and are double headed.

Girdles

No clavicle in pectoral girdle. Scapula and coracoid are well developed. The scapula is much more like that of the terrestrial mammals than the scapula of Cetacea, and is nearer that of the Seals. The spine is situated about the middle; the acromian is directed downwards. The skeleton of the arm also departs less from the ordinary mammalian type than does the Cetaceans. The radius and uina are ankylosed at their extremities. There are five digits, all of which possess the usual number of phalanges.

Pelvic girdle is extremely rudimentary and if present is represented by a pair or more of vestiges widely separated from the spinal column.

Internal Anatomy

Salivary glands are well developed.The stomach has two parts cardiac and pyloric. Caecum is also present in large intestine. The apex of heart is bifurcated. The diaphragm, like the Cetacean, is oblique and very muscular. It divides the body cavity into dorsal and ventral partitions. Brain is small and convolution is merely absent. Testes are abdominal and placentation is of zonary type. They are herbivorous and feed on large and estuarine plants.

17

Dentition in Mammals

Teeth are the first hard structures of the body to put in an appearance during vertebrate development, even before any part of the body sketeton. The structure, kind, number and arrangement of teeth are collectively known as *dentition*. The initial function alloted to the dentition, in vertebrates, is to hold the prey or to prevent the escape of prey from mouth. In mammals the teeth perform many functions like cutting, grinding, tearing and sometimes locomotion. They are also used in defence and offence. Teeth are the derivatives of stomodaeal region of the alimentary canal. Thus these integumentary derivatives are homologous with the placoid scales of Elasmobranchs. These are the exoskeletal derivatives.

In lower vertebrates including fishes and amphibians, the teeth are of *acrodont type* because they are fixed on the mucous membrane of the jaws and whenever they are worn out they don't leave any gap or socket there. In crocodiles, *Archaeopteryx*, and mammals the condition of dentition is *thecodont*. In this condition the teeth are fixed in alveolar sockets in jaws. In reptiles, a somewhat intermediate stage has been observed. Here the teeth are partly fixed on the jaw bones and partly fixed in sockets where they are placed obliquely. This stage is called the *pleurodont*.

Adaptive radiation

The most primitive eutherians-the insectivores, feed upon invertebrates specially the insects, and from these evolved other mammals like carnivores, ant-eaters, sanguivores, omnivores etc. The modern classification of eutherian mammals is based upon the trophic adaptations of their teeth. Dentition provides clue to the diet of the mammal and it also helps in deciding the pedigree or ancestory of certain mammals.

Toothless mammals

Teeth are present in most of mammal but, however, some mammals have no teeth. This category includes, the *Tachyglossus* (spiny anteater), and the giant anteater *Myrmecophaga*, a relative of the Armadillo. In *Ornithorhynchus* (duck-billed platypus) embryonic teeth are replaced by horny epidermal plates in adults. Similarily in whalebone whales foetal teeth are replaced before or soon after birth by sheets of a fibrous, stiff, horn-like epidermal derivative known as *baleen* which extends downward from the upper jaw. Baleen whales are filter feeders, straining small organisms known collectively as plankton, from the water by use of their baleen sieves.

STRUCTURE OF A TOOTH

Typically a mammalian tooth is embedded in a socket in the jaw bone, - the dental alveolus, lined by a vascular membrane, known as *alveolar membrane*. A tooth is differentiated into three parts *crown*, *neck* and *root*.

Crown

The part of the tooth which projects out of the jaw is termed as the *crown*. It is white glistening part of the tooth.

Root

The basal part of tooth that remains embedded in the alveolar socket. Its terminal part is called *root canal* that may remain either open or closed. In open rooted tooth the growth is unlimited as in the incisors of rodents, lagomorphs and elephants. And in close rooted tooth, the growth is restricted as in the majority of cases in mammals.

Neck

The part of tooth between crown and the root is the neck. It remains embeed in the gum.

The major part of a tooth is composed of hard dermal bony substance, the *dentine*. It encloses the *pulp cavity* that remains filled with *pulp* made up of connective tissues, blood vessels, nerves and mesenchyme cells or *odontoblasts*. In the crown, dentine is covered externally by a thin, very hard and shining layer of *enamel* which is the hardest part of the tooth. The dentine has fine net-work of *canaliculi* to get nourishment from blood. The root of tooth is surrounded and fixed in jaw bone by a layer of *cement* and a vascular *periodontal membrane*.

DEVELOPMENT OF A TOOTH

The embryonic origin of mammalian tooth is two fold. *Enamel* is secreted by stomodaeal ectoderm, and the rest of the tooth is formed from mesoderm. The *dentine* or *vitrodentine* is entirely of mesodermal origin but is formed under the organizing influence of an enamel organ which comes from stomodaeal ectodermal epithelium.

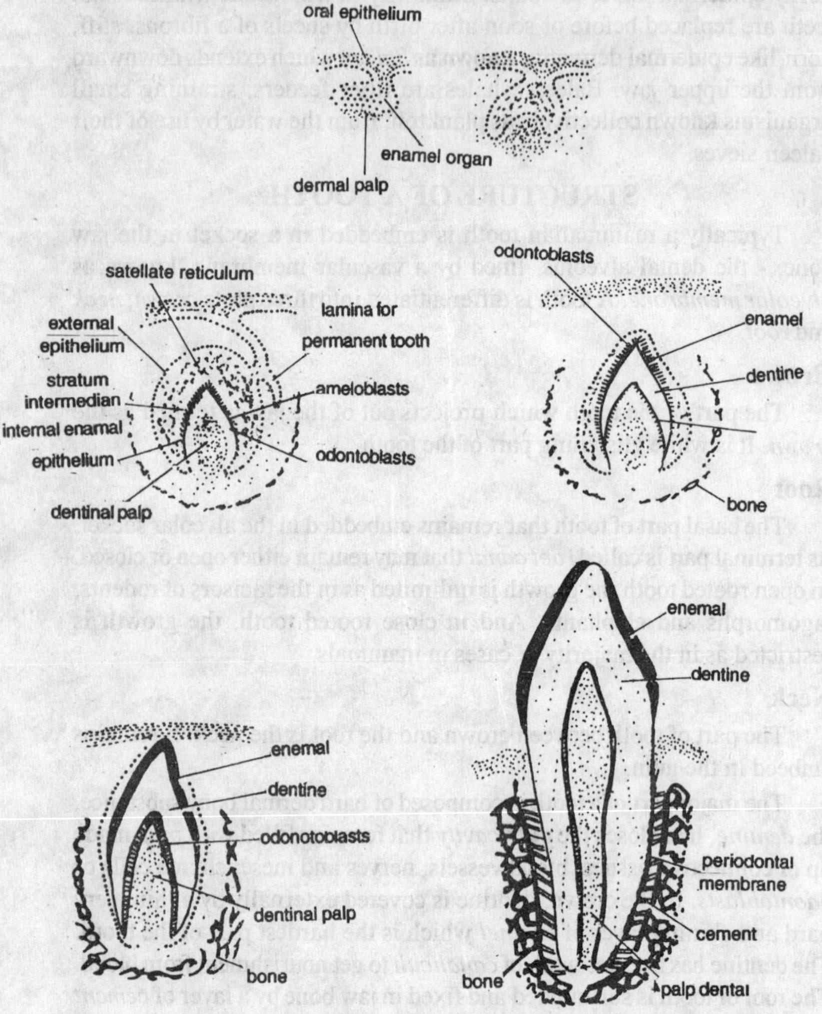

Fig. 17.1. Stages in the development of a tooth.

The first step in this direction of development is the appearance of ectodermal thickening or the *dental primordium* by a process of invagination into the surrounding mesenchyme to become the shelf like *dental lamina*. From this, at intervals, small epithelial buds proliferate, each of which develops into a *tooth gum* by multiplication of the ectodermal cells. The mesenchymal cells under the ectoderm also increase in number and push against the latter so that an inverted, cup shaped structure, the *enamel organ* takes form. This will give to the tooth that appears later on in life. The mesenchyme within the enamel organ is known as the *dental papilla.* Those cells of the dental papilla next to the enamel organ become differentiated into *odontoblasts,* which deposite a layer of dentine just under the ectodermal cells of the enamel organ. Dentine is harder than bone. Its organic and collagen content is less than that of bone.

The cells of the enamel organ become differentiated into two layers, the *outer* and *inner enamel layers*. Looser cells, making up the *enamel pulp,* lie between them. The cells of the inner enamel layer become *ameloblasts,* or enamel forming cells. Enamel is the hardest substance in the body. It is translucent and of a bluish white cast. Striae of Retzius also known as incremental lines are seen in section of enamel. These are lines of enamel growth. Enamel contains 90% inorganic and 4% organic substances.

In most cases, after a tooth has completely formed it ceases to grow since the odontoblasts fail to function any longer. A layer of peculiar histological structure, the *cementum* is formed around the root of the tooth, that part below the crown. Collagenous fibers or Sharpey's fibres anchor the cementum in the bone of the jaw.

REPLACEMENT OF TEETH

On the basis of replacement, the teeth are classified as follow :

Monophyodont

In this the teeth grow once only and are never replaced. A few mammals develop only a first set of teeth. In human beings there are 12 monophyodont teeth. These are all premolars and last molars.

Diphyodont

In most of mammals two sets of teeth develop that is why called *diphyodont*. The *lacteal* ("*milk*") or *deciduous dentition* appears first in a generally regular order from anterior to posterior and deciduous teeth are replaced by the permanent teeth. There is a definite sequence in which the teeth erupt. For example numbering the permanent set in human beings 1 to 8 from front to rear, the sequence of eruption is 6, 1, 2, 4, 5, 3, 7, 8. Eruption of number 8, the last molar, is delayed in higher primates, and this " *wisdom tooth*" is sometimes imperfect, unerupted or is missing.

Polyphyodont

Most vertebrates through reptiles have a succession of teeth, and the number of replacement during a life time is indefinite but numerous. This stage is called the *polyphyodont*. It has been estimated that an elderly crocodile may have replaced its front tooth 50 times. Polyphyodont condition does not occur in mammals.

MORPHOLOGICAL DIFFERENTIATION OF TEETH

On the basis of shapes the teeth can be distinguished as :

Homodont

When all the teeth are of a similar form or shape, the dentition is said to be *homodont*. The toothed whales are homodont mammals. Non-mammalian vertebrates are usually homodont. The initial function alloted to homodont dentition is to prevent the escape of prey from the mouth cavity.

Heterodont

When teeth are arranged in groups which differ in shape and function; the term *heterodont* is applied to this dentition. Most vertebrates below mammals that possess teeth have homodont teeth. However, there are several kinds of fishes like jackson sharks, *Heterodontus*, where heterodont condition is seen.

TYPES OF MAMMALIAN TEETH

The teeth of a generalized mammal may be designated from anterior to posterior, on each side of each jaw, as ; *incisors* (usually two to five), *canines* (never more than one), *premolars* (generally two to four), and *molars* (variable but often three).

Incisors, located anteriorly, have one horizontal cutting edge and a single root. They are best developed in herbivorous mammals, which use

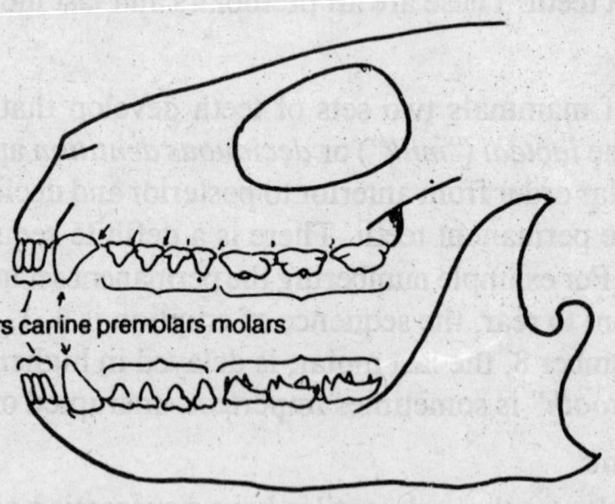

Fig. 17.2. Dentition of a hypothetical generalized eutherian mammal.

them for holding, cropping, or grazing. There are two pairs of incisors in most of mammals lodged in alveolar sockets in premaxilla. The *anterior incisors* are long and curved almost into a semicircle and the *posterior incisors* are much smaller and less curved. Incisors may be totally absent as in sloths, or lacking on the upper jaw, as in bovine. Elephant tusks are modified incisor *teeth*. In rodents and lagomorphs, incisors are open rooted and grow throughout life. In lemurs, incisors are denticulated like a comb, serving for cleaning fur.

Canines lie immediately behind the incisors. Canines are generally elongated, single rooted and with a conical sharp monocuspid crown. They are meant for piercing, tearing, and offence and defence. In carnivores the canines are spear-like and used for piercing flesh. They are also the tusk of the walrus and are used in digging molluscs and also in locomotion on ice. Canines are absent in rodents and lagomorphs and so there is a toothless interval, a *diastema*, between the last incisor and the first cheek tooth.

Cheek teeth : *Premolars* and *molars* are the *cheek teeth*. These are

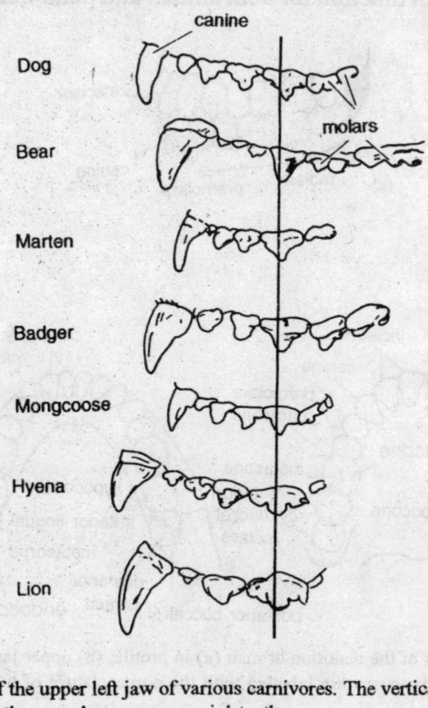

Fig. 17.3. Teeth of the upper left jaw of various carnivores. The vertical line passes through the fourth premolars, or carnassial teeth.

modified to masticate food stuffs. During mastication, the food is repeatedly worked between interlocking *occlusion surfaces* of the upper and lower dentition by the action of the mobile, sensitive tongue and a characteristic mammalian facial structure, the *cheeks*. The food thus becomes a loose pulp that readily absorbs gastric juice.

Premolars and *molars* of carnivores and herbivores are very different, those of carnivores being specialized for shearing flesh and those of herbivores for grinding. The occlusal or grinding surface is not smooth, but is worked by one to several sharp *cusps*, which interlock when the jaws close, or occlude. This cusps pattern is referred to as *tubercular* and permits both piercing and crushing of the food. On the basis of these cusps the mammalian cheek teeth are categorized into following types :

Bunodont. The cheek teeth of some mammals lack sharp ridges and pointed cusps and have, instead, low rounded cusps completely covered with enamel so that no dentine reaches the surface. These bunodont teeth wear down evenly. These are found in rhinos, some hogs, some primitive ruminants, some rodents such as the white footed mouse, and human being. These teeth function for both animal and plant materials.

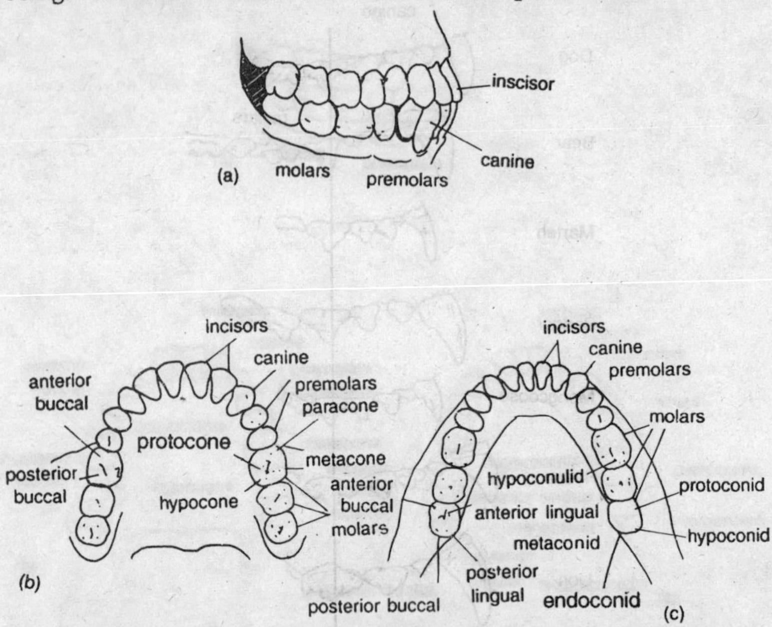

Fig. 17.4. Diagrams of the dentition of man (a) in protile; (b) upper jaw; (c) lower jaw. In b and c the cusps are labelled with the nomenclature of human anatomists on the right.

Secodont. Carnivores must be able to shear or cut away chunks of flesh from a large carcass. Hence, the cusps are sharp and knife like and present little grinding surface. In living carnivores *secodont* teeth reach their height of development in a shearing, *carnassial apparatus* of the fourth upper premolar and the first lower molar, which slide past one another like scissor blades to cut flesh.

Selenodont. Tougher plant materials such as leaves, twigs, and stems require more specialized dentition. The crowns of selenodont teeth are broad, and the enamel is disposed in vertical, crescent- shaped columns separated by dentine. Thus the crescent shaped folds of hard enamel enclose softer areas of dentine. Chewing causes the softer dentine to wear down more quickly than the enamel, there by providing sharp, crescentic, rasping ridges with a wide variety of configuration and that macerate the food during the complex side to side and forward-backword movements of the artiodactyl jaw.

Lophodont. In elephant, enormous grinding teeth are present which may measure as much as one foot in length and four inches in width. There is an intricate folding of the enamel and dentine to form transverse ridges. Such teeth are of the *lophodont* type. In elephants as well as the *Manatee* there is an almost constant succession or replacement of molar

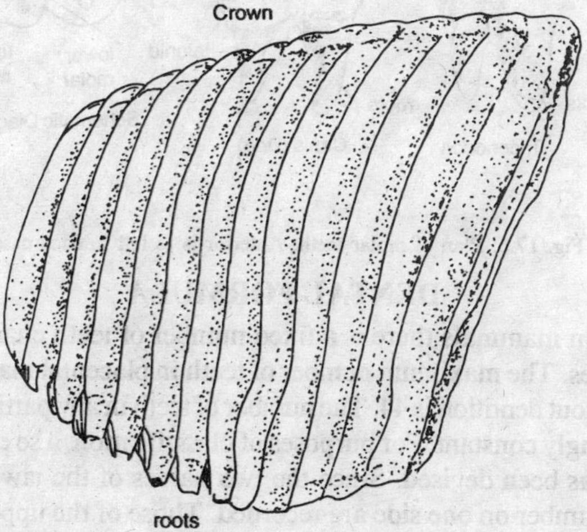

Fig. 17.5. Unerupted molar of an elephant to show formation by union of a number of separate units, each with its own pulp and root. The units are held together by cement. Those most recently formed are to the left.

teeth from behind throughout life. The front ones are pushed forward and are shed as new ones form behind. Only one fully developed molar tooth is present at a time on each side of each jaw in elephants.

***Brachydont* and *Hypsodont*.** Rodents, the largest mammalian order and with the largest variety of diets, exhibit the largest variety of teeth, some of them are low crowned with long roots (*brachydont*), as in squirrels, some high crowned and with short roots (*hypsodont*), as in wood rats. The cheek teeth of man are *brachydont*, and those of horses are *hypsodont*. Tusks are hypsodont.

***Triconodont* and *Trituberculate*.** Cheek teeth of early placentals were triconodont, having three cone like prominences arranged in a straight line. *Cynognathus* had triconodont teeth. Later on these cones of *triconodont* dentition became arranged in a triangle, resulting in *trituberculate* secodont teeth. Still later, other parts may have developed from these three original tubercles so as to form additional cusps, ridges, and folds, and thus are finally arrived at the many and varied types of mammalian cheek teeth that exist today.

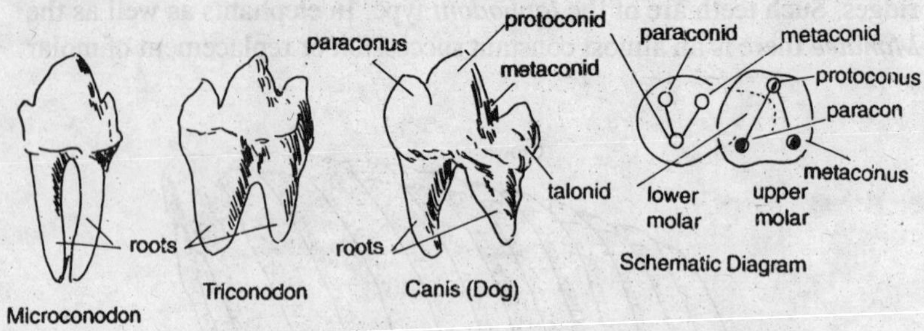

Fig. 17.6. Plan of molar teeth. Anterior is to left in each case.

DENTAL FORMULA

Only in mammals there is a fixed number of teeth characteristic of each species. The maximum number of teeth in placental mammals with the heterodont dentition is 44. The number of teeth in any particular species is surprisingly constant. For purposes of classification, a so called *dental formula* has been devised. Since the two halves of the jaw correspond, only the number on one side are recorded. Those of the upper and lower jaws are separated by a horizontal line, so that they appear in the formula as numerator and denominator. The kind of tooth is represented by the initial letters i,c,pm,m, indicating incisor, canine, premolar and molar, respectively. The number of teeth shown by a dental formula is multiplied by 2 to get the total number of teeth. Thus, the dental formula of man is i. 2/2, c. 1/1, pm 2/2, m. 3/3. In order to simplify these dental formulas, the initial letter is customarily omitted, so that for man it appears as 2/2 , 1/1, 2/2, 3/3.

When a certain type of tooth is lacking ,a zero is used to indicate this fact.

The dental formulas of some mammals are given below:

Beaver	=	1/1,	0/0,	1/1,	3/3.	=	10 × 2 = 20
Cow, Sheep and Goat	=	0/3,	0/1,	3/3,	3/3.	=	16 × 2 = 32
Cat	=	3/3,	1/1,	3/2,	1/1.	=	15 × 2 = 30
Dog	=	3/3,	1/1,	4/4,	2/3.	=	21 × 2 = 42
Mole	=	3/3,	1/1,	4/4,	3/3.	=	22 × 2 = 44
Squirrel	=	1/1,	0/0,	2/1,	3/3.	=	11 × 2 = 22
Rat	=	1/1,	0/0,	0/0,	3/3.	=	8 × 2 = 16
Horse and pig	=	3/3,	1/1,	4/4,	3/3.	=	22 × 2 = 44
Elephant	=	1/0,	0/0,	0/0,	3/3.	=	7 × 2 = 14
Kangaroo	=	3/1,	1/0,	2/2,	4/4.	=	17 × 2 = 34
Rabbit	=	2/1,	0/0,	3/2,	3/3.	=	14 × 2 = 28
Opossum	=	5/4,	1/1,	3/3,	4/4.	=	25 × 2 = 50
Lemur	=	2/2,	1/1,	3/3,	3/3.	=	18 × 2 = 36
Tarsius	=	2/1,	1/1,	3/3,	3/3.	=	17 × 2 = 34
Basic placentals	=	3/3,	1/1,	4/4,	3/3.	=	22 × 2 = 44
Bat	=	2/3,	1/1,	0/0,	4/5.	=	16 × 2 = 32
Bear	=	3/3,	1/1,	4/4,	2/3.	=	21 × 2 = 42
Skunk	=	3/3,	1/1,	3/3,	1/2.	=	17 × 2 = 34

ORIGIN AND EVOLUTION OF MOLARS

The nature of the changes in morphogenesis that have produced the mammalian molar are still obscure, in spite of long controversy. Following theories have been proposed regarding the origin and evolution of molars:

Concrescence Theory

This theory was proposed by *Rose*. According to this theory, the modern molars are the products of the fusion of a number of primitive cone shaped reptilian teeth. The prosterior teeth in the jaw of *Sphenodon* offer evidence in support of this point of view. Some compound molars, those of elephant, for instance are formed by the union during development of many, at first separate cones.

Dimer Theory

The credit for this theory goes to *Bolk* that is why it is also called the "*Theory of Bolk*".

According to this theory, each ancestral reptilian tooth carried a row of three cusps, one behind the other.Such teeth are termed *triconodont* teeth. *Bolk* suggested that each mammalian molar was formed by the fusion of two such teeth that came to lie side by side. He believed that there was evidence of this double or *dimeric* nature of the teeth in a septum. Sometimes seen in an early stage of the enamel organ. The fundamental pattern of the tooth would thus show six cusps, three on the labial and three on the buccal side. Since the remains of the molars of many of the earliest mammals show three cusps and therefore do not support Bolk's theory which requires that the most primitive molars should have six cusps.

Differential Theory or Theory of Trituberculy

It was given by *Cope* and *Osborn*. This theory is more widely accepted. The theory postulates the budding out and growth of additional contact surfaces, or *cusps*, upon the crown of an originally conical tooth.This theory is based largely upon evidence presented by the ancestral teeth of fossil mammals.

The addition of two such cusps give rise to the *tritubercular tooth* which is the typical molar of mammals generally from the earliest representatives down to *Eocene* times. Even today the forms like *Chryochloris* (mole), *Didelphys* (opposum) and some lemurs exhibit this ancestral tritubercular type.

The three cusps of a tritubercular molar are arranged in the form of a triangle. Molars of the lower jaw have a more lateral cusp, the *protoconid*, medial to which are the two secondary cusps, the *paraconid* in the anterior position and the more posterior *metaconid*. The corresponding cusps on molars of the upper jaw are *protoconus* (a medial) and two lateral *paraconus* (anterior) and a *metaconus* (posterior). The addition of extra cusps on more highly developed molars may bring the total number to a maximum of six. Molars of the lower jaw elongate some what through the development of a posterior extension, the *talonid* or heel, which may bear two or three extra cusps. The above cusps can be recognized in the molars of the most mammals and others may be added. An internal posterior cusp on the upper molar, called the *hypocone*, makes the tooth *quadrilateral*. *Protoconule* and *metaconule* added between the main upper cusps then produce a six cusped molar, from which many modern types can be derived. Futher ridges along the outer side of the tooth are known as *styles*. In the lower molar *entoconid* and *entoconulid* added to the heel also make a six cusped tooth.

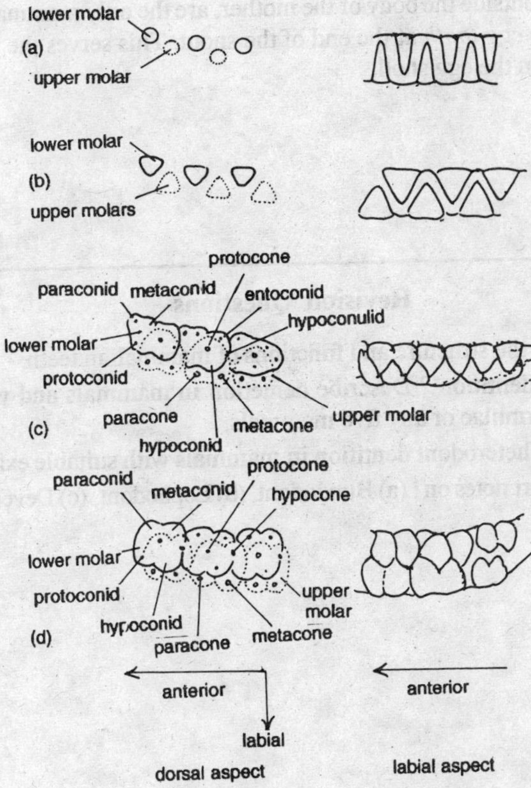

Fig. 17.7. Diagrams to show stages of arrangement of teeth and cusps.

UNUSUAL TEETH

Certain unusual teeth found in mammals deserve special mention. The *tusks* of elephant are incisor teeth with open root canals. They grow continuously throughout life. The largest known tooth is the tusk of an extinct mammoth, *Archidiskodon*. It weigh over 250 pounds and is more than sixteen feet in length. In wild boar , the tusks are formed from lower canines, while the male dugong, *Halicone*, a sea cow develops tusks from upper incisor. In both sexes of *Phacochoerus*, there are four upward curving tusks, which are the transformed canines of both jaws.

The male norwhal, *Monodon* has lost all its adult teeth except an upper left one which is prolonged enormously into a formidable twisted pikestaff that may reach seven to nine feet in length.

Embryonic monotremes, being the only mammals to develop within an egg shell outside the body of the mother, are the only mammals which have a *horny egg tooth* at the end of the snout. This serves the young in escaping from the egg shell.

Revision Questions

1. Describe the structure and functions of mammalian teeth.
2. What is dentition ? Describe dentetion in mammals and write the dental formulae of any five mammals.
3. Describe heterodont dentition in mammals with suitable examples.
4. Write short notes on : (a) Bundodont, (b) Lophodont, (c) Development of tooth.

18

Development of Rabbit

Primitive mammals lay large calcareous eggs provided with good amount of yolk as in prototherians like *Echidna* and duck- billed platypus. Their eggs are about 6 mm. in diameter and resemble those of reptiles and birds in structure and amount of yolk that is why called *polylecithal*. There is a germinal disc or blastodisc that contains cytoplasm and nuclear material. Meroblastic cleavage occurs in this disc of protoplasm. In marsupials, immature young ones are formed which are then placed into a pouch called *marsupium* on the ventral side of the abdomen as in Kangaroo, Wallaby and Wombat. Their eggs measure 0.15 to 0.25 mm in diameter. Cleavage is holoblastic and yolk sac placentation is formed during development and there is no loss of maternal tissues during parturition. The eutherians include all viviparous true placental mammals. They have minute eggs with only a least amount of yolk. Mother supplies nutrients to the developing embryo through placenta. A portion of Mullerian duct is specialized as a *brood pouch* or *uterus*, in which the eggs develop.

During evolution the yolk supply became progressively reduced from *polylecithal* to *microlecithal* that is why in mammals the development is greatly modified as compared with that of reptiles and other vertebrates. This modification is due to adaptation found in the class.

Structure of egg and sperm

In rabbit, ovulation takes place at secondary oocyte stage. It is relatively minute and contains only a little amount of yolk that is why called *microlecithal*. It is a small spherical cell, about 0.1 mm. in diameter. The nucleus occupies an eccentric position above the equator in the animal pole due to the accumulation of slightly more yolk at the vegetal pole. The true vitelline membrane is wanting. A thick membrane marked by fine, closely set radiation striation encloses the egg. This is the *zona radiata* or *zona pellucida*. There exists is a narrow space between the zona radiata and the egg, it is called the *perivitelline space*. In rabbit, the oviduct secretes a thick layer of dense albumin around the ovum. This layer of albumin is also called the *tertiary egg membrane*.

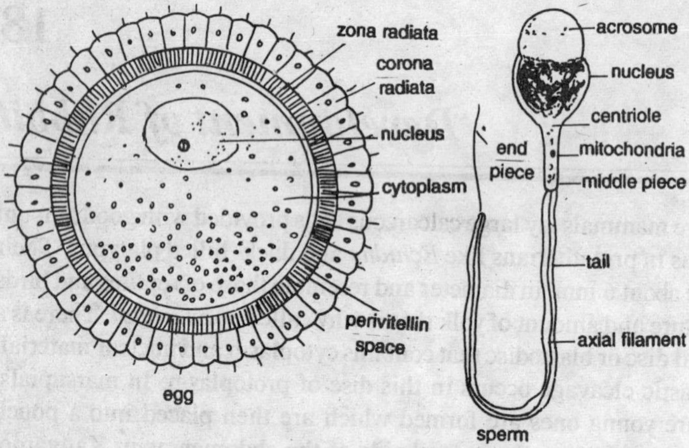

Fig. 18.1. Gametes of rabbit.

In rabbit, the sperms are motile and flagellated and each one is differentiated into head, collar and tail. Head comprises a nucleus covered by a thin layer of cytoplasm and a flattened acrosome. The middle piece is a cylindrical structure having mitochondrial spiral, centrioles and a small amount of cytoplasm. There is a long tail composed of a thin layer of cytoplasm, axial filament and end piece. The length of sperm is about 50 μ in rabbit.

Fertilization

In rabbit fertilization is internal and it takes place in fallopian tube. Sperms are stored into the vagina during coitus. From here the sperms move up the oviduct and reach the fallopian tube to fertilize the eggs. Rabbit is an induced ovulator as the ovulation occurs about 10 hours after copulation. Several eggs are released at a time. Fertilization takes place about 20 hrs after copulation. Thus the usual number of chromosomes, which is 44, is maintained. At this stage the second maturation division is completed. The fertilized egg passes down the oviduct into the uterus in about 3 days where it becomes attached to the uterine wall. The process of attachment is called *implantation*. A muscular structure is formed, through which the developing foetus gets the nourishment from the maternal blood. The structure is called *placenta*. The whole development in uterus takes about 28 days. At birth, the young produced, is hairless and its eyelids are coherent.

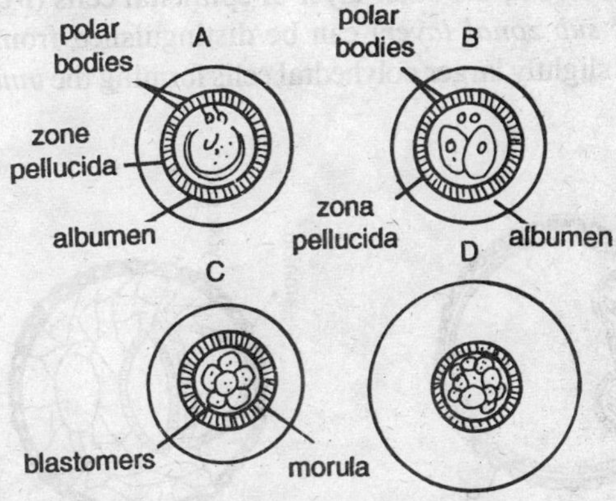

Fig. 18.2. Stages in the early development of egg of mammal.

Cleavage

Cleavage is the segmentation division and it starts soon after fertilization. It is *holoblastic* but slightly unequal. It appears about 22 hours after copulation. The *first cleavage* is vertical extending from the animal to vegetal pole and divides the zygote into two slightly unequal blastomeres. The smaller one is more opaque than the other. After about 44 hrs. of copulation the *second cleavage* occurs. It is also, vertical and occurs at right angle to the first cleavage. It results in four blastomeres. The *third cleavage* is horizontal and above the equator. It results into eight blastomeres, of which the upper four are slightly smaller than the lower four. Subsequent divisions are not quite regular and the resulting blastomeres become clustered together to form a solid ball of cells called *morula*. It attains the size of a pin's head. The ovum is still in oviduct at morula stage, but it is probably very close to the fundus of the uterus. In

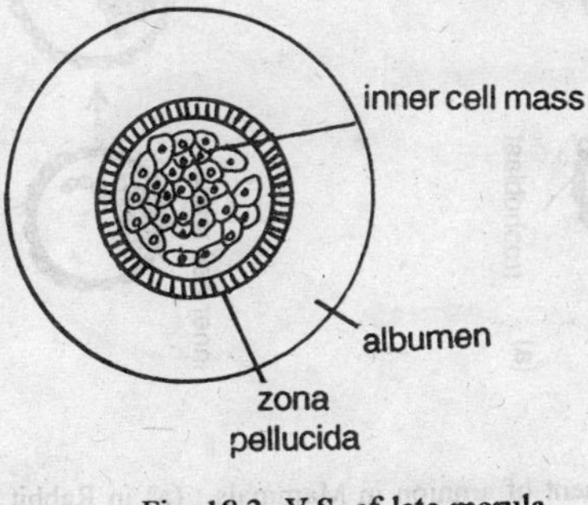

Fig. 18.3. V.S. of late morula.

a fully formed morula, the outer layer of epithelial cells (*trophoblast* or *trophoaerm* or *sub zonal layer*) can be distinguished from a compact central mass of slightly larger polyhedral cells forming the *inner cell mass.*

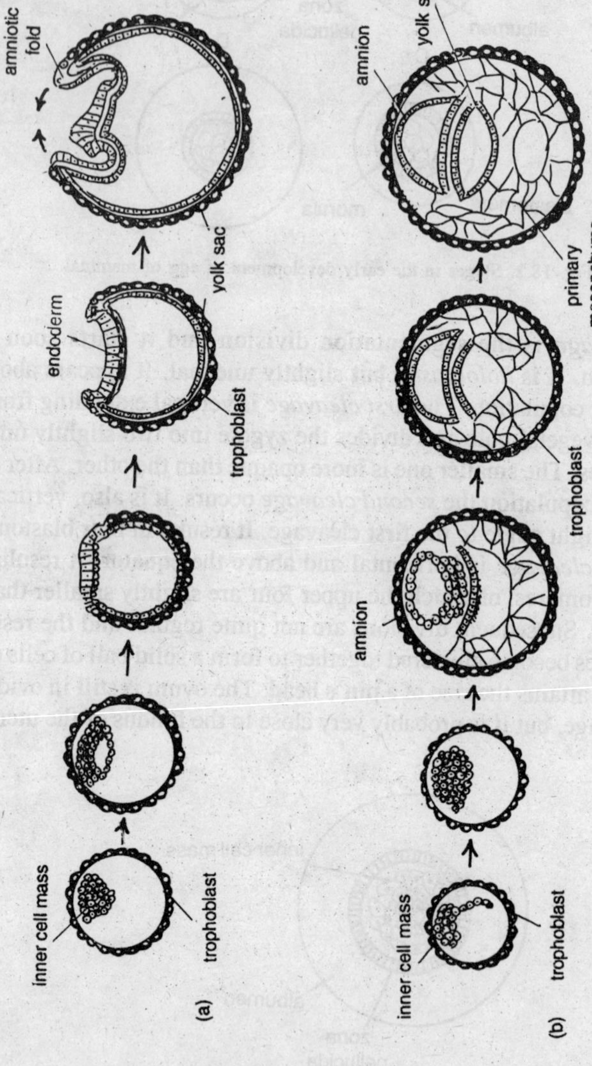

Fig. 18.4. Development of amnion in Mammals : (a) in Rabbit (b) in Man.

Blastocyst

The morula is not appreciably larger than the fertilized egg although it consists of many cells. The cells of the tropho-ectoderm stretch and flatten out and also increase in number, so that its outer surface has enlarged considerably in area. The result of the expansion is the formation of a cavity, the *blastocoel* within the morula. By this time the embryo has reached the uterus and begins to absorb the fluid secreted by the mucous membrane of uterus. It is absorbed by the subzonal layer, which is herein, after called the *trophoblast* due to its important role in the nourishment of the embryo. By continuous absorption of uterine fluid, the embryo swells rapidly along with its fluid filled cavity, the blastocoel that pushes the inner cell mass to one side which will develop into the embryo, that is why a term *embryonal knob* is given to this inner mass of cells. The trophoblast cells which lie immediately above the inner cell mass are called the *cells of Rauber* and the embryo at this stage is called the *blastocyst.* Implantation ocurs at blastocyst stage and the connection

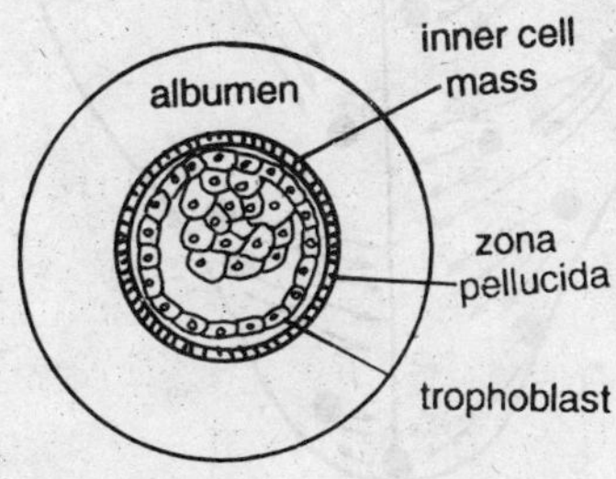

Fig. 18.5. V.S. of early blastocyst stage.

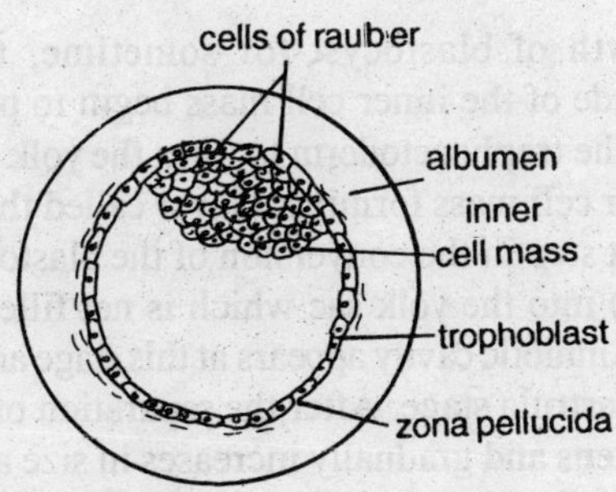

Fig. 18.6. V.S. of later blastocyst stage.

developed between trophoblast and uterine mucosa leads to the formation of the *placenta* through which the embryo exchanges nutrients and excretory products with its mother.

Fate Map

It is the representation of various *prospective* or *presumptive areas* on the embryonal disc with the help of either vital dyes or carbon particles. In rabbit, it is far from well known. Since the general pattern in further development is very much like that of a chick, it is supposed that map of prospective areas is similar to that of the chick embryo.

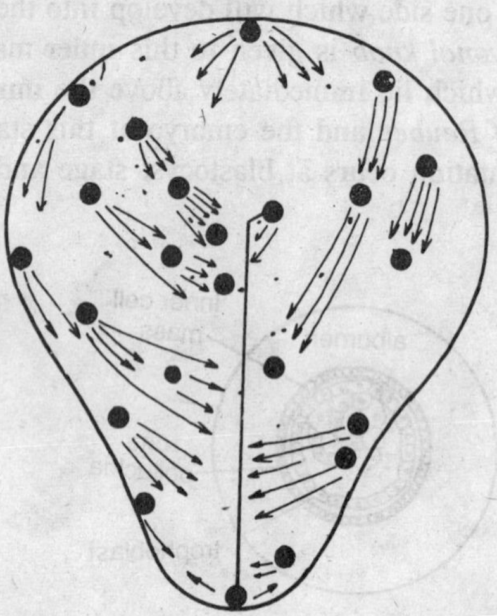

Fig. 18.7. Fate Map.

Gastrulation

After the growth of blastocyst for sometime, the inner cells (unattached) from side of the inner cell mass begin to proliferate along the inner surface of the trophoectoderm to form the yolk sac. These cells extend over the inner cell mass forming a layer called the *endoderm*. Its separation is the first step in the conversion of the blastocoel (excluding the embryonal knob) into the yolk sac which is not filled with yolk but merely with a fluid. Amniotic cavity appears at this stage and the blastocyst now represents the gastrula stage. After the separation of endoderm, the embryonal knob flattens and gradually increases in size and gives rise to the embryo hence called *embryonal disc*. At this stage, it is equivalent to the area pellucida of the blastoderm of the chick. The cells of Rauber

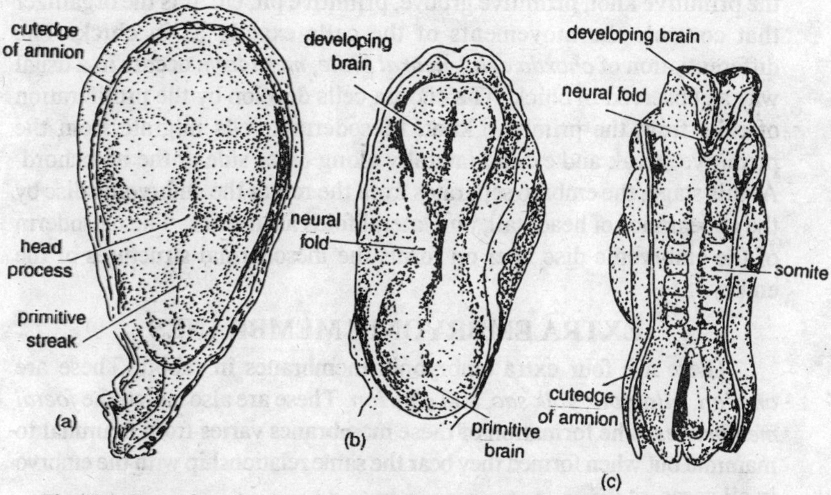

Fig. 18.8. Formation of embryo in mammal : (a) 16 days (b) 18 days (c) 20 days.

degenerate (may be absorbed by the trophoblast) and the disc becomes exposed at the surface of the blastocyst. By this time the zona pellucida of the original ovum and albuminous layers surrounding it also break and are absorbed.

Primitive streak

While the implantation is going on, all the cells of prospective areas freely migrate to take their final positions in the embryo. It is marked by the appearance of *primitive streak* that develops on the embryonal disc. It resembles the primitive streak of chick and has all its components like

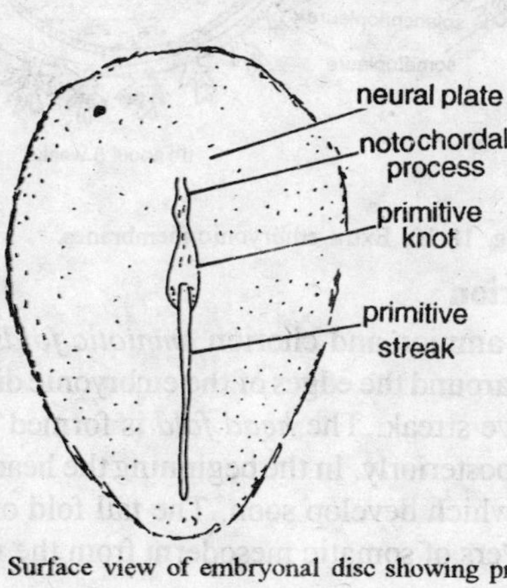

Fig. 18.9. Surface view of embryonal disc showing primitive streak.

the primitive knot, primitive groove, primitive pit, etc. It is the organizer that controls the movements of the cells exactly as in chick. The differentiation of *chorda cells, neural plate, mesoderm* occurs in a usual way as observed in chick. The chorda cells develop by the proliferation of cells from the primitive knot. Mesodermal cells migrate from the primitive streak and extend laterally along other side of the notochord. At this stage, the embryo separates from the rest of the embryonic disc by the appearance of head, tail, and lateral folds as in chick. The mesoderm of the embryonic disc later on forms the mesodermal structures of the embryo.

EXTRA EMBRYONIC MEMBRANES

There are four extra embryonic membranes in rabbit. These are *amnion, allantois, yolk sac,* and *chorion.* These are also called the *foetal membranes.* The formation of these membranes varies from mammal to mammal but when formed they bear the same relationship with the embryo in all cases.

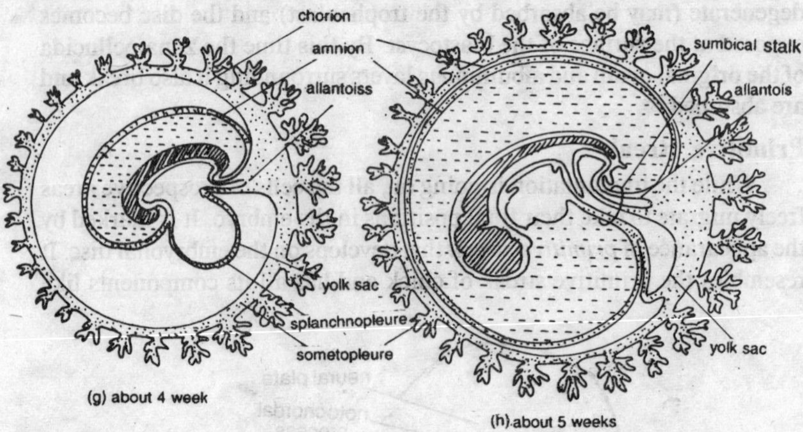

Fig. 18.10. Extra embryonic membranes.

Amnion and Chorion

To give rise the amnion and chorion *amniotic folds* are developed from the trophoblast around the edges of the embryonic disc, but after the formation of primitive streak. The *head fold* is formed on the anterior side and the *tail fold* posteriorly. In the beginning the head fold is without mesodermal layers, which develop soon. The tail fold of the amnion is provided with the layers of somatic mesoderm from the very beginning, and is larger. Each fold encloses a cavity, the *extra embryonic coelom.* The outer layer which is known as *chorion* or *serosa* is formed of an outer ectoderm and inner somatic mesoderm whereas the inner layer which is known as *amnion* is formed of an outer somatic mesoderm and inner ectoderm. The head and tail folds grow over the embryo which finally meet and fuse so as to enclose the embryo in an ectoderm lined amniotic cavity. As the tail fold is larger the *seroamniotic connection* lies above the anterior region of the embryo. After the fusion of trophoblast of the chorion develops villi, the *chorionic villi,* like those of the lower half of the blastocyst, which penetrates into the walls of the uterus to draw the nourishment.

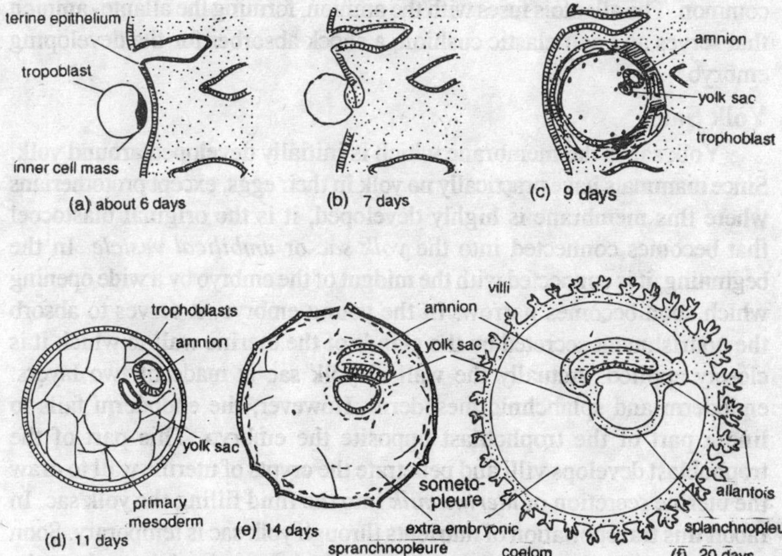

Fig. 18.11. Mammalian extra embryonic membranes.

The amnion protects the embryo from shock and injury, and its fluid prevents its dessication. On the other hand, the chorion provides a large space for the growth of the allantois. In addition to its protective function, a part of the chorion contributes to the formation of the placenta for the transportation of metabolites.

Allantois

The allantois appears before the amniotic cavity has become closed or the amniotic folds meet. It arises as an outgrowth from the hind gut of the embryo that is why allantois consists of endoderm inside and splanchnic mesoderm outside. It enlarges rapidly and extends into extra embryonic coelom between the amnion and chorion. As it grows outside the amnion, it develops blood vessels in its wall. With further development some of these blood vessels become larger forming *umbilical* or *allantoic arteries* and *veins*. As the allantois enlarges, it gets fused with the chorion over a small disc shaped area thus forming- *allanto-chorion* or *chorio-allantois*. It consists of four layers: ectoderm, or trophoblast, two layers of mesoderm, one of amnion and other of chorion, and endoderm, the inner most. These layers play important role in respiratory and excretory processes of the developing organism. In addition, it forms the major part of the placenta.

Protection of the embryo is the function of all foetal membranes in common. The allantois fuses with the amnion, forming the allanto- amnion that serves as a soft elastic cushion, a shock absorber for the developing embryo.

Yolk Sac

Yolk sac is the membrane which is initially developed around yolk. Since mammals have practically no yolk in their eggs, except prototherians where this membrane is highly developed, it is the original blastocoel that becomes connected into the *yolk sac* or *umbilical vesicle*. In the beginning, it is connected with the midgut of the embryo by a wide opening which soon becomes narrow. In the young embryo, it serves to absorb the nourishment secreted by the glands of the uterine wall to which it is closely applied. Actually the wall of yolk sac is made of two layers: endoderm and splanchnic mesoderm. However, the endoderm fails to line a part of the trophoblast opposite the embryo. This part of the trophoblast develops villi and penetrate the crypts of uterine wall to draw the uterine secretion or *uterine milk* into the fluid filling the yolk sac. In rabbit this transportation of nutrients through yolk sac is temporary. Soon it is replaced by the *allantoic placenta*, which is retained throughout the remaining gestation period. Thus with the gradual development of allantois, it starts reducing and finally it is exposed neutrally and the *uterine milk* may move directly to the gut. The stalk of the yolk sac and that of the allantois together with their blood vessels constitute the *umbilical cord* that helps in the transportation of metabolites.

19

Placentation in Mammals

All living mammals are viviparous with the exception of prototherians. The eggs of prototherians are provided with good amount of yolk particles. In such cases the development is similar to that of reptiles. The metatherians present a wide variety of conditions. Their eggs though minute are somewhat larger than those of the placental mammals. The embryo has a brief period of uterine gestation, though no fixed for nor definite uterine attachment is, as a rule, established. Metatherian mammals such as kangaroos give birth to immature young ones. The eutherians are strictly viviparous and their eggs are microscopic containing least amount of yolk (*microlecithal*). The development of such eggs is not possible till they get continuous supply of food materials from any other source. This is done by developing a connection in between the wall of the embryo and the wall of mother's uterus. This connection is called the *placenta*. By means of placenta the developing embryo obtains nutrients and oxygen and gets rid of carbon dioxide and metabolic wastes. The blood of the mother and foetus do not mix at all in the placenta or in any other place.

Placenta is commonly present in mammals though in different shapes and sizes. It is also developed in non- mammalian forms like *Peripatus*, *Salpa*, *Mustelus*, *Chameleon*, etc. The only group of mammals where placentation does not occur is the Monotremata or Prototheria. These animals resemble the reptiles in their anatomy as well as in their morphology.

IMPLANTATION

Implantation is the process where the embryo becomes attached to a nutritional substrate i.e. the wall of uterus. The blastocyst remains free within the uterus for about four days and comes in direct contact with the uterine *epithelium* or *endometrium* and makes further growth possible. At about 11th day, the developing embryo in human is completely inside the uterine wall. And the original point of entry into the uterine wall is sealed with a fibrous and cellular plug known as the *closing coagulum*. The implantation of the blastocyst may occur in one of the following manners:

(i) Central Implantation

It is also known as *superficial implantation* and in this the embryo remains within the lumen of the uterus and the extra embryonic membranes make a superficial attachment to the uterine mucosa. This type of implantation is developed in pig, rabbit, cow, cat, dog, sheep etc.

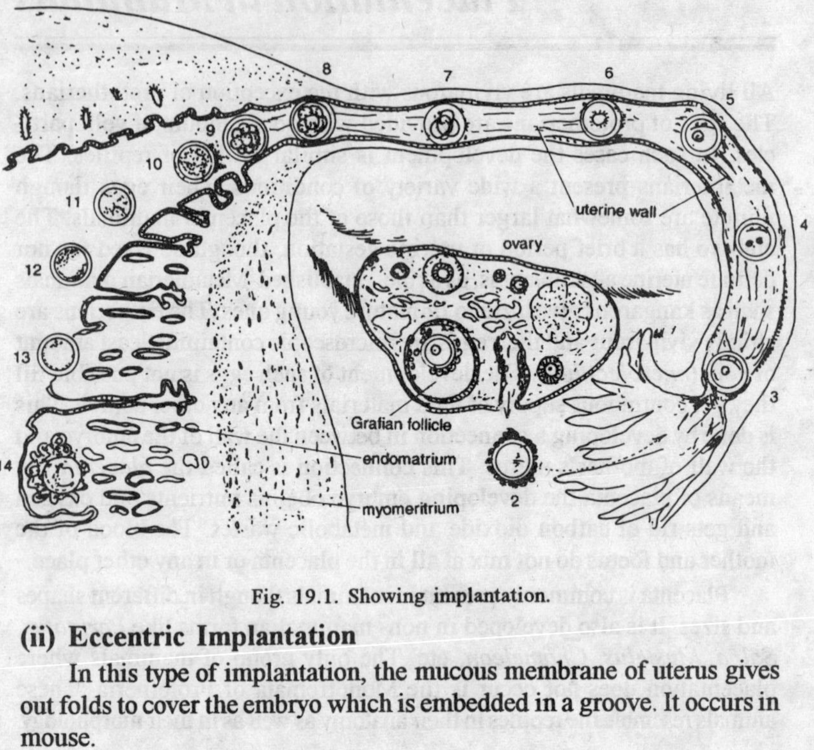

Fig. 19.1. Showing implantation.

(ii) Eccentric Implantation

In this type of implantation, the mucous membrane of uterus gives out folds to cover the embryo which is embedded in a groove. It occurs in mouse.

(iii) Interstitial Implantation

In this type the embryo burrows into the uterine mucosa below the epithelium and becomes surrounded completely by the endometrial tissues of the uterus. It occurs in guinea pig, man and chimpanzee.

TYPES OF PLACENTATION

There are two main types of placenta as given in the following heads:

1. Yolk Sac Placenta

In some cases the yolk sac establishes a close connection with the uterine wall forming the yolk sac placenta. It is confined to a small group of marsupials (kangaroos and its allies). In this the yolk sac grows very large and almost surrounds the embryo. It develops vitelline blood vessels for carrying materials absorbed from the uterus to the foetus. In this, allantois it either rudimentary or absent.

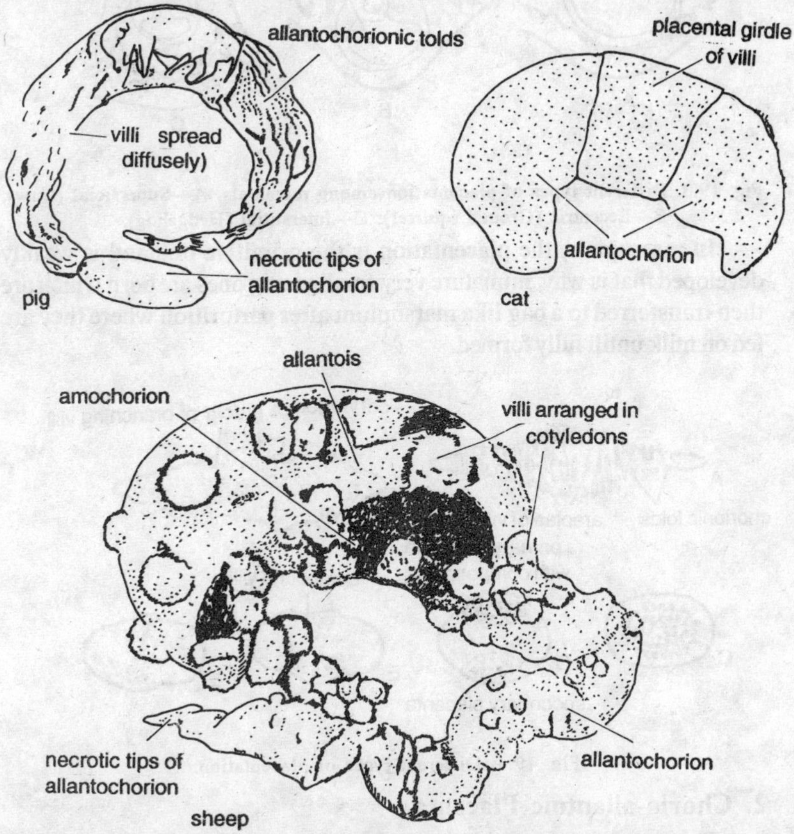

Fig. 19.2. Different types of placentation.

In the forms like *Didelphis virginiana*, the North American opossum the primitive yolk sac placenta is formed. In this a loose connection between the blastocyst and the wall of uterus is developed to absorb the uterine milk secreted by the endometrium. In *Dasyurus*, the marsupial cat, still advanced yolk sac placenta is developed. Here by the erosion of the uterine wall, the blastocyst sinks into it, and pushes the chorionic wrinkles into the uterine tissue. The contact is made more conspicuous with the formation of more folds of the chorion and in this way nourishment as well as oxygen may also be absorbed from the maternal blood.

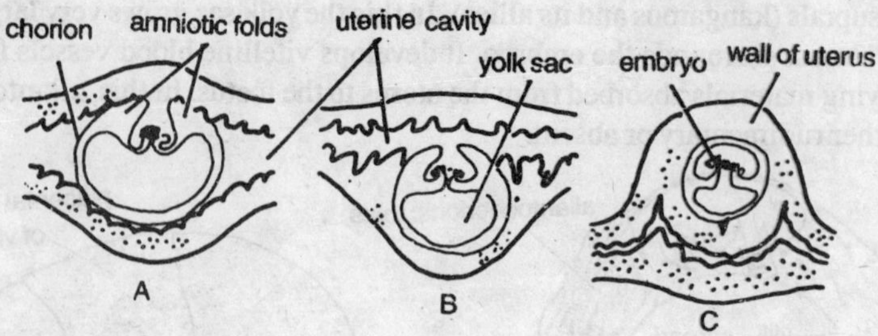

Fig. 19.3. Different types of placentation among mammals. A—Superficial (Cow); B—Eccentric (Ground squirrel); C—Interstitial (Hedgehog).

In marsupials, the placentation is the primitive one and is weakly developed that is why, immature very small young ones are born which are then transferred to a bag like marsupium after parturition where they are fed on milk untill fully formed.

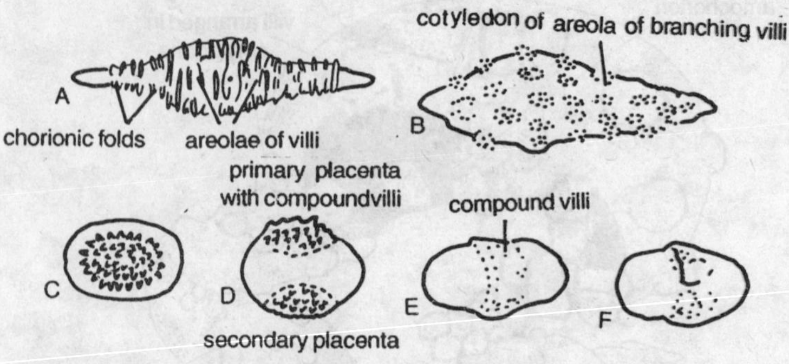

Fig. 19.4. Different types of placentation.

2. Chorio-allantoic Placenta

This type of placentation is developed in all eutherians, however, its primitive form is developed in the marsupials like *Perameles*, the bandicoot, it also has an efficient yolk sac placentá. In eutherians the allantois out grows from the hind gut of the embryo as an endodermal sac covered externally by mesoderm. The allantois grows and spreads in the extra embryonic cavity, its mesoderm fuses with that of the chorion over a some what restricted region. The layer formed by fusion of allantois and chorion is termed *allanto - chorion*. The trophoblast of this region forms vascular processes or *villi* which invade and burrow into corresponding depression or crypts of the wall of uterus whose epithelium and connective tissue break down. This complicated structure is called *allantoic placenta* that serves for the *respiration, nutrition*, and *excretion* of foetus.

CLASSIFICATION OF PLACENTA

The placenta can be classified variously. The classification is based on three criteria :

I. According to the cennection between maternal and foetal tissue on this basis 3 types of placenta are seen

1. Non-deciduate Placenta

The non-deciduate placenta is more simple, and the chorionic villi are simple and unbranched and establish a rather loose connection with the uterine wall. Thus at the time of birth, maternal tissues are not torn from the uterine mucosa. The chorionic villi are easily withdrawn from the uterine crypts, like the fingers from the gloves. Hence no bleeding occurs. The nondeciduate placenta is met with ungulates, cetaceans, sirenians and lemur.

2. Deciduate Placenta

In deciduate placenta, the union between chorion and the uterine mucosa or the endometrium is much more intimate. The superficial layer of the uterus grows extensively over the blastodermic vesicle and is pushed away from the uterine wall. This structure is called *decidua*. The chorionic villi are richly branched and arise from the decidua like root system of a tree. Thus during parturition there is a loss of decidua with the shedding of blood. Example : dogs, cats etc.

3. Contra-deciduate

In certain animals, like mole (*Talpa*) and bandicoot (*Perameles*), the foetal villi and uterine crypts are so intimately connected that during parturition, even most of the chorionic placenta is left behind in the uterus which is later on digested by the maternal leucocysts.

II. According to distribution of villi

1. Diffuse type

In this placenta, the chorionic villi are uniformly distributed all over the surface of the blastocyst but are absent at the extreme end of the blastodermic pit. It occurs in horse, pig, and some other ungulates.

2. Cotyledonary type

In this type the villi are not distributed uniformly all around the foetus. They are confined to particular bunches or tufts called *cotyledons*. These are received by the uterine wall by specially thickened areas called the *caruncles*. This type of placenta is developed in cow, sheep and deer.

3. Intermediate type

As the name suggests, it is an intermediary between the diffuse and cotyledonary nondeciduate placenta. It shows a dual distribution of villi by having single villi scattered between the cotyledons. Examples are giraffe and camel.

4. Zonary type

The zonary placenta bears villi in one or two transverse bands around an elongated blastocyst. The villi are in close contact with the maternal tissues and during parturition much of uterine layer is lost with the placenta. It is developed in elephants and carnivorous mammals.

5. Discoidal type

In this type the villi are restricted to a circular disc or plate on the dorsal surface of blastocyst. The part of uterine tissue that encloses the blastocyst is called the *deciduate capsularis*. It occurs in rabbit, bats, insectivorous and rodents.

6. Metadiscoidal type

In this type of placenta the early blastocyst is entirely buried in the uterine wall, and forms villi all around it. Later on, it projects into the uterine cavity, and the villi disappear from the free surface, persisting on a small disc like area, attached to the uterine wall. It occurs in human beings, apes and monkeys.

III. Histological Types of Placenta

With regard to the intimacy in the relationship between the foetal and maternal parts of placenta, there are five types of placenta as given in the following lines:

1. Epithileo-chorial placenta

This is the simplest type of placenta found in the pig and horse. Here the allantois and chorion fuse together and are supplied jointly with allantoic vessels. The allanto-chorionic membranes come in contact with uterine lining and the chorionic villi fit in the uterine mucosa. In this placenta all the six components take active part. These are uterine epithelium, uterine connective tissues, endothelium of uterine capillaries, trophoblast of allanto-chorion, connective tissues of allanto-chorion and endothelium of foetal capillaries. Examples are pig, horse etc.

2. Syndesmo-chorial placenta

In this, only five barriers are present and the uterine epithelium is eroded and thus the trophoblast comes in direct contact with uterine connective tissues. The chorional villi occupy deeper pits in the uterine tissues. Moreover there is no bleeding during parturition. This type of placenta is developed in cow, sheep, goat, buffalo, camel etc.

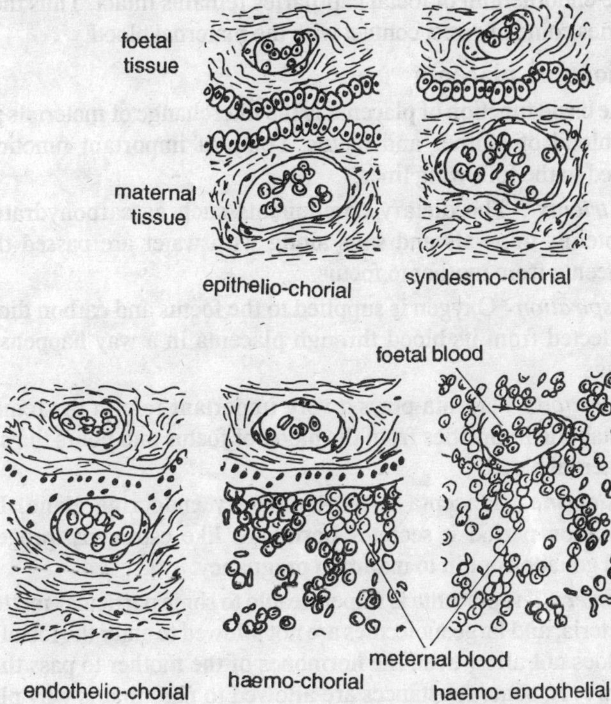

Fig. 19.5. Histological types of placentation.

3. Endothelio-chorial placenta

This type of placenta is formed in carnivorous like dog, cat, tree shrew, mole etc,. There is a breakdown of uterine epithelium and uterine connective tissues so only four barriers take part. The trophoblast comes in direct contact with the maternal blood vessels.

4. Haemo-chorial placenta

In this, all the three maternal barriers, viz, *uterine epithelium*, *uterine connective tissue* and *endothelium* of uterine blood capillaries are eroded, and the foetal barriers remain intact. The foetal villi are, thus directly bathed in maternal blood flowing in lacunae. Examples: man, apes, monkeys, some insectivorous mammals, and some rodents.

5. Haemo-endothelial placenta

This type of placenta is developed in rat, guinea pig and rabbit etc. In this five barriers including all the three maternal barriers and two foetal (trophoblast and connective tissue of allanto-chorion) are eroded and only the endothelium of foetal capillaries remains intact. Thus the foetal capillaries come in direct contact with the maternal blood.

Functions of placenta

The basic function of placenta is the interchange of materials present in the blood of mother and foetus. Some of important functions are described in the following lines.

(i) *Nutrients* : The dietary components such as carbohydrate, fats, proteins, minerals and salts along with water are passed through placenta from mother to foetus.

(ii) *Respiration* : Oxygen is supplied to the foetus and carbon dioxide is collected from its blood through placenta in a way happens in the lungs.

(iii) *Excretion* : Placenta plays a very important role in the removal of metabolic impurities from the blood of foetus and pours the same in maternal blood.

(iv) *Endocrine* : Placenta is the temporary endocrine gland. During gestation period it secretes hormones like estrogens, progestrone and gonadotrophin to maintain pregnancy.

(v) *Barrier* The placenta is impermeable to some particular matter. The bacteria, and large molecules are not allowed to enter the foetal blood. It does not allow even the hormones of the mother to pass through. However, some substances are allowed to pass that is why placenta is called the *selective barrier*.

Table 19.1. Placental Types

	Maternal uterine mucous membrane						Foetal endothelium		
Type of Placenta	Maternal blood	Maternal endothelium	Maternal endothelium connective tissue	Maternal epithelium	Foetal epithelium	Foetal mesoderm connective tissue	Foetal epithelium	Foetal food	Example
Epithelio-chorial	+	+	+	+	+	+	+	+	Horse, pig, donkey
Syndesmo-chorial	+	+	+	—	+	—	+	+	Cow, sheep, goat
Endothelio-chorial	+	+	—	—	+	+	+	+	Dog, cat
Haemo-chorial	+	—	—	—	+	+	+	+	Primates, some
Haemo-endothelial	+	—	—	—	—	—	+	+	Some rodents and rabbits

Revision Questions

1. What is placenta ? Describe various types of placentae found in mammals.
2. What is implantation ? Describe various types of impla ntation in mammals.
3. Describe the importance of placenta to the foetal growth.
4. Describe various functions of placenta.
5. Write short notes on : (a) Hemochorial placenta, (b) Syndesmochorial placenta, (c) Deciduous placenta, (d) Implantation.

20

Endocrine Glands

The various physiological activities of the body are controlled by two systems: *nervous* and *endocrine*. In man as in all other mammals, the *endocrine system* consists of about ten different glands located in particular parts of the body. These glands have no ducts and liberate their secretions, known as *hormones*, directly into the bloodstream. For this reason the endocrine glands are also referred to as the ductless glands.

A hormone may be defined as a "specific product (organic substance) of an endocrine gland secreted into the blood which carries it to some part of the body where it produces a definite physiological effect." This effect may be either *excitatory* or *inhibitory* in its action. Thus, hormones are not only the "chemical messengers" that pass from the glands via the bloodstream to the target organ or some process; but they are important regulating substances that control virtually every aspect of the metabolism in living cells.

Chemical nature

All hormones are organic substances of varying structural complexity. Chemically, they may belong to any of the following categories :

(a) *Amino acid derivative* : e.g., thyroxin

(b) *Catecholamine* : e.g., adrenaline, noradrenaline

(c) *Polypeptide or proteins* : e.g., oxytocin, vasopressin, prolactin, adrenocorticotropic hormone, somatotropin (growth hormone), insulin, glucagon, secretin, relaxin etc.

(d) *Glycoproteins* : e.g. thyrotropin, follicle-stimulating hormone, luteinizing hormone.

(e) *Steroids* : eg., cortisone, aldosterone, testosterone, estrogen, progesterone, etc.

The endocrine system consists of the following glands in a vertebrate.

1. Pituitary Gland
2. Pineal gland

3. Thyroid
4. Parathyroid
5. Adrenal
6. Pancreas
7. Gonads
8. Thymus

1. PITUITARY GLAND OR HYPOPHYSIS

Hypophysis is the chief center of the endocrine system. On one hand it is in direct connection with the central nervous system through the hypothalamus, while on the other almost all endocrine glands are under the regulatory influence of its trophic hormones. Thus, pituitary forms an important link between the nervous and the endocrine systems and acts as a transductor maintaining their functional integration. Considering its important position in the neuroendocrine system it was also referred to as *master gland*, however, this concept is completely discarded owing to the

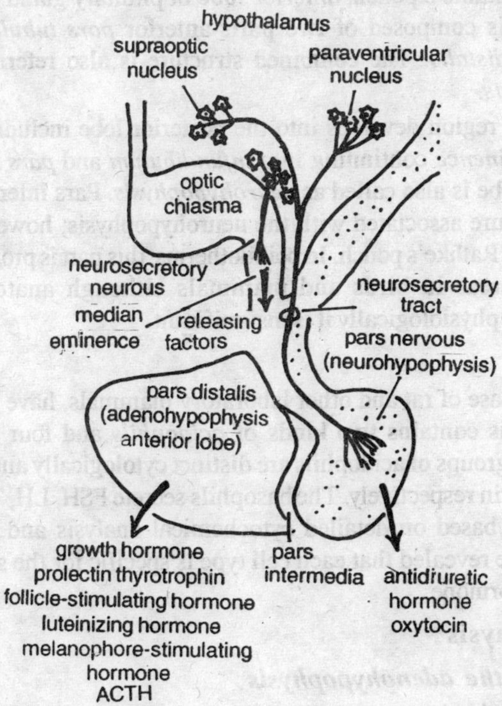

Fig. 20.1. Hypothalamus and pituitary.

fact that it is subservent to the nervous system and even to some of the endocrine glands.

Structure

The pituitary gland is a small, nut-like structure situated at the base of the brain. It is in communication with the floor of third ventricle by a stalk, the *hypothalamus*. In human beings, it weighs about 0.5 gm. In women, during pregnancy the gland increases both the size and weight reaching up to 1 gm. Morphologically, it is a compound gland of internal secretion composed of three parts derived from two embryonic primordia.

The body of pituitary develops from two embryonic sources first is an ectodermal glandular diverticulum-*Rathke's pouch* which is an inward invagination of the primitive buccal cavity. It meets with a similar neural down growth from the floor of the third ventricle. The connection of buccal cavity disappears during later stages of the development; however, neural connection persists throughout the life as the hypothalamus.

From the Rathke's pouch, *anterior lobe* of pituitary gland develops which in turn is composed of two parts-anterior *pars tubularis* and posterior *pars distalis*. The combined structure is also referred to as *adenohypophysis*.

The neural region develops into the posterior lobe including parts like *median eminence* continuing into *infundibulum* and *pars nervosa*. The posterior lobe is also called as *neurohypophysis*. Pars intermedia is one more structure associated with the neurohypophysis; however, it is derived from the Rathke's pouch. In poikilotherms, this part is prominently developed whereas in birds and mammals although anatomically distinguishable, physiologically it is insignificant.

Histology

Studies in case of rat and other laboratory mammals, have revealed that pars distalis contains two kinds of *acidophils* and four types of *basophils*. Two groups of acidophils are distinct cytologically and secrete STH and prolactin respectively. The basophils secrete FSH, LH, TSH and ACTH. Studies based on detailed cytochemical analysis and electron microscopy have revealed that each cell type is specific for the secretion of a particular hormone.

Adenohypophysis

Hormones of the adenohypophysis

Adenohypophysis secrets six different hormones with distinct physiological effects. Chemically all the adenohy-pophysial hormones are proteins or polypeptides and three of them, FSH, LH and TSH, contain carbohydrate conjugated with polypeptide (Glycoproteins).

Depending on their functional significance, they can be grouped into two categories: (1) tropic hormones, and (2) gonadotropins. The tropic hormones are produced to activate another endocrine glands or target organs. Further, their deficiency brings about functional impairment of the specific glands or organs. Gonadotropins are also tropic hormones concerned with normal functional state of gonads and accessory reproductive organs.

Following will be the generalized discussion of a hormone, its physiological actions and malfunctions because of hypo- or hyper-functioning.

1. Thyroid stimulating hormone(TSH) or Thyrotropin

Biochemically it is a glycoprotein with estimated molecular weight ranging from 10,000 to 30,000. Ade- nohypophysis synthesizes TSH under the influence of releasing factors from the hypothalamus. There exists a negative feedback between circulating level of thyroxin and the hypothalamic releasing center.

TSH acts on the thyroid influencing the biosynthesis of thyroxine. On hypophysectomy, the secretion of TSH and its circulating level falls down. During such conditions thyroid becomes completely atropic, The colloid (hormone precusor) becomes depleted and follicles become abnormally enlarged.

2. Adrenocorticotropic hormone (ACTH)

Biochemically it is a straight chain polypeptide composed of 39 amino acid residues and molecular weight about 4,500.

ACTH acts on adrenal cortex influencing its synthetic activity. On hypophysectomy the adrenal cortex undergoes a marked degeneration. Furthermore, to such a hypophysectomized animal if exogenous ACTH is injected, the synthesis of cortical steroids is restored.

There exists a negative feedback, relationship between circulating level of the cortical steroids and hypothalamic releasing centers.

3. Somatotropin (STH) or Growth hormone

It is a protein with a molecular weight ranging between 21,500 and 48,000 in different species of animals. Human STH is composed of about 200 amino acid residues. It is also called as growth hormone because of the fact that its secretion during growth of an animal is considerably high but once full growth is attained, declines to a low value. The concentration of STH in children is about 300 micrograms per liter of plasma which drops by about 30 per cent in adults. Its secretion continues throughout the life of an animal.

STH enhances all the metabolic processes related with the growth of the body. It increases protein synthesis and other anabolic processes. Fats are readily utilized for the energy requirements, however, there is a decrease in the rate of carbohydrate utilization throughout the body.

The anabolic effect of STH in terms of gain in body weight is clearly evident in laboratory animals and man. This can be well illustrated by comparing weight gain in case of a laboratory rat injected with STH with that of a normal rat of the same age and kept under similar physiological conditions. The growth effect, in general, is marked and demonstrable on the linear growth of the skeleton system. In general, growth ceases in the late adolescence because on the closure of epiphysial growth centers of the long bones of skeleton. The growth centers cease to exist when sufficient level of the hormones is established in the circulation.

Ateliotic (or Lorain) dwarfism is a resulting from deficiency of STH during the childhood. The dwarf in this case is called as *midget*. It is normally proportionate but child size individual never attaining maturity (development of secondary sexual characters and attainment of puberty).

Gigantism is overgrowth resulting from STH hyperactivity. The growth of a giant is quite proportionate but unlimited reaching up to 9 feet height in man. However, the individual cannot survive as a result of other physiological disturbances.

The deficiency of STH after attaining adulthood although is not so fatal still may cause certain malfunctions as loss of some weight. On the other hand, STH hyperactivity in adults produces a syndrome known as *acromegaly*. In these adults STH produces increased thickness of the bones of hand, feet, hips making them abnormally wide and heavy. Similarly, supra-orbital ridges of the skull and mandibles become noticeably prominent. This growth appears after closure of the growth centers.

STH as a biological synergist : Adenohypophysial tropic hormones like TSH. ACTH, LH, FSH have been shown to be less effective when STH level falls below normal. From this observation the concept has been emerged that STH must be a biological synergist which creates a responsive environment in which the target organs or glands exhibit maximum response to different hypophysial hormones.

4. Prolactin or Lactogenic hormone or Luteotropin

The prolactin is one more adenohypophysial hormone existing diverse biological actions. It is found to be present in the pituitary from all classes of vertebrates. Biochemically it is a straight chain polypeptide with 205 amino acid residues and a molecular weight about 25,000.

It exerts a lactogenic action in birds and mammals. In birds like pigeon and doves, it enhances the production of crop milk by a process of desquamation. In mammals, usually after parturition, i.e. birth of an infant, it brings about secretion of milk from the mammary alveoli and ductules.

In general, prolactin during pregnancy helps in maintaining functional state of corpus luteum (Luteogenic effect) and after parturition it influences the mammary glands which produce milk (Lactogenic effect).

In addition to this, prolactin also induces changes in the maternal behavior, in some birds it promotes nesting behaviour in both the sexes. Similar, enhancement in the reproductive behaviour has been found in salamander. On administration of prolactin,the terrestrial animal migrates to water for spawning.

5. Follicle stimulating hormone (FSH)

It is a water soluble glycoprotein with molecular weight ranging between 30,000 and 67,000.

Under the influence of FSH, young ovarian follicles start developing a number of granulosa and antra layers, whereas in case of testes it has a marked influence on the initial stages of the spermatogenesis.

6. Luteinizing hormone (LH) or Interstitial stimulating hormons (ICSH)

Biochemically it is a conjugated protein containing carbohydrates, with a molecular weight ranging between 28,000 and 30,000.

In females, it causes ovulation, i.e. release of a mature ovum from the ovary. It is also involved in the development of corpus luteum - a mass of cells developed in the empty follicle after ovulation. The corpus luteum acts as a secondary endocrine source elaborating ovarian hormones implicated in the maintenance of pregnancy.

In males, interstitial cell stimulating hormone (ICSH) activates interstitial cells of the testes, (cells of Leydig) to function as a secondary endocrine source producing testicular androgens. The androgens are involved in the maintenance of accessory reproductive organs and secondary sexual characters.

Although apparently similar gonadotropins, FSH and LH, are secreted by the pituitary of both male and female, still their functional significance varies owing to the fact that ultimately the hypothalamus is sexually dimorphic and brings about different pattern of pituitary release.

Regulation of adenohypophysis

What regulates the release of various tropic hormones of the adenohypo- physis was a puzzle for a long time. However, an important discovery of hypothalamo-hypophysial portal system has solved it. It is a well established fact that specific tropic releasing factors (RF) synthesized in the hypothalamus are carried by the hypothalamo-hypophysial portal system to the adenohypophysis where they influence synthesis of a specific tropic hormones.

Pars Intermedia

It is prominently developed in poikilotherms, whereas in homeotherms although it is anatomically disguishable and possesses potential for secreting hormones, still seems to have little functional significance.

It secretes a group of polypeptides designated as *melanophore stimulating hormones* (MSH). So far two MSHs are identified from the pituitaries of vertebrates, a-MSH and b-MSH. The MSH peptides were named on the basis of their influence on melanophores; nevertheless, they also affect other kinds of chromatophores. They influence chromatophore system by exerting an influence on either concentration or dispersion of variously colored granules in the chromatophores, ultimately giving them characteristic colour patterns. Thus, pars intermedia plays an important role in physiological color responses. In higher vertebrates, i.e. birds and mammals chromatophores are completely absent, however, their pituitaries are capable of secreting these hormones. It is further evident from the fact that pituitary extract of these animals has got a marked chromatophortropic effect on the chromatophore system to poikilothermic vertebrates.

Neurohypophysis or Posterior Lobe

Neurohypophysis or posterior lobe of the pituitary is posterior continuation of the hypothalamus which subsequently comes in contact with adenohypophysis, originating from pinched off Rathke's pouch, to form the body of pituitary gland.

Unlike adenohypophysis, neurohypophysis is a *neurohaemal organ* where neurohormones produced in the specialized neurosecretory nuclei of the hypothalamus are stored. Neurohaemal nature of the neurohypophysis is further evident from the fact that its removal does not impair the normal functioning of neurohypo- physial hormones. Moreover, if it is transcended below the infundibulum there appears a marked accumulation of neurosecretion on the cut surface.

In higher vertebrates neurohypophysial hormones are synthesized by groups of specialized neurosecretory cells of the hypothalamus. The neurohormones are subsequently conveyed to the neurohypophysis by the axonal transport where they are merely stored. Whether the neurohypophysis merely stores the neurohormones or there is any modification before their subsequent release is not known.

Two hormones have been identified from the neurohypophysis, however, there exists a considerable overlap in their biological actions. The principle hormones are: *Antidiuretic hormone* (ADH) synonymous with *vasopressin*, and *Oxytocin*.

1. Antidiuretic hormone (ADH)

The ADH plays an important role in the osmoregulation, i.e. water balance of the body. It affects all the sites of water metabolism and organs concerned with water exchange. In this regard ADH has a prominent action on the kidneys. Under the influence of its higher circulating level highly concentrated urine is produced, the effect being called as *antidiuretic*. At cellular level, the hormone acts on epithelial cells of the distal portion of the rertal tubule. It is further evident from the fact that extremely concentrated urine is produced on exogenous injection of ADH or neurohypophysial extract. The concentration is also accompanied by reduced urinary volume. Hypothalamic lesions destroying supraoptic nucleus and supraoptico-hypophysial tract produce a clinical manifestation in the laboratory animals, known as *diabetes insipidus*. It is characterized by the excretion of large volumes of extremely dilute urine. Such diabetic animals consume large quantities of water (*polydipsia*) and eliminate a large volume of urine (*diuresis*). This condition can be corrected by administration of vasopressin. The effect of ADH at cellular level is on the cells of the distal segment of the nephron where it selectively increases or decreases the membrane permeability for water according to the osmotic state of the body.

2. Oxytocin

Oxytocin plays an important role in the female reproductive physiology, particularly at the time of parturition. Two main functions have been assigned to it: (1) to facilitate the ascent of spermatozoa in the female tract after copulation, and (2) to expel the foetus at the time of parturition.

The oxytocin acts on the uterine musculature which undergoes involuntary contractions aiding ascent of sperms after coitus and delivery or expulsion of foetus from the uterus at the time of parturition. Thus in viviparous animals, a normal circulating level of oxytocin is essential for normal delivery.

Like viviparous animals, in oviparous vertebrates like birds and reptiles, it plays an important role in the reproductive physiology. It induces oviposition in hens by contractions of the shell gland and the vagina. In fishes, there is a marked effect on reproductive behaviour.

After parturition oxytocin brings about milk ejection from the mammary glands. This is one of the best established functions of the oxytocin *Galactogogic effect*. In this response the hormone acts on the branching myoepithelial cells around the mammary alveoli resulting in an increase in milk pressure and its subsequent flow through the teats.

PINEAL BODY

It is a tiny object lying deep in the groove between the cerebellum and the cerebral hemispheres. Occasionally, a tumor developed in it, and the sex glands then appeared to develop precociously. However, the removal of the pineal, in animals, had no such effect, in fact, no visible change in their development occurred.

Although thought by the ancients to be the seat of the soul, it is probable that the pineal is no more than an evolutionary vestige of the medial eye, an eye on the back of the head which evolved among certain of our reptilian ancestors.

THYROID

The embryologic origin of the thyroid as a tube growing out of the mouth cavity. At that stage, the thyroid is an exocrine gland, emptying its secretion into the mouth; however, the duct disappears and the thyroid then be- comes an endocrine grand, emptying its secretion directly into the blood. This probably explains why thyroxin can be effectively given by mouth, this is true of few other hormones. It is not even necessary that an extract be given; desiccated thyroid, in the preparation of which thyroid glands are extracted with ether to remove the fat, dried, and ground, is usually adequate.

Each lobe of the thyroid is supplied by two arteries. The blood supply is very generous, in fact, the thyroid receives more blood per gram of weight than any other organ in the body. (In the adult, the thyroid weight about 25 gm. and receives from 125 to 150 ml. of blood per minute).

Histologically, the thyroid consists of *alveoli*, spherical bodies lined with thyroid cells, the center is filled with a pink-staining jelly-like mass, the so-called *colloid*. It is thought to be stored thyroxin combined with a protein. As needed, the thyroxin leaves the colloid and enters the blood. Between two alveoli are present *C-cells or parafollicular*, cells which produce *calictonin*.

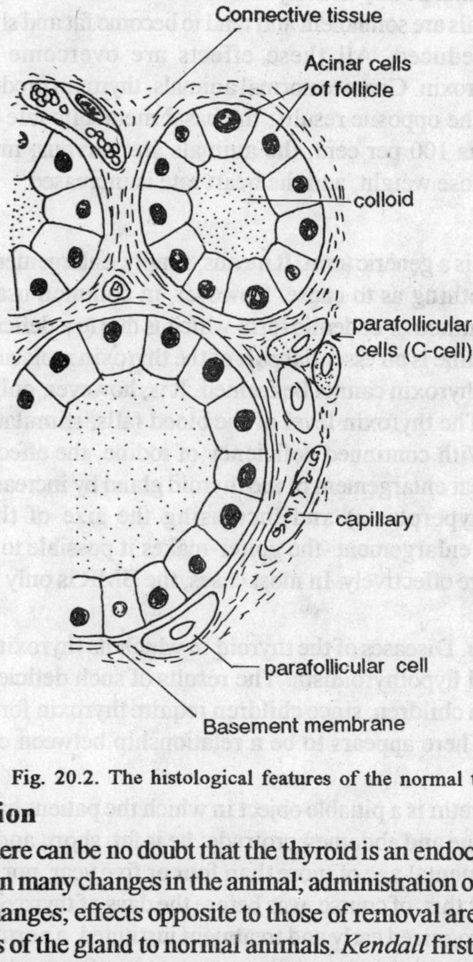

Fig. 20.2. The histological features of the normal thyroid gland.

Function

There can be no doubt that the thyroid is an endocrine gland. Removal results in many changes in the animal; administration of thyroxin overcomes such changes; effects opposite to those of removal are produced by giving extracts of the gland to normal animals. *Kendall* first obtained crystalline thyroxin after having worked on literally tons of thyroid glands. The structural formula was worked out by *Harrington*, who later synthesized thyroxin. As has been said, synthetic thyroxin is little more than a laboratory curiosity.

When an animal's thyroid is removed, many things happen, but all are explainable on the basis of an extreme reduction of his ability to utilize food i.e. his basal metabolic rate is greatly reduced. This is usually expressed as a reduction in his oxygen consumption, but, after all, the purpose of the oxygen is to burn food. If thyroidectomy is done to the young animal, the animal does not grow and fail to develop either mentally or sexually.

In the adult animal bodily activity is decreased when the thyroid is removed. Such animals are somnolent and tend to become fat and sluggish; the heart rate is reduced. All these effects are overcome by the administration of thyroxin. Given to normal animals, thyroxin produces, as might be expected, the opposite results; the basal metabolic rate may be increased as much as 100 per cent, the animals are nervous; muscular tremors occur, they lose weight, and the heart rate is increased.

Endemic Goiter

The word goiter is a generic term. It means, simply, enlargement of the thyroid, and says nothing as to cause. However, in common usage, the term refers to the common or endemic form which is due to a deficiency of iodine in the diet. Iodine is an essential part of the thyroxin molecule, and, in its total absence, thyroxin cannot be formed. It is, however, only rarely completely absent. The thyroxin level of the blood falls, stimulating the secretion of TSH. With continued deficiency of iodine, the effect of the TSH is to cause a great enlargement of the thyroid gland by increasing the number of cells (hyperplasia) and increasing the size of the cells (hypertrophy). This enlargement -the goiter-makes it possible to use the available iodine more effectively. In most cases, the BMR is only slightly reduced, if at all.

Hypothyroidism. Diseases of the thyroid in which its thyroxin output is reduced are called hypothyroidism. The results of such deficiency are much more severe in children, since children require thyroxin for growth and development. There appears to be a relationship between endemic goiter and *cretinism*.

The complete cretin is a pitiable object in which the patient has a very stupid look, his tongue and abdomen protrude; he is fat, short, and stocky. He never reaches a mental age of more than four or five year, nor does he develop sexually. All this, of course, was before the days of thyroxin. Now, if the condition is recognized early and treatment instituted, a normal child will result. Early recognition is especially important in reference to mental development, since the cells of the nervous system develop rapidly, and the alert child's multiple experiences of early learning cannot be compensated in later life.

Myxedema is adult hypothyroidism. It is marked by sluggishness, both mental and physical, and a puffiness of the skin, showing itself especially in bags under the eyes. This puffiness is due to the deposition of protein in a thin, jelly-like form under the skin. All reflexes which go through the brain are slowed; mental processes are also retarded. The basal metabolism is frequentely as low as minus forty or fifty. The heart rate is very slow, and the person always feels cold. Treatment of myxedema is the easiest thing in the world, one tablet of dessicated thyroid several times a week does the job perfectly.

Hyperthyroidism

The commonest type of hyperthyroidism is called *exophathalmic goiter.* Since this is the reverse of myxedema, the symptoms can be predicted: loss of weight, extreme nervousness, a fast heart; the patient is always hot, and the BMR may be as high as plus fifty or sixty. Many times, the nervous system symptoms are very severe, and patients suffer from hallucinations and other psychotic manifestations.

Until recently, the only treatment of exophthalmic goiter was surgical removal of the entire thyroid gland. If only a portion were removed, the remainder would rapidly hypertrophy and the symptoms reappear. Surgeons dreaded the operation, which was extremely bloody; for another thing, the parathyroids had to be spared. Also the aftermath of the operation was often a tragedy that has never been satisfactorily explained.

Control of Secretion

Thyroid secretion is controlled largely, but not entirely, by a hormone from the anterior lobe of the pituitary called *thyrotropin*, or "*thyroid-stimulating hormone*" (TSH). If the secretion of thyroxin by the thyroid is controlled by the secretion of TSH by the pituitary, one is bound to ask, "What stimulates the pituitary to secrete TSH?"

We are here dealing with a homeostatic mechanism. There should be a certain amount of thyroxin secreted; if there is, the basal metabolic rate is normal, and all process depending on it are normal, too. The anterior lobe is peculiarly sensitive to the amount of thyroxin circulating in the blood. If the amount falls, the anterior lobe increases its output of TSH, which stimulates the thyroid to increased activity. If the amount of thyroxin in the circulating blood rises the opposite effect is produced: the output of TSH falls, and the thyroid in turn becomes less active. This mutual control is represented schematically above.

While removal of the thyroid results in a fall of 50-60 per cent in the basal metabolic rate, removal of the anterior lobe results in a fall of only 30-40 per cent; it seems, therefore, that there must be an additional source of stimulation. What it may be is not known.

PARATHYROIDS

In the human, there are usually four tiny masses of cells, two on each side, buried within the thyroid gland. These are the parathyroids. They are not actually buried: the capsule of the thyroid extends beneath them, and they have their own blood supply, so that it is possible to remove the thyroid and leave at least the upper parathyroids intact. In many animals, such as the rat and the rabbit, there is a good deal of accessory parathyroid tissue extending along the trachea, sometimes even into the thorax: such animals rarely develop tetany following removal of the parathyroids.

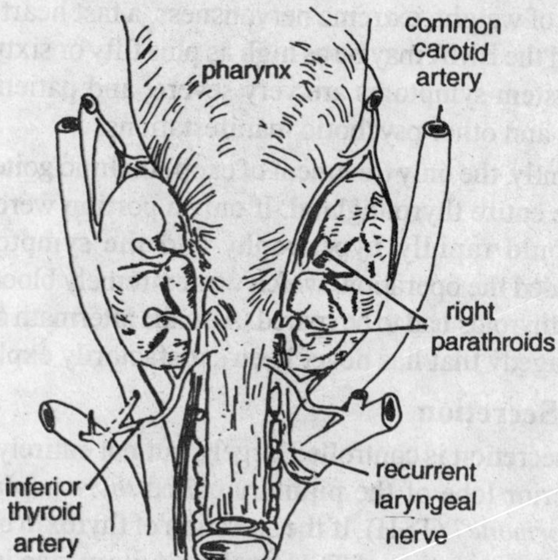

Fig. 20.3. The human parathyroid glands.

The function of the parathyroids was discovered almost accidentally when it was found that many patients after thyroidectomy developed tetany. On removal of the parat-hyroids in the dog the calcium level in the blood plasma from a normal of 10 mg. per 100 ml. decreased to about half that. Exactly the same result occured in the human when, inadvertently, his parathyroids were removed along with his thyroid gland.

The function of the parathyroids is to maintain the calcium level in the blood at the normal level. Just how they do this is to certain, but one effect of the administration of *parathormone* (the hormone of the parathyroids) is to greatly increase the number of osteoclasts. These, it will be remembered, are the cells which destroy bone; it seems, therefore, that parathormone is able, should the blood calcium level fall to add calcium from bones to the blood.

The secretion of parathormone is, so far as is known, controlled exclusively by the level of calcium in the blood. During pregnancy and lactation, when the mother's blood level of calcium may fall because of the demands of the baby, the size of the parathyroids- and, presumably their activity is greatly increased. This is also true in rickets, where, due to failure of calcium absorption, the blood level of calcium also tends to fall. On the other hand, if much calcium is taken in the diet, the blood level tends to rise, and the size of the parathyroids decreases accordingly.

Ordinarily, hypoparathyroidism is rare. There are, however, a number of conditions in which-whether the parathyroids are responsible or not-the blood calcium is low. Infantile tetany is not uncommon: this is not true tetany, but is marked by muscular twitchings (Chvostek's sign) and spasms (Trousseau's sign). There is also a tropical disease called *sprue* with similar symptoms, where absorption of calcium from the intestine is decreased.

The condition of a low calcium level in the blood, such as occurs in the diseases mentioned, is called *hypocalcemia*. The opposite condition *hypercalcemia*, also occurs. This happens when there is a tumor of the parathyroids, the cells of the tumor are active parathyroid cells, and the secretion of parathormone is increased. Just as a decreased secretion results in a fall in blood calcium, so on increased secretion tends to produce a rise; the excess calcium is, however, eliminated by the kidneys and through the intestine. This means a constant drain on the body's calcium reserves, which are, of course, the bones. As earlier mentioned, parathormone increases the activity of the osteoclasts; the bones become weak and fragile; such people suffer fractures of the bones very frequently; a mere bump against the corner of a chair or table is sufficient. The disease is called *osteitis fibrosa*.

THE ADERNAL OR SUPRARENAL GLANDS

The adrenal glands are situated one on each side of the vertebral column, closely applied to the upper poles of the kidneys : hence the name *supra-renals*. The adrenal glands are surrounded by a capsule of areolar tissue containing fat.

Structure

The glands are composed of two distinct parts which differ both anatomically and physiologically. The outer part (derived from mesoderm) is known as the *cortex* and the inner part (derived-from neural crest) as the *medulla*.

I. Cortex

It is composed of three layers of cells

(i) *Zona glomerulosa*. The outer layer zona glomerulosa, is made up of comparatively small thickly set ovoid groups of cells. These secrete mineralocorticoids which regulate salt and water balance.

(ii) *Zona fasciculata*. The middle layer, zona fasciculata is the widest layer which is made up of polyhedral cells arranged in radiating columns. This layer secretes glucocorticoids affecting carbohydrate metabolism.

(iii) *Zona reticularis*. The inner layer, zona reticularis is made up of an irregular network of rows of cells. These secrete sex hormones.

II. Medulla

The medulla is completely surrounded by the cortex. In man this region is thin, comprising only 5-10 per cent of the gland. The cells of the medulla assemble in rounded groups or short anastomosing columns with many intermingling blood capillaries. The medulla is composed of sympathetic ganglion cells which have no postganglionic fibres. Medullary cells are essentially neurosecretory cells because they are stimulated by preganglionic sympathetic fibres to produce the hormones *adrenaline* and *noradrenaline*. Medullary cells have a special affinity for chromium compds such as $K_2Cr_2O_7$, and Chromic acid, and they are, therefore, also referred to as *chromaffin cells*.

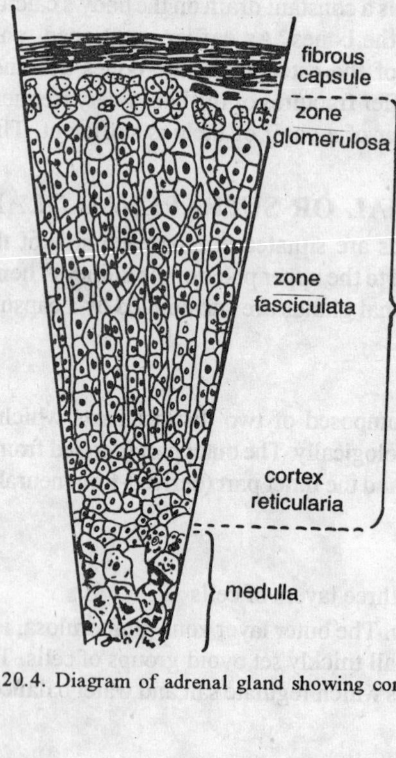

Fig. 20.4. Diagram of adrenal gland showing cortex and medulla.

Functions of Adrenal cortex

The adrenal cortex produces a number of potent hormones all of which are steroid derivatives:

1. The Mineralocorticoids

These are associate with the maintenance of electrolyte balance in the body and distribution of water in tissues. Specific examples are *aldosterone* and *deoxycorticosterone*. The most potent mineralocorticoid is aldosterone. Deoxycorticosterone is only 4% as potent as aldosterone.

The mineralocorticoids promotes the reabsorption of sodium and chloride ions by renal tubules. Retention of these in the blood keeps its osmotic pressure high, as a result of which water as also reabsorbed. This in turn assures normal blood volume and pressure. Increases excretion of potassium ions.

The amount of aldosterone produced is influenced by the sodium level in blood. When the sodium blood level falls, more aldosterone is secreted and more sodium reabsorbed. Aldosterone secretion is stimulated by the angiotensin produced by kidneys.

Hyposecretion of aldosterone causes *Addison's disease*, characterised by excessive loss of sodium chloride in the urine and elevated levels of potassium in the serum. It helps in lowering of blood pressure, body temperature and BMR. Muscular weakness, hypoglycemia, loss of appetite, vomitting and gastro-intestinal disturbances. Brownish pigmentation of bronzing or the skin especially the exposed parts, for example, the face and hands due to deposition of melanin.

2. The Glucocorticoids

These primarily affect metabolism of carbohydrate, proteins and lipids. Specific examples are *corticosterone*, *hydrocortisone* or *cortisol* and *cortisone*. Their secretion is stimulated by ACTH from the anterior lobe of pituitary.

The glucorticoids are metabolically antagonistic to insulin. Under their influence glycogen is changed to glucose in the liver, raising the blood sugar level (hyperglycemic action). During stress, they promote the conversion of fats and proteins to glycogen that is ultimately converted to glucose (gluconeogenesis).

They have antinflammatory and antiallergic properties. Cortisol is used in the treatment of rheumatoid arthritis when it is even injected inside the diseased joint. It is a life saving drug in anaphylactic or adverse reactions to certain drugs-like reaction to the injection of penicillin and, in severe attacks of asthma. It is also useful in certain autoimmune diseases, as well as in the form of ointments for skin and eyes. In recent years, this hormone has been utilized to suppress the phenomenon of rejection in transplantation of organs.

Hypersecretion of cortisol in adults results from one of the two cases:-

1. Adrenocortical hyperplasia initiated by increased production of ACTH due to hyperactivity of basophil cells in the pituitary gland.
2. Benign or malignant tumours of the adrenal cortex.

The term *Cushing's disease* has been restricted to those cases which are of pituitary origin whereas *Cushing's Syndrome* denotes adrenocortical hyperfunction directly involving the adrenal glands.

Due to hyperadrenocorticism (Cushing's disease and Syndrome) include hyperglycemia and glycosuria (diabetogenic effect), excessive deposition of fat over the face, back of the neck and abdomen, muscular weakness due to potassium depletion through the kidneys, and wasting of the muscles due to protein anti- anabolic effect and gluconcogenesis.

3. The Sex hormones

The primary adrenal androgens are *Dehydroepiandrosterone* (DHEA) and *Adrostenedione*. These cause retention of nitrogen chloride. If present in excessive amounts, they also lead to masculinization in the female. Adrenal estrogens influence the development and maintenance of the secondary sex characters in females. The hypersecretion of androgenic hormones is results in overgrowth of hairs, enlargement of penis and increased sexual desire in males. In female hairs may grow more on the face, chest, limbs, breast may atrophy, voice may become harsh and manstruation may cease. This phenomenon is called adrenal virilism (presence of male characters in female).

II. Medulla

The adrenal medulla is a derivative of the sympathetic part of the autonomic nervous system. When stimulated by preganglionic sympathetic nerve fibres, it secretes two hormones : *adrenaline* (*epinephrine*) and *noradrenaline* (*norepinephrine*). These hormones belong to a class of substances known as catecholamines that are derivatives of amino acid tyrosine.

Functions of Noradrenaline

It is a precursor of adrenaline which does not possess a methyl group (-CH_3), as is found in the adrenaline. Nor adrenaline produces an overall vasoconstriction (except in coronary arteries), but otherwise its effects on metabolism are rather inconspicuous.

Functions of Adrenaline

1. Causes vasodilation of the arterioles of the skeletal muscles increasing the supply of oxygen and nutritional materials for a sustained muscle activity.
2. Increases heart rate, cardiac output and causing vasoconstriction of the arterioles of the skin, mucous membranes and splanchnic viscera, directing the blood away from them to the skeletal muscles, brain, coronary artery and liver.
3. Dilates trachea and bronchi to permit a greater volume of air to enter the lungs at each inspiration.
4. Slows down peristalsis in the digestive tract and limits the flow of saliva.
5. Increases the tone of the anal and urethral sphincter muscles, thus inhibiting micturition and defaecation.
6. Stimulates the conversion of liver glycogen stored in liver and muscles to glucose that is ready for oxidation.
7. Decreases insulin, thereby preventing the glucose from being taken up by peripheral tissues and preserving it for the CNS.

The net result of such changes is that an increased quantity of blood is pumped faster to heart, muscles and brain ; it is well oxygenated and rich in nutrients. These preparations are valuable for the body in providing a rapid physiologic response to emergencies such as fatigue, shock, fear, excitement and danger. In this sense, it mobilises what has been termed the "fight or flight" mechanism i.e., the emergency function, as suggested by *Cannon*.

PANCREAS

Pancreas is a compound gland comprising exocrine and endocrine parts. The exocrine portion is composed of acini producing pancreatic juice, whereas the endocrine portion consists of small aggregations of epithelial cells called as *islets of Langerhans*. Human pancreas contains a million or more individual islets scattered widely throughout the acinar tissue. The cells of the islets are separated by a very rich system of capillary vessels or sinusoids.

Pancreas as an endocrine gland secretes two hormones, *insulin* and *glucagon*, that are involved in the glucose homeostasis. Both of these hormones act mainly, but not exclusively, on the liver as it is the main site of carbohydrate metabolism.

Three types of cells are identified in the pancreatic islets. First type, the *alpha cells* are less abundant and tend to arrange at the periphery of the islets. They are the source of a hyperglycemic principle, *glucagon*. *Beta cells* constitute the second cells type and are the source of a hypoglycemic principle, *insulin* which is the most studied hormone because of its involvement in the most common endocrine disorder *diabetes mellitus* known to man. Many investigators have described a third cell type, C cells or Y cells. They are few in number and secrete *somatostatin* hormone.

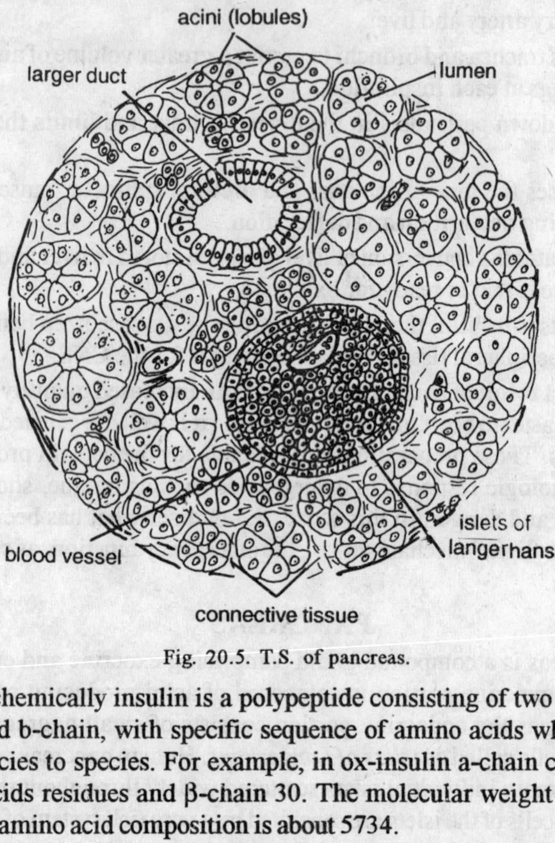

Fig. 20.5. T.S. of pancreas.

Biochemically insulin is a polypeptide consisting of two chains. α-chain and b-chain, with specific sequence of amino acids which varies from species to species. For example, in ox-insulin a-chain contains 21 amino acids residues and β-chain 30. The molecular weight calculated from the amino acid composition is about 5734.

The glucagon molecule is a straight chain polype-ptide-containing 29 amino acids residues and has a molecular weight of 3485. The peculiarity of glucagon molecule is the complete absence of disulphide bonds.

The somatostatin contains 14 amino acids.

Glucose metabolism

In the body glucose is the most readily available source of energy. In the circulation, normally its level ranges between 90 and 140 mg/100 ml of plasma. The level consequently also forms general cellular and renal threshold for glucose. Further, any rise in it leads to dehydration of cellular compartments (glycosuria) and urinary loss of glucose (polyurea). These are the symptoms of hyperglycemia. On the contrary, whenever glucose level falls below the normal value (hypoglycemia) cells are starved and vital constituents of body like proteins are mobilized to satisfy glucose needs of the body.

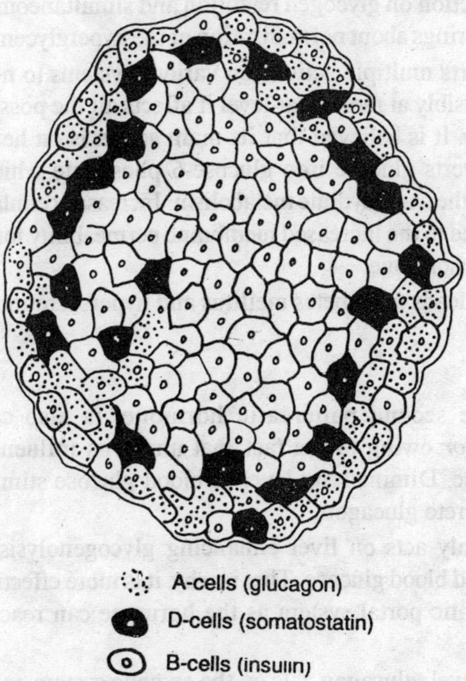

Fig. 20.6. The typical cellular composition of an islet of Langer-hans to show the distribution of the different cell types

1. Insulin

Rising level of blood glucose (hyperglycemia) stimulates b-cells of the islets to secrete more and more insulin which subsequently normalizes the hyperglycemia. At molecular level insulin affects all the possible sites involved in the glucose metabolism.

It normalizes hyperglycemia by enhancing glucose utilization, deposition and conversion. In this process primary effect is increased utilization of glucose by the tissues. It is believed that the action of insulin is on the membrane system which becomes readily permeable to glucose. Secondly, excess of glucose is converted into some other form by a process of gluconeogenesis. It enhances protein synthesis so also excess of glucose is converted into glycogen in the liver and muscles (glycogenesis), at the same time glycogenolysis in the liver is suppressed. Thus, increased cellular oxidation of glucose in the tissue, its utilization for the synthesis of fat and glycogen encourage its removal from the circulation. Insulin also enables extraordinary retention of glycogen in the liver. In this way be exerting bilateral action on glycogen retention and simultaneous glucose utilization insulin brings about normalization of the hyperglycemia.

As insulin exerts multiple actions on various systems to normalize hyperglycemia, possibly at molecular level it affects all the possible sites of cellular anatomy. It is believed that its main action is on hexokinase system which converts glucose into glucose-6 phosphate which is the rate limiting step in the carbohydrate metabolism. Increased cellular uptake of glucose is assigned to the increased membrane permeability for it under the influence of the hormone.

Hyposecretion leads to diabetes mellitus and hypersecretion leads to insulin shock.

2. *Glucagon*

Glucagon, the second pancreatic hormone, is also called as *hyperglycemic factor* owing to the fact that under its influence blood glucose tends to rise. Diminishing level of blood glucose stimulates a-cells of Islets to secrete glucagon.

Glucagon mainly acts on liver enhancing glycogenolysis thereby normalizing elevated blood glucose. That is why, it is more effective when injected in the hepatic portal system as the hormone can reach site of action directly.

At molecular level, glucagon acts on the enzyme system engaged in hepatic glycogenolysis, particularly phosphorylase system which converts glycogen into glucose-l-phosphate which is the rate limiting step in glycogen mobilization.

Like hypoglycemia which is totally the effect of insulin, glucagon is not the only hyperglycemic factor and a number of other endocrine principles can mimic its effects.

GONADS

The gonads secrete sex hormones

I. Male sex hormones

In mammalian testes, the interstitial (Leydig) cells lying scattered in between the seminiferous tubules synthesize male hormones, the *androgens*. The principal male hormone is *testosterone*, which is synthesized from cholesterol. Other hormones are 15-hydroxytestosterone and 6-hydroxy-testosterone.

Of the synthetic products, *methyl testosterone* and *testosterone propionate* are important members.

Functions of Testosterone

1. Promotes the growth and functions of the epididymis, vas deferens, prostate, seminal vesicles and penis.
2. Stimulates the development of male secondary sex characters- (i) the voice deepens (ii) hair begins to grow on the face and on the upper lip; in the axillae and in the pubic region. (iii) there is a greater skeletal and muscular growth.
3. Influences spermatogenesis and seminal plasma secretions.
4. Exerts a feedback inhibitory effect on pituitary LH secretion.
5. It has a general anabolic effect on the body by stimulating protein synthesis.

II. Female Sex hormones

Two main types of female hormones are secreted by the ovary: the *estrogens* produced by the cells of de- veloping graffian follicle and the *progesterones* derived from the corpus luteum that is formed in the ovary from the ruptured follicle after ovulation.

Functions of Estrogens

The principle estrogenic hormone in the blood circulation is *estradiol* which is secreted by theca interna cells of the graffian follicle. The estradiol is excreted as *estrone* or *estriole*.

1. Promotes the development of female secondary sex characteristics. At the start of the adolescence (puberty) the mammary glands (breasts) develop, chiefly by proliferation of ducts, the pelvis becomes broader, voice stays high pitched, the genitalia enlarge and there is growth of hair around them and in the axillae, and development of fat deposits in subcutaneous tissues and other particular regions to make a typical feminine body (characterised by rounded body contours) are seen.
2. Prepares the uterine mucosa for the later action of progesterone i.e., proliferative growth of the lining of the endometrium, deepening of uterine glands, and increased vascularity.

3. Influences growth of fallopian tubes and stratification of vaginal epithelium.
4. Suppresses the production of pituitary FSH.

Functions of Progesterone

After ovulation, the discharged follicle cells become transformed into a characteristic body known the corpus luteum, a temporary endocrine structure that secretes the hormone, *progesterone*. It is a steroid which is synthesised from its immediate precursor, pregnenolone.

1. Causes extensive development of the endometrium, preparing the uterus for the reception of the embryo and for its nutrition.
2. The hormone suppresses manustral cycle, ovulation and the production of pituitary LH which originally stimulated corpus luteum formation.
3. Stimulates the mammary glands.
4. Maintains the foetus by forming placenta and inhibits uterine muscles to contract during pregnancy.

Relaxin. In addition to progesterone, corpus luteum of some mammals like guinea pig, mouse, rabbit, dog and cow, produce a second hormone termed relaxin, which relaxes pubic symphysis and thus facilitates birth.

THE THYMUS

Located in the upper part of the thorax, the thymus is quite large in the young animal, occupying most of the upper third of the thorax, but as the animal grows, the gland atrophies. By the time adulthood is reached, it is no more than a pair of small lobes lying on either side of the trachea. Histologically the thymus does not have the appearance of an endocrine gland, it is mainly fat and lymphoid tissue. However, it does contain certain unique structures called *Hassal bodies*, which are small masses of onion-shaped cells, to which some ascribe a secretory function.

These Hassal bodies are present in the medulla. The outer part is called cortex which is made up of closely packed lymphocytes but no Hassal bodies.

Thymus secretes three hormones *Thymosin*, *Thymosin* I and *Thymosin* II.

The function of Thymosin is yet to be known. The thymus is primary centre for the formation of lymphocytes during early stages. The lymphocytes migrate to the peripheral lymphoidal tissue and by multiplication form secondary source of lymphocytes.

Probably it secretes sex-gland inhibitory hormone which, as long as the thymus remained large and functional, inhibited sex-gland development,

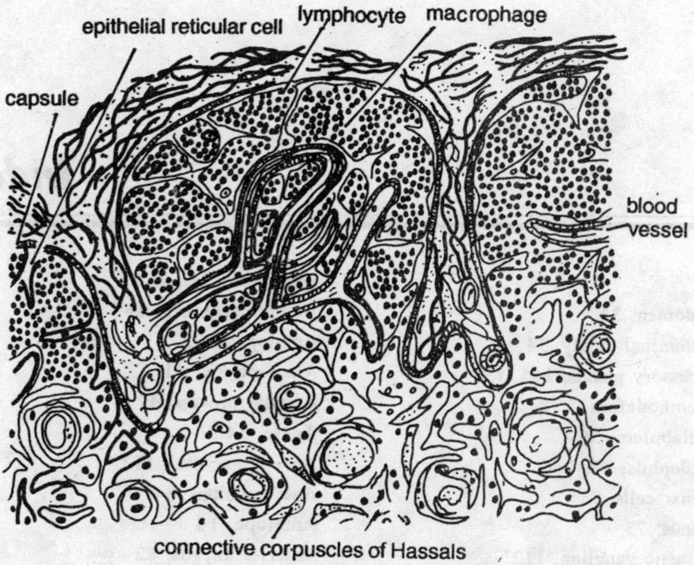

Fig. 20.7. Structure of Thymus.

but with atrophy of the thymus, this hormone is no longer secreted, and the sex-glands are permitted to develop.

Revision Questions

1. What is a hormone ? Describe the hormones of adenohypophysis emphasising the functions of each hormone.
2. Describe the structure and functions of hormones secreted by Adrenal gland.
3. Describe the structure of thyroid gland ? Discuss the formation of thyroxine hormone and its functions.
4. Describe the structure of pancereas. Discuss the hormonal disorders induced by the endocrine components of pancreas in a mammal.
5. Describe the structure and hormones of parathyroid gland.
6. Write short notes on : (a) Adrenalin, (b) Insulin, (c) Aldosterone, (d) Antidiuretic hormone, (e) Adrenal medulla.

Index

N

O